KornShell Programming Tutorial

KornShell Programming Tutorial

Barry Rosenberg

Addison-Wesley Publishing Company
Reading, Massachusetts • Menlo Park, California • New York • Don Mills, Ontario
Wokingham, England • Amsterdam • Bonn • Sydney • Singapore • Tokyo
Madrid • San Juan • Seoul • Milan • Mexico City • Taipei

The publisher offers discounts on this book when ordered in quantity for special sales. For more information, please contact:

Corporate & Professional Publishing Group
Addison-Wesley Publishing Company
Route 128
Reading, Massachusetts 01867

Library of Congress Cataloging-in-Publication Data

Rosenberg, Barry, 1958–
KornShell programming tutorial / Barry Rosenberg.
p. cm. - - (Hewlett-Packard Press series)
Includes index.
ISBN 0-201-56324-X
1. KornShell (Computer program language) I. Title. II. Series.
QA76.73.K67R67 1991
005.13'3--dc20 91-13003
CIP

Cover design by Joyce Weston
Typeset by the author in 10-point Times
Printed on recycled and acid-free paper

11 12 13 14 15 16 17 MA 00 99 98 97

11th Printing November, 1997

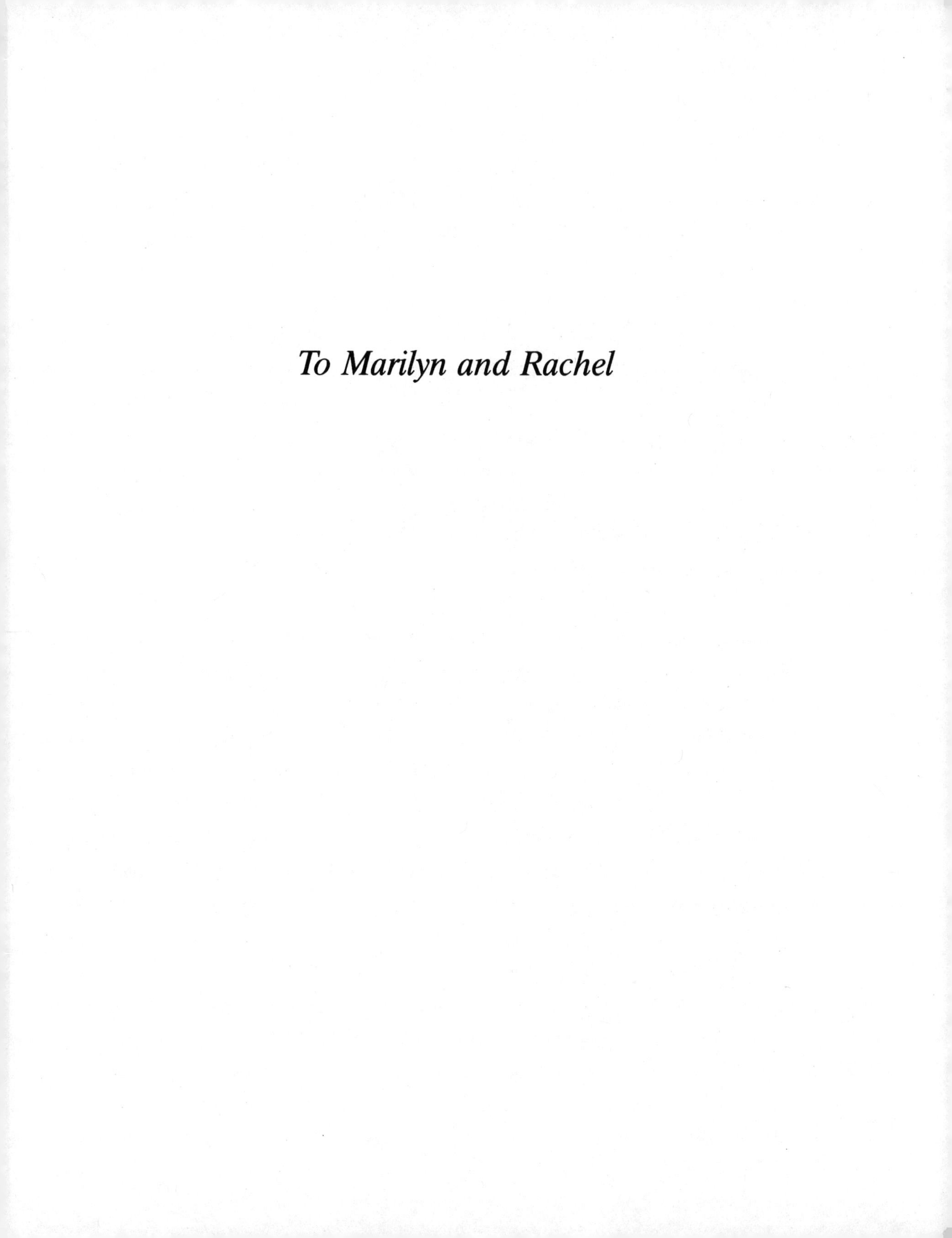

To Marilyn and Rachel

Short Table of Contents

Contents

Chapter 1 Before Writing Your First Kornshell Scripts

Chapter 2 Getting Started

Chapter 3 Data Types

Chapter 4 Math

Chapter 5 Pattern Matching

Chapter 6 Conditions

Chapter 7 Loops

Chapter 8 Creating Menus

Chapter 9 Command Line Arguments and Positional Parameters

Chapter 10 Functions

Chapter 11 Start–Up Scripts and Environments

Chapter 12 Input and Output

Chapter 13 Manipulating Strings

Chapter 14 Kornshell Reserved Variables

Chapter 15 Foreground, Background, and Signaling

Chapter 16 Kornshell Applications

Chapter 17 Command Line Editing and the History File

Appendix Statement and Alias Quick Reference

Figures

Tables

Preface That No One Will Ever Read

Research indicates that virtually no one actually reads prefaces in computer books. In fact, this preface could be about the Loch Ness Monster for all most readers care.

But why don't people read prefaces? Is it because prefaces sometimes get too personal? ("...and I want to thank Sal, who made this book possible.") Is it because the sentiments of nerdy authors can be a bit repulsive? ("...Sal, my MicroVAX, was always there when I needed her.") Is it because they are predictably self-deprecatory in an ironic way? ("...and I want to thank: [list of 250 noted experts goes here] for reviewing drafts of this manual. Naturally all mistakes are my own.") No, when it comes right down to it, people avoid prefaces because they're boring.

It is also de rigueur for the nerdish author to explain, folksinger style, why he or she decided to write this piece. I guess this book sort of came to me while I was camping out in the glorious Rocky Mountains. I was gazing at pristine waterfalls and awe-inspiring sunsets when I said to myself, "This land must be preserved. I shall write a KornShell book." Possessed by a demonic ecological fervor, I roared down that mountain in a snowmobile, fired up a 1200 watt workstation, and wrote it all down for you. I only ask that you use the power of the KornShell for good, rather than evil.

Actually, I've been writing programming manuals for many years under the pen name "Apollo Computer Inc." Recently, my agent insisted that I change it to "Hewlett-Packard Company," presumably because it sounded less ethnic. Through the years, I've been lucky enough to get lots of feedback from my readers. What do you think they ask for? More text? No. More syntax? Definitely not. When it comes right down to it, readers consistently ask for only one thing: *more examples*.

So, I listened to them and based this tutorial entirely on examples.

I feel that short, focused examples are more valuable than long, detailed examples, and I've written the book accordingly. The purpose of the book is not to make me look clever; it is to make you look clever. Nevertheless, I've sprinkled a few lengthy examples into the mix for those of you who enjoy that sort of thing.

When I was a mere lad my family doctor pointed to a massive encyclopedia of pharmaceuticals and told me that he could treat 90% of all patients with only six different medicines. Similarly, although the KornShell is a very rich language, my goal is to focus on the common script ailments and to leave the beriberi treatment to specialists.

Beginners may be wondering, "Is this book too hard for me?" No, probably not. Programmers experienced in various languages, though not in the KornShell, are probably wondering, "Is this book too wimpy for me?" No, probably not. To help guide both kinds of readers through the book, I've marked certain sections as being more appropriate for one group or the other. Beginners don't need an explanation of traps and experienced programmers already know what loops are.

Here's how I've organized the book:

Chapter 1 introduces the KornShell and its features.

Chapter 2 contains some simple KornShell scripts to get you started.

Chapter 3 discusses data types.

Chapter 4 shows you how to do simple math.

Chapter 5 illustrates pattern matching.

Chapter 6 explains how to evaluate conditions.

Chapter 7 shows you how to set up loops.

Chapter 8 describes how to create simple menus.

Chapter 9 explains how to evaluate command line arguments.

Chapter 10 illustrates functions.

Chapter 11 has a lot of conceptual stuff in it about environments and inheritance. It also contains some sample start-up scripts.

Chapter 12 examines input and output.

Chapter 13 focuses on string manipulation.

Chapter 14 describes the many variables that are part of the KornShell.

Chapter 15 describes various advanced features of the KornShell. (This chapter is aimed at the sophisticated programmer.)

Chapter 16 contains a half-dozen lengthy KornShell examples.

Chapter 17 explains command line editing and the history file.

Appendix contains a syntactic quick reference. This appendix will become more valuable to you as your KornShell experience increases.

Since the KornShell runs on all sorts of operating systems, I've tried to keep operating system dependencies to a bare minimum. Nevertheless, my sense is that the majority of KornShell users are either working under the UNIX* operating system or are at least marginally familiar with it. Therefore, in the examples that do contain commands, I've picked UNIX commands.

---

* UNIX is a registered trademark of UNIX System Laboratories Inc.

It is now time for the obligatory nod to the tools that made this book possible. I used the \fB**troff**\fR .mm macro package to format drafts of this book (an experience akin to running blindfold through nettles) and then came to my senses and converted the whole thing to Interleaf TPS. //cascade, my trusty Apollo DN4000 workstation, was always there when I needed her. It practically goes without saying that I created camera-ready copy for the book on a Hewlett-Packard laser printer.

My three primary reviewers were KornShell gurus David Korn, Steve Sommars, and Glenn Fowler, all of whom gave fantastic and diplomatic criticism.

I also received important criticism and help from Tom Barstow, Dave Beckedorf, Bart Hanlon, Warren Johnson, Ed Johnston, Mark Keil, Mike Kong, Alice Lynch, Dave Penfield, Will Roaf, Frank Rubinsky, John Weiss, Daryl Winters, Teri Witham, and other people whose names I have no doubt forgotten to list. Eric Eldred and Quentin Sullivan found so many bugs in early drafts that, and I mean this as a compliment, they should have a brand of insecticide named after them.

Judy Tarutz is my long-suffering editor. In person, Judy is a kind, gentle soul with an outrageous sense of humor. Give her a red pen though, and she turns into Conan the Barbarian. Her savage red pen cut a bloody swath through early drafts of this book. If we should chance to meet up one day, dear reader, I'll tell you all the "weak" jokes she made me take out.

I'd also like to thank the members of the Academy.

A consortium of great minds—those minds owned and operated by Ted Ricks, John Wait, Jack Danahy, and Steve Spicer—led me to the KornShell and helped me define the material for this book.

Finally, I'd like to thank the person who really made this book possible: my wife and best friend, Marilyn.

Whoops, almost forgot. Naturally, all mistakes are my own.

Chapter 1

Before Writing Your First KornShell Scripts

Some people learn best from pure reference material. These people like a meticulous, dirt-free, syntactic representation of all known program features. These people prefer their world broken down into squiggly braces and italicized symbols. These people not only can spell "Backus Naur" correctly, they can pronounce it correctly, too.

Avoid these people.

This book, on the other hand, is a tutorial for people who prefer to learn through examples. In fact, the book is approximately 50% examples.*

Warning! This book does not detail every single amazing nuance of the KornShell. The KornShell is very rich in features, but my intention is to focus on the features that will get you started at the expense of the "Gee whiz, Harry, just look at the neat way you can do this" sorts of features.

Second warning! I've broken a treasured UNIX tradition by attempting to write an easy-to-use book. In fact, you don't have to know too much about the UNIX system or its culture in order to understand this book. If this offends you, complain to **/dev/null**. (Sorry, couldn't resist.)

I will now attempt to answer a few of the more common beginner's questions.

---

* This book is sold by weight, not by volume. Some settling of examples may occur during shipping.

"What is a shell?"

Just about every operating system provides at least one shell. Typically, the operating system invokes a shell when you log in. After the shell starts up, it waits for you to enter commands. For example, if you were a UNIX user who wanted to know the names of the files in a directory, then you would probably type the command **ls** inside a UNIX shell. The UNIX shell will *interpret* the **ls** command, which means that it will figure out what command you typed ("oh, you want to execute an **ls** command") and then invoke the command. By contrast, Apple Macintosh users typically don't use a shell program; instead, they command the operating system by clicking a mouse button and selecting commands from menus.

For many users, the only purpose of a shell is to enter operating system commands.

"Can a shell do anything besides executing operating system commands?"

Yes. Most shells support a special shell programming language. Some of these shell programming languages are fairly primitive. Others rival high-level languages like C or FORTRAN in their complexity.

One way of looking at a shell is that it is a high-level language from which it is very easy to invoke operating system commands.

"What can I do with this shell programming language?"

That really depends on the shell programming language you're using and on your skill as a programmer. The KornShell's programming language lets you perform many of the same feats that you can in C or FORTRAN. In addition, you can often write a KornShell *script* in a fraction of the time it would take you to write a C program. A KornShell script is a program, stored in a text file, written in the KornShell's special shell programming language.

"What is the KornShell?"

The KornShell is a shell invented by David Korn of Bell Laboratories. The KornShell is available on most UNIX systems. It also runs on DOS, OS/2, and VMS.

"How does the KornShell compare to the other UNIX shells?"

The Bourne shell is the original UNIX shell. It was invented in the early seventies. The syntax of the Bourne shell programming language resembles the syntax of an old language called ALGOL.

The C shell was invented in the late seventies. It contains many features not found in the Bourne shell. The syntax of the C shell programming language resembles that of the C programming language.

The KornShell was invented in the mid-eighties. It is a superset of the Bourne shell, meaning that it supports every feature of the Bourne shell plus many new ones. In addition, the KornShell incorporates some of the best features of the C shell.

"If I already know the Bourne shell, why should I bother learning the KornShell? After all, doesn't every Bourne shell script run under the KornShell?"

That's like saying, "I already know how to ride a tricycle. Why should I bother learning how to ride a bicycle?" True, both the Bourne shell and KornShell will get you to the same place, but you'll arrive there faster and more comfortably in the KornShell.

For all you C programmers out there: going from the Bourne shell to the KornShell is a little like going from C to C++. Sure, all your C programs will compile under C++, but wouldn't you miss out on a lot of goodies if you never learned C++'s special features?

Ten Reasons to Use the KornShell for Your Next Script

1. Has all sorts of fancy pattern matching constructs not found in other shells.
2. Has cute name; rhymes with "Bourne."
3. Lets you easily parse complex strings. Really hard to do comparable feats with C language.
4. Runs on many different platforms.
5. Gradually obsoleting Bourne shell.
6. Supports powerful, yet easy–to–use tests on files and directories.
7. Lets you specify different data types.
8. Runs many scripts faster than Bourne shell.
9. Supports functions.
10. Really fun to use.

"I've heard that there are different revisions of the KornShell. Which revision does this book describe?"

David Korn customarily releases a new revision of the KornShell every two or three years. KornShell users usually identify these revisions by the year in which Korn releases them. This book describes the KornShell revision that came out in 1988, generally known as **ksh.88**. Each KornShell revision builds on the features of the previous ones. So, the next version of the KornShell will contain the features described in this book plus a few new ones.

If you aren't sure which revision of the KornShell you are currently using, then try issuing the following command:

```
$ what ksh
```

With a little bit of luck, the preceding command will produce output that looks something like this:

```
ksh:
                Version 11/16/88e
```

The number **88** in the output tells you that you are using a KornShell revision that came out in 1988. If you see the number **86** or **84**, then you are using an earlier KornShell revision. If that's the case, then many of the examples in this book won't work as shown.

"What do I have to do before I start writing KornShell scripts?"

You don't *have to* do anything before writing a KornShell script. However, you should eventually learn how to create an effective KornShell start-up script. (See Chapter 11.)

"What is the best way to use this book?"

In general, people remember only a small percentage of what they read but a high percentage of what they do. Therefore, I'd like to encourage you to play with the examples. That is, type them in as is, and then use them as a springboard for your own experiments. I'm sure you'll get frustrated from time to time, but I do hope that you'll have fun.

"How much do I have to know about programming in order to use this book?"

Well, to be honest, the more you know about programming and the UNIX operating system, the more you'll get out of this book. Nevertheless, even rank beginners should be able to get through at least the first nine chapters.

"If I'm still hungry for more KornShell after I digest this book, what else can I read?"

You can read the definitive KornShell reference manual, which is:

> Bolsky, Morris and David Korn. *The KornShell Command and Programming Language.* New Jersey: Prentice-Hall, 1989.

Chapter 2
Getting Started

This chapter shows you how to write and execute very simple KornShell scripts.

A KornShell script is simply a text file. To create a text file you'll need a text editor. You can use any ASCII text editor on your system. For example, UNIX users may wish to use the **vi** editor or perhaps **emacs**. Choose whatever text editor you like.

Here is a KornShell script to help get you started. Use your text editor to create a file named **first.ksh**. Then enter the following single line of text into this file:

```
echo $RANDOM
```

When you've finished entering the text, save the file.

Executing This Script

To execute a KornShell script, simply enter the pathname of the file in which it is stored. For example, assuming that the file **first.ksh** is stored in your current directory, you'd execute it by typing

```
$ ./first.ksh
12752
$
```

For those of you unacquainted with UNIX names, **./first.ksh** means the file named **first.ksh** that is stored in the current directory. The dollar sign ($) is the default KornShell prompt. Actually, you can define any KornShell prompt you want (see Chapter 14), but I use a bland old dollar sign throughout the book just for the sake of capitalistic simplicity. If, after typing the pathname of the script, the system displays a random integer followed by the KornShell prompt, then congratulations, you are in the KornShell and are ready to write KornShell scripts. However, if the system does not display an integer, then please read the next section.

What Shell Is Executing My Script?

If the KornShell is the only shell on your computer system, then you can ignore this page and the next one. However, the system on which you are currently working may support more than one kind of shell. For example, the Apollo workstation on which I am typing these words can run four different shells simultaneously: the KornShell, the Bourne shell, the C shell, and the Domain/OS Aegis shell. Since so many different shells are available, I have to ensure that it is the KornShell, and not one of these other shells, that is executing my KornShell scripts. Unfortunately, the shell in which you are working is rarely willing to scream out its identity without some prodding.

The **first.ksh** script, simple as it is, can help you identify the type of shell that is executing your script. As I mentioned before, if the script outputs a random integer, then the KornShell is executing the script. If, however, executing the script produces a blank line, for example:

```
$ ./first.ksh

$
```

then the Bourne shell is probably executing your script.

If executing the script produces an error message like this:

```
$ ./first.ksh
RANDOM: undefined variable
```

then the C shell or some other shell is probably executing your script.

When you log in or boot your machine, many operating systems will start up a shell for you. What shell will it start up? Well, that depends on the operating system; different operating systems pick different default shells. Usually though, the operating system allows you to specify which shell to start up at login. To learn how to do this, see a book that describes your operating system or talk to your system administrator.

Suppose you can't figure out how to specify the KornShell as your login shell. In this case, you can usually start up the KornShell from within the other kind of shell. To do this, you have to remember that the KornShell itself is simply a program file named **ksh**. If you're in a UNIX shell, you can execute the program by simply typing its pathname; for example:

```
% ksh
$
```

If you're lucky, this simple command will snap you into the KornShell. However, if it doesn't work, you may have to specify the full pathname at which the **ksh** program is stored. For example, the **ksh** program is often stored in pathname **/bin/ksh**, so here's a possibility:

```
% /bin/ksh
$
```

If your login shell is not a UNIX shell, you may have to specify the name of a command that will execute the program. For example, in the VMS shell, you execute programs by specifying the command **ex** followed by the pathname. So, the following command might get you out of the VMS shell and into a KornShell:

```
VMS Shell: ex ksh
```

Now for the confusing part: you can execute a KornShell script without actually being in a KornShell. There are two ways to do this.

One way is to specify the pathname of the **ksh** itself followed by the pathname of your KornShell script. For example, suppose you are in a C shell but want to execute the KornShell script stored at pathname **./first.ksh**. In this case, you'd issue the following command:

```
C Shell: ksh ./first.ksh
```

There is a second way to execute a KornShell script without actually being in a KornShell, but this second way isn't standard. That is, although some operating systems use the following convention, I can't guarantee that yours will. In this method, you specify the pathname of the executing shell on the first line of the script. You usually precede the shell name with the two characters **#!** and these two characters must be flush left. So, for example, if you add the **#!** preamble to script **first.ksh**, the script will contain:

```
#!/bin/ksh
echo $RANDOM
```

You can execute this script from any kind of shell. For example, suppose you are working in the C shell. When you type

```
C Shell: ./first.ksh
```

the operating system will read the **first.ksh** line of the script, then have the KornShell stored at pathname **/bin/ksh** execute the remainder of the script.

Operating System Commands in a Shell Script

Suppose that you execute two UNIX operating system commands, **date** and **df**, as follows:

```
$ date
Sat Feb 16 15:16:10 EST 1991
$ df
/dev/dsk/W0d0s1   (//node_2707c):     73309 blocks    (N/A) i-nodes
```

The **date** command prints the current date and time and the **df** command tells you how much disk space you have available. (The **df** command generates different information on different implementations of the UNIX operating system, so the output you see may not look like the above.)

Instead of issuing these two commands individually, you can bundle them into a KornShell script. KornShell scripts often contain one or more operating system commands. The following script consists solely of operating system commands. Please use your text editor to type this script into a file named **starting.ksh**.

```
date
df
```

Executing This Script

Assuming that you are working in a KornShell, you execute a KornShell script by entering the pathname of the file in which it is stored. For example, assuming that **starting.ksh** is stored in your current directory, you would type

```
$ starting.ksh
Sat Feb 16 15:17:10 EST 1991
/dev/dsk/W0d0s1   (//node_2707c):     73308 blocks    (N/A) i-nodes
$
```

(If typing **starting.ksh** doesn't work, try typing **./starting.ksh**.)

When a script finishes, the KornShell will display a new prompt (here represented as **$**) and await your next command.

! BEWARE: Are You Allowed to Execute This Script? !

Some operating systems permit users to deny other users the chance to execute a script. There may be good reasons to prevent certain scripts from falling into the wrong hands. However, we're not here to debate the ethics of computer security or explain how these protections work. Please refer to documentation on your operating system for a complete description of file protection.

It is rather important that you know about a common problem. Suppose you try to execute a KornShell script named **sample.ksh**, but the operating system returns an error message similar to the following:

```
$ sample.ksh
/bin/ksh: sample.ksh: cannot execute
```

or perhaps this:

```
$ sample.ksh
/bin/ksh: sample.ksh: permission denied
```

The preceding messages tell you that you don't have permission to execute this script. If you are working on the UNIX operating system, try issuing the following command:

```
$ chmod +rx sample.ksh
```

The preceding command will give you permission to execute the script *if* you are the owner of the script. If you don't own the script, you cannot give yourself execute permission. A possible way to circumvent this restriction is to copy the script into a directory that you do own and then give yourself the appropriate permissions.

To invoke a typical compiled program (like **a.out**), you only need execute permission. However, to invoke a script you usually* need both read and execute permission.

```
$ sample.ksh               # need execute and read permission for sample.ksh
```

There is a way around this problem, too. An alternate way of invoking a KornShell script is by specifying the pathname of the KornShell itself followed by the script name; for example:

```
$ /bin/ksh sample.ksh      # need read permission for sample.ksh
```

If you invoke a script this way, you only need read permission. That is, you don't need execute permission.

* UNIX systems that install **/etc/suid_exec** do not need read permission.

Comments

Here is an example that shows how to put comments into your script. Using a text editor, type the following into a file named **comments.ksh.**

```
# The KornShell permits you to write comments that take up an entire
# line or just part of a line.  To tell the KornShell that you are
# making a comment, precede your comment with a # sign.

# Some scripts contain an operating system directive like this
# on the first line:
#     #!/bin/ksh
# However, in that special situation, the # does not indicate
# a comment; it indicates the name of the shell program that will
# process the script.

 date         # this UNIX command returns the date and time
 df           # this UNIX command tells you how much disk space is
              # currently available

# This script contains some blank lines.  The KornShell ignores blank
# lines.  Use blank lines and other white space to make your program
# easier to read.

# We're going to place comments at the start of every sample shell
# script in the book.  These comments will explain what the script is
# demonstrating.
```

Executing This Script

Assume that this shell script is stored in file **comments.ksh.** To invoke it, you issue the following command:

```
$ comments.ksh
Sat Feb 16 16:02:10 EST 1991
/dev/dsk/W0d0s1   (//node_2707c):     73305 blocks    (N/A) i-nodes
$
```

(From now on, I'm going to omit the trailing prompt **$.**)

! BEWARE: Picking a Bad Name for Your Script !

Sometimes you will write the perfect KornShell script, invoke it, and then NOTHING HAPPENS! Worse yet, perhaps you invoke the script and SOMETHING TOTALLY UNEXPECTED HAPPENS! What now?

If you are absolutely certain (and you never will be) that your coding is good, you might try to change the filename of the script. Perhaps you've inadvertently given the script a name reserved for some other KornShell use. For example, suppose you put your script in a file named **test**. If you type **test** at the shell prompt, the KornShell will not invoke your shell script; rather the KornShell will try to perform a **test** statement because, by coincidence, **test** is also the name of a KornShell statement. You can find a list of KornShell statements in the Appendix.

Another possibility is that your script name matches an operating system command name. For example, suppose you name a script **cat**. That name is perfectly legal; however, **cat** also happens to be the name of a UNIX command. You have to ask yourself a question. If you type **cat** on the command line, which **cat** will get executed—your script or the UNIX command? I'll answer that in a moment, but it should be clear to you by now that you don't want to get in that situation. In other words, try to avoid script names that match other names on the system.

Now, which **cat** gets executed? That depends on your **PATH** variable, which is described in Chapter 14. To find out what your **PATH** directories are, type:

```
$ print $PATH
```

Briefly, the KornShell starts looking for a file named **cat** in the ordered list of **PATH** directories. If the directory containing your shell script (for instance, ./) precedes the directory containing the **cat** command, then the KornShell executes your script. However, if the directory containing your shell script comes after the directory containing the **cat** command, then the KornShell executes the **cat** command. Incidentally, a way to ensure that your **cat** script gets executed is to specify its full pathname when you execute it; for example:

```
$ cat                  # too vague
$ ./cat                # right
$ /usr/newmar/cat      # right again
```

A good convention to follow is to append the suffix **.ksh** to every filename that contains a KornShell script. So, for example, instead of naming the file **cat**, name it **cat.ksh** instead. This convention will make it easier for you to identify files containing KornShell scripts.

Another problem with names is picking one that's too long. Most operating systems impose rather severe limits on the number of characters in a filename. On some operating systems, the limit is 32 characters, which isn't much of a burden on the script namer. However, most implementations of the System V UNIX operating system impose a limit of 14 characters. DOS imposes a limit of 8 characters (not including a **.ksh** suffix). All script names in this book conform to the 8–character limit; however, the software instructor inside of me wants to remind you that long, descriptive names are better than short, cryptic ones. So, with regards to naming you might remember the axiom: "short will port, but longer is stronger."

The Usage Line

Each KornShell script in the rest of this book contains a *usage* line that describes the proper way to invoke the script. In the early chapters, the usage lines will be pretty bland, but in later chapters we'll see that usage lines can become quite elaborate. For example, a more complex usage line might specify the names of possible options to enter on the command line. We'll also see how to print the usage line if the user improperly invokes the script.

```
USAGE="usage: sample.ksh" #this line tells you how to start the script

 date    # this UNIX command returns the date and time
 df      # this UNIX command tells you how much disk space is
         # currently available
```

Executing This Script

Assume that this shell script is stored in file **sample.ksh**. To invoke it, you issue the following command:

```
$ sample.ksh
Sat Feb 16 16:04:50 EST 1991
/dev/dsk/W0d0s1  (//node_2707c):    73304 blocks   (N/A) i-nodes
```

From now on, information on invoking the script will be presented in each script's usage line.

By the way, specifying a usage line has a hidden benefit; namely, a user can issue a **grep** command to find out how to invoke the script. **grep** is a UNIX command that finds occurrences of specified words inside a specified file. For example, if the user wants to find out how to run **sample.ksh** without resorting to trial-and-error, the user can type the following UNIX command:

```
$ grep USAGE sample.ksh
USAGE="usage: sample.ksh" #this line tells you how to start the script
```

This **grep** command displays all lines in **sample.ksh** that contain the word **USAGE**.

Simple Output

The KornShell supports two output statements: **echo** and **print**. Since **print** is more versatile than **echo**, the book concentrates on **print**. See Chapter 12 for complete details on output.

```
USAGE="usage: output1.ksh"  # simple uses of the print statement

 echo  "Hello world."       # the last echo in the book
 print                      # prints a blank line

# Use print to output text.  Although you don't have to surround your
# text in single or double quotes, it is a good idea to get into that
# habit.  That's because the double quotes will preserve all white
# space within your output. See "Beware: The Quotes from Hell" at the
# end of this chapter.
 print  Hi        earth.    # okay
 print "Hi        earth."   # better

# By default, the print statement ends each line with a newline
# character.  In other words, the output of two consecutive print
# statements will appear on separate lines.  If you don't want the
# print statement to end each line with a newline, use the -n option.
 print -n "Bon"         # -n inhibits the newline here...
 print -n "jour "       # ...and here
 print    "le monde."   # no -n; therefore, print a newline

# The \n is an explicit order to print a newline character.
 print "hi\nto\nyou"    # print a single word on each line

# Use \t within your text to print a tab.
 print "\tBuenos dias al mundo."
```

Executing This Script

```
$ output1.ksh
Hello world.

Hi earth.
Hi        earth.
Bonjour le monde.
hi
to
you
     Buenos dias al mundo.
```

Variables

As in algebra, a KornShell variable is a symbol that represents a value. For example, the variable **x** might represent a numerical value like 365 or a textual value like "earth cycle." Actually, naming a variable **x** isn't very evocative. It's better to pick descriptive names for your variables, like **length_of_a_year**.

Variable names can contain any combination of

- Letters (uppercase or lowercase)
- Digits
- Underscores (_)

However, a variable name cannot begin with a digit nor have spaces between words. Here are some examples of legal and illegal variable names:

```
tears_of_a_clown      # legal variable name
tears of a clown      # illegal because of white space between words
eighty_six            # legal variable name
86                    # illegal because it starts with a digit
eighty6               # legal
```

Variable names can be as long or as short as you desire. In other words, unlike most high-level languages, the KornShell does not impose a limit on the length of variable names.

You can use as many variables as you like within a KornShell script. In addition to the variables that you create, the KornShell comes with a few variables of its own. To get a list of all variables and their values, type

```
$ set
```

To find out what these variables mean, see Chapter 14.

Variable names are case sensitive. For example, the KornShell views **DOG**, **dog**, and **Dog** as three distinct variable names. So you won't get confused, it's usually a good idea to avoid uppercase letters in variable names. For example, **dog** is probably a better choice than **DOG** or **Dog**.

Chapter 3 details variable declaration and variable data types.

Simple Input

Use the **read** statement to perform input. The **read** statement is very versatile; you can use it for entering numbers or text. The syntax of **read** is simpler than comparable input statements of other high-level languages. You don't need to supply any fancy **A7** directives (as in FORTRAN) or **%d** specifiers (as in C). See Chapter 12 for complete details on input; in particular, you should pay extra attention to the **-r** option of **read.**

```
USAGE="usage: input1.ksh"  # read statement

# The read statement gathers one line of input and assigns it to one or
# more variables.
 print -n "Enter a number, letter, word, phrase, or sentence: "
 read user_input

# Here, the read statement gathers one line of input and assigns it to
# three different variables.
 print -n "Enter three numbers: "
 read first second third
# If the user enters 10 15 20, then read will assign 10 to variable
# first, 15 to variable second, and 20 to variable third.
```

Executing This Script

When you invoke **input1.ksh**, the script will pause whenever it reaches a **read** statement and wait for you to type something. After you type some information and press the <RETURN> key, the script will assign your input to the appropriate variable or variables. By the way, sample input appears in **boldface** so that you can distinguish it from the `script's output`.

```
$ input1.ksh
Enter a number, letter, word, phrase, or sentence: Rachel Elisa
Enter three numbers: 10 15 20
```

The KornShell will assign the value "Rachel Elisa" to variable **user_input**. Then, the KornShell will assign the value 10 to variable **first**, the value 15 to variable **second**, and the value 20 to variable **third.**

Writing the Value of a Variable

Use this syntax to find the value of a variable:

$*variable*

That is, specify a dollar sign **$** in front of the variable name. Therefore, to output the value of a variable, use this syntax:

print "**$***variable*"

The following script demonstrates how to output the value of a variable. See Chapter 12 for more information about the **print** statement.

```
USAGE="usage: var_out.ksh"  # writing the value of a variable

 print -n "Enter a number, letter, word, phrase, or sentence: "
 read x               # assign to x whatever user enters
 print                # print a blank line

# Contrast the following three print statements:
 print "x"            # prints the letter x
 print "$x"           # prints the value of variable x
 print "x = $x"       #
```

Executing This Script

```
$ var_out.ksh
Enter a number, letter, word, phrase, or sentence: Marilyn Tucker

x
Marilyn Tucker
x = Marilyn Tucker
```

Newlines, Semicolons, White Space, and Other Information for Inquiring Minds

Anybody who has been around the block a few times with programming languages wants to know the answers to several simple questions.

"Can I put more than one command on the same line?"

You can put multiple commands on the same line if you separate the commands with semicolons; for example:

```
date  df                    # wrong
date; df                    # right
```

"Can I spread a single command over more than one line?"

In general, commands should start and end on the same line. However, some commands can span more than one line; for example, this is okay:

```
print "hi
there"     # writes "hi" on one line and "there" on the next
```

"Do I need to put white space between different parts of a command?"

The KornShell is obsessive about *white space* (space, tab, and newline). Sometimes, white space is required; sometimes, white space is forbidden. In general, though, you should place white space between the different parts of a command; for example:

```
print -n "Hi"               # right
print-n "Hi"                # wrong, need white space between print and -n
```

but there are plenty of exceptions (which will be described throughout this book). For example, certain assignment statements forbid white space:

```
x=10                        # right
x = 10                      # wrong, can't have white space
```

In general, you do not need to place white space next to any of the following characters:

```
(  )  &  |  <  >  ;
```

"Do commands have to start in a particular column (as in FORTRAN or many assembly languages)?"

No. The column in which you start a command has absolutely no influence on how the KornShell will execute that command.

Assigning a Value to a Variable

The KornShell supports many ways of assigning a value to a variable. However, the easiest method is to specify the name of a variable, then the equal sign =, and then the value you are assigning to the variable. So, for example, the following line assigns the value 100 to variable **test_score**:

```
test_score=100
```

You may assign a value of any length to a variable (unless that variable is declared as an integer; see the next chapter for details).

```
USAGE="usage: assign.ksh" # assigning values to variables

# Here are four ways to assign a numerical value to a variable.
 n=100           # I prefer this syntax; no space before or after =
 let n=100
 let "n = 100"
 ((n = 100))
 print "The value of n is $n"

# You can assign a letter, word, or phrase to a variable by specifying
# the variable name, an equal sign, and the value; for example:
 letter="Q"
 word="elephant"
 phrase="The rain in Spain."
 print "letter = $letter;  word = $word;   phrase = $phrase"

# Use the equal sign to assign the value of one variable to another
# variable; for example:
 x=$n            # assign the value of variable n to variable x
 print "x = $x"

# While we're on the subject, let's print out the usage line
 print "$USAGE"
```

Executing This Script

```
$ assign.ksh
The value of n is 100
letter = Q;  word = elephant;   phrase = The rain in Spain.
x = 100
usage: assign.ksh
```

! BEWARE: Common Mistakes When Assigning Variables !

Variable assignment often frustrates beginning KornShell programmers because the KornShell is so sensitive to white space. For example, consider the following two variable assignments:

```
y = 100
title = "Mountains of Norway"
```

They both look wholesome enough; however, both will cause a KornShell error because of improper use of white space. For example, the first assignment might cause an error like this:

```
y: not found
```

The correct way to write these assignments is as follows:

```
y=100
title="Mountains of Norway"
```

Don't put any white space on either side of the equal sign. The only proper place for white space in an assignment statement is within the double quotes.

Now consider another kind of variable assignment mistake, one involving improper use of the dollar sign. The following lines assign the value 50 to variable **dog** and then show the right and wrong ways to assign the value of **dog** (50) to another variable named **bear**:

```
dog=50              # assign 50 to variable dog
bear=dog            # mistake 1: assigns the word "dog" to bear
$bear=$dog          # mistake 2: don't put a $ in front of bear
bear=$dog           # right: assigns value of dog to bear
```

Mistake 1 is particularly bothersome because the KornShell will not warn you about it. The KornShell thinks you want to assign the word "dog" to a variable named **bear** and sees nothing wrong with that. (The KornShell cannot guess your intentions.) Mistake 2, on the other hand, will cause the following KornShell error message:

```
dog=50:  not found
```

Finding Your Mistakes

If your KornShell script isn't working properly, there are two ways to figure out what's wrong:

- You can stare intently at the terminal until large vats of sweat pour down your brow.
- You can run the script (or part of it) in debug mode.

To run the entire script in debug mode, invoke it like this:

```
$ ksh -x name_of_script
```

For example, to run the script **input1.ksh** in debug mode, issue the following command:

```
$ ksh -x input1.ksh
+ USAGE=usage: input1.ksh
+ print -n Enter a number, letter, word, phrase, or sentence:
Enter a number, letter, word, phrase, or sentence: + read user_input
Rachel Elisa
+ print -n Enter three numbers:
Enter three numbers: + read first second third
10 15 20
```

The + is the default debug mode indicator. As the KornShell executes a command, it prints the + followed by the command itself, allowing you to trace the execution of your program. Those lines not preceded by a + are the script's input and output. In other words, if you ran the script normally (not in debug mode), you'd see every line not preceded by +.

A script running in debug mode often runs very slowly and produces volumes of output. To diminish these downsides you can limit the range of debug mode. That is, you can run regions of the script in debug mode and other regions in normal mode. Place the directive **set -x** just before the line at which you want debug mode to start. To stop debug mode, place the directive **set +x** at the point where you want normal mode to start. You can place any number of **set -x** and **set +x** pairs in your script. In the following script, the debug region covers the two statements between **set -x** and **+x**. Statements outside of the debug region are in normal mode.

```
print "hello there."   # normal mode (not in debug mode)
set -x                 # start debug mode
y=10                   # in debug mode
z=$y                   # in debug mode
set +x                 # stop debug mode, start normal mode
print "bon jour la"    # normal mode (not in debug mode)
```

Ordinarily, if you've placed at least one **set -x** inside the script then you shouldn't specify **ksh -x** when you invoke the script; instead, just type the name of the script.

! BEWARE: Confusing + and - !

Most beginners expect the + to turn something on and the - to turn something off. However, by convention, the KornShell sees the + and - the other way around.

The Quotes from Hell

Research indicates that people tend to remember facts best when the facts are presented at the very beginning or the very end of a communication. Here, on the final pages of Chapter 2, I present something very important, something vital to your mental health and well-being. For it is here that I explain the difference between the single quote ´ and the double quote ".

The following characters have special meaning to the KornShell:

```
$  \  #  ?  [  ]  *  {  }  +  &  |  (  )  ;  \  "  ´
```

For example, in the following expression, note the significance of the dollar sign ($):

```
print  x    # output the letter x
print  $x   # output the value of variable x
```

In most instances, you will want the special significance of these characters; after all, the KornShell provides these characters to simplify programming. However, there are some instances in which you will want the KornShell to *turn off* the special significance of these characters. For example, there may come a time when you will want the dollar sign to mean just a plain old dollar sign rather than "the operator that evaluates variables."

For this purpose, the KornShell provides the following features:

- A pair of single quotes ´...´ turns off the special significance of *all* enclosed characters.
- A pair of double quotes "..." turns off the special significance of all enclosed characters, except

```
$  `  "  \
```

Let us now consider several examples to illustrate these somewhat confusing principles. For example, suppose you want to print the value of variable **y**. In the following example, the single quote turns off the special significance of the dollar sign, but the double quote does not:

```
y=50
print  $y     # right;         Output -- 50
print "$y"    # right again;   Output -- 50
print ´$y´    # wrong;         Output -- $y
```

Suppose you want to use the UNIX command **rm** to delete a file named **stain**. In this case, since the filename contains no special characters, quotation marks are irrelevant.

```
# The following three commands are synonymous:
rm  stain
rm ´stain´
rm "stain"
```

Suppose, however, that the file was named **$stain** rather than **stain.** In this case, you must somehow tell the KornShell to turn off the special significance of the dollar sign. If you don't turn it off, the

KornShell will interpret **stain** as meaning the value of variable **stain**. Here are a few good and bad ways to remove **$stain**:

```
rm $stain    # wrong, because KornShell will try to evaluate stain
rm '$stain'  # right
rm '$'stain  # right also
rm \$stain   # right also
rm "$stain"  # wrong, because the value of "$stain" is null.
```

The backslash character (\) shuts off the special meaning of the character immediately to its right. Thus, **\$** in the preceding example is equivalent to **'$'**.

Use either single quotes or double quotes to preserve white space within a string. That is, if you don't enclose a string within single or double quotes, then the KornShell will eliminate all extra white space between the words.

```
print  hi        there     # output -- hi there
print 'hi        there'    # output -- hi        there
print "hi        there"    # output -- hi        there
```

Since the single quotes and double quotes themselves have special meaning, you may be wondering how to print them. Consider the following examples:

```
print 'Welcome 'Home''      # output -- Welcome Home
print 'Welcome "Home"'      # output -- Welcome "Home"
print "Welcome 'Home'"      # output -- Welcome 'Home'
print "Welcome "Home""      # output -- Welcome Home
print "Welcome \"Home\""    # output -- Welcome "Home"
```

By the way, do not confuse the grave accent ` (also known as the tick or the backquote) with the single quote '. Although they look quite similar, they have different meanings. As a rule of thumb*, you can usually find the single quote ' on the same key as the double quote ". Also, do not confuse the backslash \ with the slash /.

Finally, when using single or double quotes, remember to "pair" them. That is, if you place only one double quote on a command line, there's a good chance that the KornShell will mark that command as an error. If you are working at the KornShell command line and forget to pair your quotes, then the KornShell will probably present you with a line continuation prompt. For example, the following line looks perfectly correct until you notice that there's only one double quote, instead of the requisite two:

```
$ print "Let me introduce a man who needs no introduction
>
```

The > is the default KornShell line continuation prompt. This prompt tells you that the KornShell could not see the end of the command on the previous line. To end it, you'll need to provide a second double quote; for example:

```
$ print "Let me introduce a man who needs no introduction
> "               # end the print statement
```

* Actually, it's more a rule of right pinky if you're a touch typist.

Chapter 3
Data Types

This chapter explains data types in the KornShell.

If You're New to Programming...

A variable holds a value. The *data type* of a variable specifies the kind of values that the variable is allowed to hold. That is, a variable with a certain data type can hold certain kinds of data. If you assign the wrong kind of data to a variable, the KornShell will issue an error.

If you don't explicitly declare the data type of a variable, the KornShell gives the variable the data type known as *string*. A string consists of zero or more letters, numbers, or punctuation marks. For example, here are seven different string values:

```
elephant
Q
Cat in the Hat
/usr/users/einstein
537
^#@2Y
Call me at 555-1212
```

A string is the least restrictive data type. That is, a string variable can hold any sort of value; the KornShell won't issue an error message even if you assign something bizarre to a string variable. The vast majority of variables used in KornShell scripts have the string data type. For this reason, most beginners need only a cursory understanding of data types.

The *integer* data type indicates that a variable can hold an integer value only. If you intend to use a certain variable in mathematical calculations, you should consider declaring it as an integer data type. If you're a little rusty on math, let me remind you that an integer is a number without a fractional (decimal) part. Numbers with fractional parts are called *real numbers*. For example, the following numbers are integers:

```
8              537            -9000          125
```

but the next group are real numbers:

```
8.2            537.914        -9000.529      125.0
```

Some implementations of the KornShell do support real numbers but the "standard" KornShell does not. Therefore, this book is going to ignore real numbers.

By the way, did you notice that 537 appears as an example of both an integer and a string? How is that possible? Several examples in this chapter explain this dichotomy.

Another data type, the *array,* is a collection of string values or integer values. Each value in the collection is stored in a separate cell. That is, the array is made up of multiple cells, each cell containing one value. Each cell is numbered. The first string value is stored in array cell number 0, the second string value is stored in array cell number 1, and so on. Since the cells are numbered, you can easily store and retrieve specific values. An array is a great place to store related information. For example, Table 1 illustrates an array that holds familiar quotations. The first cell of the array, cell number 0, holds the quotation, "To be or not to be." The second cell holds the quotation "Be there. Aloha.," and so on. This array consists of five cells.

Table 1. An Array Is a Way of Organizing Related Information

Cell number	**Value stored in this cell**
0	To be or not to be.
1	Be there. Aloha.
2	Do be a doo–bee.
3	Can I have another slice of apple pie, Aunt Bea?
4	Let it be.

Finally, you can specify *constants*. A constant is like a variable in that both a constant and a variable each have a name and each can hold a value. However, unlike a variable, the value of a constant cannot change. That is, you assign a value to a constant when you declare it, and from that point on, you cannot change its value.

If You're an Experienced Programmer...

Programming in a high-level language is, to a large extent, an exercise in declaring data types and then using them correctly. By contrast, most shell scripting languages don't support any data types.

Programming in the KornShell falls somewhere between these two extremes. That is, the KornShell supports some data types; however, you do not usually have to explicitly declare the data type of any variable before using it. Good data type declaration can make your KornShell scripts run faster. On the other hand, ignoring data types can cause KornShell errors.

As an experienced programmer, you probably have certain expectations about data types. Please be warned that KornShell data types do not always work the same way that data types in other high-level languages do. In fact, data types in the KornShell can have a certain Twilight Zone edge to them. For example, in a KornShell script, you can declare a variable as an integer and then change the data type, mid-script, into a string.

You should feel more comfortable knowing that the KornShell supports the following three familiar data types:

Strings — By default, all variables are strings. In other words, if you do not specify the data type of a particular variable, the KornShell implicitly types it as a string. KornShell strings are a little different from strings you may be familiar with in other programming languages. For example, you can do mathematical operations on KornShell strings. KornShell strings can be of arbitrary length; you do not ordinarily specify the length of a string when you declare it. A KornShell string variable can hold a string value of any length (including a null or empty string). Chapter 13 describes several string *attributes*; for example, you can specify that a string cannot contain any uppercase letters or that a string is always right-justified.

Integers — The KornShell supports the integer data type. Declaring variables as integers speeds up mathematical operations. Chapter 4 explains several integer attributes; for example, you can specify that an integer is to be represented in base 2 or perhaps that an integer must have exactly four digits. Integers are stored as signed 32-bit values.

Arrays — As in most high-level languages, the KornShell supports arrays. By default, an array variable holds an array of strings; however, you can specify an array of integers instead. Unlike most high-level languages, the KornShell does not support a way to set the size of an array. Depending on your implementation, the size of an array will always be either 512 or 1024* elements. All arrays are one-dimensional.

In addition, you can declare constants.

You declare data types and constants with the **typeset** statement or one of its aliases.

By default, all variables are global; however, it is possible to declare a local variable within a KornShell function (see Chapter 10).

---

* Future implementations of the KornShell may increase the size limit or may provide another way of specifying array sizes.

Declaring Strings

By default, every variable is a string. That is, unless you tell the KornShell otherwise, every variable that you use in your script is automatically considered a string. In the following script, variables **letter**, **sentiment**, **book**, **numerical_string**, and **phone_message** are all strings, simply because you don't declare them. See Chapter 13 for more details on string attributes.

```
USAGE="usage: decl_str.ksh"  # how to declare strings

# Assign a value to five different string variables.
 letter="A"
 sentiment="always"
 book="Cat in the Hat"
 numerical_string="537"
 phone_message="Call me at 555-1212"

 print "Here are some string values: "
 print "$letter, $sentiment, $book, $numerical_string, $phone_message"

 print -n "Enter anything -- "
 read z
 print "Here is another string: $z"

# For clarity, you can explicitly declare a variable as a string with
# the typeset statement.
 typeset st
 st=$z
```

Executing This Script

```
$ decl_str.ksh
Here are some strings values:
A, always, Cat in the Hat, 537, Call me at 555-1212
Enter anything -- concrete noun
Here is another string: concrete noun
```

Declaring Integers

You can declare an integer variable in either of the following equivalent ways:

> **typeset –i** *variable_name*
> **integer** *variable_name*

The following script explores the integer data type.

```
USAGE="usage: decl_int.ksh"  # how to declare integers

 integer y       # declare y as an integer
 y=100           # assign an integer value to y
 print "y = $y"
# Now that y is an integer, you cannot assign a string value to it.
# y="Cat in the Hat"  # will usually cause an error

# Put an integer value into a string variable.
 x=150           # x is a string because you didn't declare it otherwise
 print "x = $x"
 x="Cat in the Hat"  # okay to assign non-numerical value to x
 print "x = $x"

# You can also initialize a variable when you declare it, as follows:
 integer z=1
```

What's the difference between **y** (the integer) and **x** (the string)? By specifying **y** as an integer, you are sacrificing the ability to perform a lot of useful string manipulation. On the other hand, doing math with **y** is faster than doing math with **x**. (The next chapter details math.) So, a good rule of thumb is to declare a variable as an integer if you intend to use it in mathematical operations only. Otherwise, let it stay a string.

Executing This Script

```
$ decl_int.ksh
y = 100
x = 150
x = Cat in the Hat
```

Declaring Constants

You declare constants with the **-r** (readonly) option of the **typeset** statement or with the **readonly** statement. Once you declare a constant, also known as a readonly variable, you cannot change its value.

```
USAGE="usage: decl_con.ksh" # how to declare constants

# Declare legs_per_dog as a constant.
 typeset -r legs_per_dog=4
 print "legs_per_dog = $legs_per_dog"
# legs_per_dog=6              # illegal to reassign its value

 print                        # print a blank line
# Declare greeting as a constant.
 typeset -r greeting="Ohio"
 print "greeting = $greeting"
# It is illegal to reassign the value of a constant, but let's try it
# anyway just to see what happens.
 greeting="Kohneecheewa"
```

Executing This Script

```
$ decl_con.ksh
legs_per_dog = 4

greeting = Ohio
decl_con.ksh[14]: ksh: greeting: is read only
```

By the way, the "14" that appears in the error message tells you that the error occurred at line number 14.

Declaring Arrays and Assigning Values to Them

The KornShell supports one-dimensional arrays of strings or integers. You cannot explicitly declare a variable as an array. Instead, the KornShell creates an array the first time you assign a value to it. Also, you cannot explicitly declare the size of an array; each array automatically holds up to 1024 values (or 512 values on some older KornShell implementations).

The first cell in an array is numbered 0. Therefore, array cells are numbered from 0 to 1023.

The following script creates two arrays—an array of strings called **animal** and an array of integers called **test_scores**—and assigns values to both arrays. You cannot explicitly declare the base data type of an array. By default, all arrays are arrays of strings. However, if you declare a variable as an integer and then use that variable as an array, then you've essentially created an array of integers.

```
USAGE="usage: decl_ary.ksh"  # declaring arrays and filling them
# Create an array of strings and assign some values to it.
 animal[0]="dog"          # the KornShell creates an array named animal
                          # and puts the string value "dog" in cell #0
 animal[1]="horse"        # put "horse" into cell #1
 animal[2]="pigeon"       # put "pigeon" into cell #2
# You don't have to assign values to all cells in the array.
# Here, skip cells 3, 4, and 5, and then assign a value to 6.
 animal[6]="monkey"       # put "monkey" into cell #6
# Note that cells 3, 4, and 5 contain the "null" value.

# Create an array of integers and assign some values to it.
 integer test_scores      # test_scores is now an integer
 test_scores[0]=100       # test_scores just became an array of integers
 test_scores[1]=95        # put 95 into cell #1
 test_scores[2]=97        # put 97 into cell #2
 print -n "Enter the score on the final exam: "
 read test_scores[3]      # have user assign value of cell #3
# test_scores[4]="pigeon"# illegal to put pigeon into array because
                          # pigeon isn't an integer value

# An alternate way to assign values to an array is to use the set -A
# statement.  For example, the following line creates an array of
# strings named flowers and assigns three values to it:
 set -A flowers gardenia "bird of paradise" hibiscus
# Not all implementations of the KornShell support set -A.
```

Executing This Script

```
$ decl_ary.ksh
Enter the score on the final exam: 96
```

Printing Values in an Array

The following script illustrates how to print an entire array or a specific value of an array.

```
USAGE="usage: pr_ary.ksh"  # printing array values

# Create an array of strings and assign four values to it:
 set -A flowers gardenia "bird of paradise" hibiscus rose

# Print individual cells of the array:
 print "Cell #0 contains ${flowers[0]}"
 print "Cell #1 contains ${flowers[1]}"
 cell_number=2
 print "Cell #$cell_number contains ${flowers[$cell_number]}"
 print       # blank line

# Print all the elements of an array like this:
 print "The entire array contains -- ${flowers[*]}"
# or like this:
 print "The entire array contains -- ${flowers[@]}"
# See Chapter 9 for the distinction between these two ways of printing
# all the elements of an array.
```

Executing This Script

```
$ pr_ary.ksh
Cell #0 contains gardenia
Cell #1 contains bird of paradise
Cell #2 contains hibiscus

The entire array contains gardenia bird of paradise hibiscus rose
The entire array contains gardenia bird of paradise hibiscus rose
```

! BEWARE: Common Array Mistakes !

The pair of braces { } confuses a lot of array users. Don't use the braces when the name of the array appears on the left side of the assignment operator (=); for example:

```
array[2]="tulip"          # right
${array[2]}="tulip"       # wrong
```

However, you must use the braces when the name of the array appears on the right side of the assignment operator; for example:

```
flower=${array[2]}        # right
flower=array[2]           # wrong
```

Putting the two sides together, the following statement assigns one element of an array to another:

```
array[3]=${array[2]}      # right
```

In general, you should use the braces when printing an array element. For example, suppose you assign the value "tulip" to **array[2]**. Here are the right and wrong ways to print that value:

```
  array[2]="tulip"        # assign a value to array[2]
  print "${array[2]}"     # right; the KornShell will print "tulip"
# print "array[2]"        # wrong
# print "$array[2]"       # wrong
```

By the way, the expression **$array** means the value of the first element of **array**. In other words, **$array** is a synonym for **array[0]**.

Chapter 4
Math

This chapter explains how to perform mathematical operations.

If You're New to Programming...

The KornShell supports simple math. You can perform addition, multiplication, subtraction, and two kinds of division.

The important thing for beginners to remember is that the KornShell does math only on integer values. The KornShell cannot perform math on floating-point (real) values. (Actually, there are a few KornShell versions that do support floating-point values, but since this isn't a standard feature, we're going to ignore it.)

Also, if you've never programmed before, you may try to be overly polite and use commas (or periods in some countries) to break up large numbers. Don't do it. For example, here are some right and wrong ways to represent the integer ten thousand:

```
10000  # right
10,000 # wrong
10.000 # wrong
```

If You're an Experienced Programmer...

The KornShell supports the fundamental mathematical operations you'd expect to find in any popular compiler language. However, it doesn't go much beyond the basics. You can add, subtract, multiply, and divide integers, but you can't perform any transcendental functions (like cosines) or perform any floating-point operations. The KornShell provides math features as a simple convenience. After all, your script may need to perform an occasional math operation. Realistically though, the KornShell would not be a good choice when you need to average a million integers. When you need to tackle a mathematically intensive problem, use a compiled language. Simply put, math operations run much more slowly in a KornShell script than in a compiled program. On the other hand, averaging a hundred integers might take a KornShell script only a second or two longer than a comparable FORTRAN program. And since you can usually code and debug KornShell scripts faster than FORTRAN programs, the extra second might be a small price to pay.

Beyond the basic mathematical operations, the KornShell lets you specify a variety of integer bases. For example, you can specify hexadecimal output. The KornShell also supports five bit operators.

The range of values that can be stored in an integer variable is machine dependent. All KornShell implementations store integers in at least 16 bits; most store integers in 32 bits. By default, all integers are signed.

Table 2 lists all the mathematical operators.

Table 2. Summary of Math Operators

Operator	Operation	Example of operation	Result
+	Addition	((y = 7 + 10))	17
–	Subtraction	((y = 10 - 3))	7
*	Multiplication	((y = 5 * 6))	30
/	Division	((y = 37 / 5))	7
%	Modulo division	((y = 37 % 5))	2
<<	Left shift bits	((y = 2#1011 << 2))	2#101100
>>	Right shift bits	((y = 2#1011 >> 2))	2#10
&	Bitwise AND	((y = 2#1010 & 2#1100))	2#1000
^	Bitwise exclusive OR	((y = 2#1010 % 2#1100))	2#1010
|	Bitwise OR	((y = 2#1010 | 2#1100))	2#1110

* You can call a desk calculator program (like the UNIX utility **bc**) in order to perform floating-point operations or transcendental functions.

Addition, Subtraction, and Multiplication

This script demonstrates addition, subtraction, and multiplication. In general, you should perform math operations inside a pair of double parentheses; for example:

```
((answer = 15 + x))  # assign the sum of 15 and x to variable answer
```

You can place any amount of white space inside the double parentheses. Extra white space may make your script easier to read.

```
USAGE="usage: math1.ksh"  # demonstrates +, -, and *
# Declare variables x, y, and z as integers.
 integer x=5              # assign 5 as the starting value of x
 integer y=7              # assign 7 as the starting value of y
 integer z

 ((z = x + y))            # add x and y and assign the sum to z
 print "$x plus $y is $z"

 ((z = x - y))            # subtract y from x and assign the sum to z
 print "$x minus $y is $z"

 ((z = x * y))            # multiply x and y and assign the product to z
 print "$x times $y is $z"

# You can also perform mathematical operations on string variables;
# that is, you don't have to declare a variable as an integer in
# order to use it in a mathematical operation.
 print -n "\nHow many tigers does the zoo have? "
 read tigers    # tigers is a string variable
 print -n "How many lions does the zoo have? "
 read lions     # lions is a string variable
 ((cats = tigers + lions))  # cats is a string variable.
 print "The zoo has a total of $cats cats."

# Most implementations of the KornShell let you perform math operations
# inside the print statement.
 print "The zoo has a total of $((tigers + lions)) cats."
```

Executing This Script

```
$ math1.ksh
5 plus 7 is 12
5 minus 7 is -2
5 times 7 is 35

How many tigers does the zoo have? 20
How many lions does the zoo have? 30
The zoo has a total of 50 cats.
The zoo has a total of 50 cats.
```

By the way, the dollar sign ($) is optional within ((...)) operations such as:

```
((y = y + 50))
```

By omitting the dollar sign, you are telling the KornShell to do straight integer mathematics. If you had written the statement this way instead:

```
((y = $y + 50))
```

the KornShell would have temporarily converted the value of **y** to a string, done the addition, and then converted **y** back to an integer. The moral of the story is to avoid the dollar sign within ((...)) operations.

Division

Do you remember learning long division? Before you knew anything about fractions and decimals, you learned that each division problem yielded two answers: a quotient and a remainder. For example, if your teacher asked you what 16 divided by 3 is, you answered, "The quotient is 5 and the remainder is 1."

The KornShell has a similarly simplistic view of division. Since each division answer has two parts, the KornShell provides two division operators: one for the quotient (/) and one for the remainder (%). The % operator is often called the *modulo division operator*.

```
USAGE="usage: division.ksh"  # two kinds of division operations

 print -n "How far did you run (in meters)? "
 read distance

 ((kilometers = distance / 1000))
 ((remaining_meters = distance % 1000))

 print "You ran $kilometers kilometers and $remaining_meters meters."
```

Executing This Script

```
$ division.ksh
How far did you run (in meters)? 2700
You ran 2 kilometers and 700 meters.

$ division.ksh
How far did you run (in meters)? 700
You ran 0 kilometers and 700 meters.
```

! BEWARE: Floating–Point Numbers !

The KornShell cannot perform mathematical operations on floating–point numbers. However, if you specify a floating–point number in a KornShell script, the KornShell will not issue an error message. Instead, the KornShell will convert the floating–point number to an integer.

The KornShell converts a floating–point number to an integer by truncating it. Thus, if you specify the value 7.9 in a script, the KornShell will convert it to the integer value 7 as in the following example.

```
x=7.9
y=2.4
((z = x + y))
print "$x + $y is $z"
```

Executing the preceding script produces the following output:

```
7.9 + 2.4 is 9
```

If you must do floating–point calculations, use a high–level language or a utility (like the UNIX **awk** utility) that can handle floating–point numbers.

Some KornShell implementations can perform floating–point arithmetic; however, this capability is not yet standard.

Grouping Mathematical Operations

As in algebra, the KornShell lets you use a pair of single parentheses to group mathematical operations. For example, consider the following attempt to convert a Fahrenheit temperature to centigrade:

```
((centigrade = fahrenheit - 32 * 5 / 9))        # wrong
```

Which of the three math operations (–, *, or /) will the KornShell execute first? In fact, the KornShell will do the multiplication first, the division second, and the subtraction third. The result of all that math will be a wrong answer.

Let's try it again. This time we'll use pairs of parentheses to force the correct order of operations. The following statement causes the KornShell to do the subtraction first, the multiplication second, and the division third:

```
((centigrade = ((fahrenheit - 32) * 5) / 9))   # right
```

```
USAGE="usage: math_grp.ksh"  # grouping math operations

 tigers=20
 lions=30
# Tell the KornShell to add tigers and lions together and then multiply
# that sum by 4.
 ((cat_legs = (tigers + lions) * 4))
 print "There are $cat_legs cat legs in the zoo."

# Calculate a percentage.
 print -n "\nHow many are in favor: "
 read favor
 print -n "How many oppose: "
 read oppose
 ((percent_who_favor = (favor * 100) / (favor + oppose) ))    # right
# Although the next statement is algebraically equivalent to the
# previous one, the next statement will almost certainly assign the
# incorrect answer 0 to variable percent_who_favor.
# ((percent_who_favor = (favor / (favor + oppose)) * 100) )) # wrong
 print "Percent in favor is %$percent_who_favor."
```

Executing This Script

```
$ math_grp.ksh
There are 200 cat legs in the zoo.

How many are in favor: 723
How many oppose: 534
Percent in favor is %57.
```

! BEWARE: Common Mistakes in Math Operations !

Here now are antidotes for a few common mathematical poisons.

First, don't forget that you have to enclose the entire mathematical operation within a double pair of parentheses. A single pair of parentheses has a completely different meaning to the KornShell.

```
(z = x + y)                  # wrong
((z = x + y))                # right
```

Second, if you do use pairs of single parentheses to group mathematical expressions, then make sure that the number of opening parentheses equals the number of closing parentheses. For example, carefully count the opening and closing parentheses in the following two operations:

```
((z = (x + y) * (a + b))      # wrong, missing one )
((z = (x + y) * (a + b) ))    # right
```

Don't be afraid to use extra white space inside the double parentheses to clarify your script.

Third, the KornShell cannot hold an infinitely high positive number or infinitely low negative number. In fact, the legal range of integer values is –2,147,483,648 to +2,147,483,647 (a tad over two billion). The KornShell will not issue an error message if you exceed one of these limits; however, when you examine the results of the operation, you'll see bizarre numbers. For example, if you multiply two billion by three, you'd expect the answer (stored in variable **debt**) to be six billion.

```
((debt = 2000000000 * 3))
```

However, the actual value stored in **debt** will be the nonsensical number 1705032704.

Fourth, printing negative numbers is a little tricky. For example, you'd certainly expect the KornShell to print the value –2 as a result of these two statements:

```
((loss = 5 - 7))
print "$loss"                # wrong
```

but the KornShell actually prints this message instead:

```
ksh: print: bad option(s)
```

The root of this puzzling problem is that all KornShell options start with a minus sign –; therefore, the KornShell thinks that you are trying to specify –2 as an option to the **print** statement. Use **print –R** instead of just plain **print** to correct this problem; for example:

```
((loss = 5 - 7))
print -R "$loss"             # right
```

Finally, note that = is an assignment operator. However, it is pretty easy to confuse the assignment operator with the equality operator. (Chapter 6 explains this distinction.)

Binary, Octal, Hex, etc.

The following script demonstrates how to specify integers in various bases. By default, the KornShell assumes that all input and output numbers are base 10 (decimal) integers. The following four statements illustrate how to declare integer variables of different bases. Incidentally, you can specify any base from 2 to 36 inclusive.

```
USAGE="usage: base.ksh"  # integers in different bases

 typeset -i   x      # declares x as a base 10 integer (default)
 typeset -i2  y      # declares y as a base 2 (binary) integer
 typeset -i8  z      # declares z as a base 8 (octal) integer
 typeset -i16 h      # declares h as a base 16 (hexadecimal) integer

# Here, we convert an integer value between these bases.
 print -n "Enter an integer: "
 read x
 h=z=y=x # assign the value of x to y, z, and h
# The KornShell outputs nondefault bases with the syntax
#
#       base#number
#
# Note that the # sign is not a comment in this context. In fact,
# the # sign is never a comment when preceded by a number.
 print "Translated into base 2, $x is $y"
 print "Translated into base 8, $x is $z"
 print "Translated into base 16, $x is $h"
```

Executing This Script

```
$ base.ksh
Enter an integer: 125
Translated into base 2, 125 is 2#1111101
Translated into base 8, 125 is 8#175
Translated into base 16, 125 is 16#7d

$ base.ksh      # notice on next line that user inputs a binary value
Enter an integer: 2#11011
Translated into base 2, 2#11011 is 2#11011
Translated into base 8, 2#11011 is 8#33
Translated into base 16, 2#11011 is 16#1b
```

Outputting a Certain Number of Digits

You can use the syntax

typeset -Z*n*

to specify the number *n* of digits for **print** to output. Paradoxically, you can use the **-Z** attribute only on strings. In other words, you can't use it to control the output of variables declared as integers.

Here's a script that uses **typeset -Z5** to set the number of output digits at five.

```
USAGE="usage: digits.ksh"    # control number of output digits

 typeset -Z5 salary       # variable salary will contain exactly
                          # five digits when output
 print -n "Enter a salary: "
 read salary
 print "salary = $salary"
```

Executing This Script

```
$ digits.ksh
Enter a salary: 32500
salary = 32500

$ digits.ksh    # assign a value having fewer than five digits
Enter a salary: 7154
salary = 07154
```

If you try to assign a value that has more than five digits, the **print** statement will display only the last five digits; for example:

```
$ digits.ksh    # assign a value having more than five digits
Enter a salary: 123456
salary = 23456
```

Chapter 5

Pattern Matching

This chapter explains how to specify patterns that you can use in certain KornShell commands or statements.

If You're New to Programming...

An overly used (and macabre) joke says that "Close only counts in horseshoes and hand grenades." Well, it turns out that "close" also counts in the KornShell. For example, the word "elephant" obviously matches the word "elephant." But if you desire, you might tell the KornShell that the words "elephants" and "elephantine" are also sufficiently close enough to "elephant" to count as matches. You might even tell the KornShell that any word starting with the letter "e" counts as a match.

You define "close" in the KornShell by specifying a *pattern*. You can then use the KornShell to determine whether or not a given string matches a pattern.

You use one or more *wildcards* to specify a pattern. The term wildcard should remind you of card games like poker. If "deuces are wild" in a poker hand, you can pretend that the deuce is some other card. Similarly, the KornShell wildcard ? matches any single character. Unlike poker though, the KornShell supports many different kinds of wildcards. For example, the KornShell wildcard **[a–m]** matches any lowercase letter from **a** to **m**.

If You're an Experienced Programmer...

Suppose you had to write code to answer the following question: Given a variable-length string, does the string start with the letters **ch**, contain at least one digit, and end with a consonant?

You would probably find it rather difficult to answer that question with your average workaday high-level language. Oh sure, you might be able to call a library routine that would search for substrings. That might help a little. But, admit it, unless you're using a special-purpose pattern-matching language, you'd probably be better off with a shell language than with FORTRAN or C. Among the shell languages, the KornShell is particularly rich in pattern-matching constructs.

Longtime UNIX users will be comforted to learn that the KornShell supports the familiar *****, **?**, and **[ ]** wildcards of other UNIX shells. However, the KornShell also supports the following five additional wildcard forms:

?(*pattern1* | *pattern2*... | *patternN*)	matches zero or one of the specified patterns.
@(*pattern1* | *pattern2*... | *patternN*)	matches exactly one of the specified patterns.
*(*pattern1* | *pattern2*... | *patternN*)	matches zero, one, or more of the specified patterns.
+(*pattern1* | *pattern2*... | *patternN*)	matches one or more of the specified patterns.
!(*pattern1* | *pattern2*... | *patternN*)	matches any pattern except one of the specified patterns.

For Everyone

Note that this chapter does not contain any complete KornShell scripts. That's because the wildcards are building blocks of other statements and commands described later in the book. More specifically, you can use wildcard(s):

- As arguments to certain operating system commands (such as the UNIX commands **rm** and **ls**).
- Within a **case** statement or a **[[...]]** condition to compare a string to a pattern. See Chapter 6 for examples.
- Within a **for** or **select** statement to expand a pattern into a set of pathnames. See Chapter 7 and Chapter 8 for examples.
- Within a **set** statement to expand arguments into the set of positional parameters. See Chapter 9 for examples.
- Within string manipulation statements. See Chapter 13 for details.

?

Matches exactly one character. The character could be any single ASCII value.

Pattern: `car?`
Matches: any four-character string whose first three characters are **car**
Possible Matches: `card, cart, cara, carA, car2`
Does Not Match: `car, carts, car54`

Pattern: `ca?e`
Matches: any four-character string whose first two letters are **ca** and last letter is **e**
Possible Matches: `cave, ca3e, cabe, caRe`
Does Not Match: `cae, ca54e, caves`

Pattern: `?ab?e`
Matches: any five-character string whose second and third letters are **ab** and last letter is **e**
Possible Matches: `cable, table, 5abTe`
Does Not Match: `abe, babe, tables`

Pattern: `???`
Matches: any three-character string
Possible Matches: `act, now, 532, NBA, N5t`
Does Not Match: `am, acts`

[char1char2...charN]

Matches exactly one character from a specified set of characters.

Pattern: `car[det]`
Matches: the three letters **car** followed by **d**, **e**, or **t**
Only Matches: `card, care, cart`

Pattern: `[aeiouAEIOU]`
Matches: any one vowel
Only Matches: `a, e, i, o, u, A, E, I, O, U`

Pattern: `[0-9]`
Matches: one digit; that is, this pattern matches any character from 0 to 9
Only Matches: `0, 1, 2, 3, 4, 5, 6, 7, 8, 9`

Pattern: `[2-9][0-9][0-9]`
Matches: any integer between 200 and 999
Possible Matches: `235, 762, 987`
Does Not Match: `185, 2000`

Pattern: `[a-z][a-z][a-z][a-z]s`
Matches: any five-letter lowercase string ending in **s**
Possible Matches: `cards, lakes, boats, glbxs`
Does Not Match: `CARDS, Lakes, bo3ts`

Pattern: `[a-zA-Z][a-zA-Z][a-zA-Z]`
Matches: any three-letter string
Possible Matches: `rat, Rat, RAT, raT`
Does Not Match: `123, r3t`

Pattern: `car[!det]`
Matches: any four-character string whose first three letters are **car** and whose last character is anything other than **d**, **e**, or **t**; (the **!** means don't match these next characters)
Possible Matches: `cars, carb, cara, carn, car3, carD`
Does Not Match: `card, care, cart`

Pattern: `st[\-\]\!\\]`
Matches: any three-character string whose first two letters are **st** and whose last character is **–**, **]**, **!**, or ****; (the **** preceding each of these characters is the escape character which turns off the special meaning of the character that follows it)
Only Matches: `st-, st], st!, st\`

*

Matches zero or more characters. That is, the * matches a null pattern or any other pattern.

Pattern: `car*`
Matches: the three letters **car** followed by no characters, one character, or many characters
Possible Matches: `car, cars, car54, carbohydrate, carOB`

Pattern: `*`
Matches: just about anything (see bottom of page for exceptions); this is the wildest of wildcards
Possible Matches: `care, 15adfaseEEAS, 154, Tedwardo`

Pattern: `*.bak`
Matches: any string ending in **.bak**
Possible Matches: `153.bak, card.bak, Apple.bak`

Pattern: `c*r*s`
Matches: any string starting with **c**, ending with **s**, and containing **r**
Possible Matches: `crs, cars, cr3s, cards, chairs, charbroilers, c3r35234s`

! BEWARE: Matching Filenames !

To the KornShell, just about everything is a string. For instance, a pathname is a string. You can use wildcards to match any kind of string. For example, the pattern **A*** would match any string, pathname or not, beginning with uppercase A. However, the rules for matching a pattern to a pathname are slightly different from the rules for matching a pattern to a string that isn't a pathname. In particular, when you're comparing patterns to pathnames

- Wildcards do not match pathnames that start with a dot (.). For example, the pattern * (by itself) would not match pathname **.startup** because **.startup** begins with a dot. To match the dot portion of the pathname, you must explicitly specify a dot as part of the pattern. Therefore, the pattern **.*** would match **.startup**.
- Wildcards do not match pathnames containing the slash (/) character. To match the slash portion of the pathname, you must explicitly specify a slash as part of the pattern. For example, the pattern * would not match pathname **flo/jo**; however, the pattern */* would.

?(pattern1 |pattern2... |patternN)

Matches zero or one of the specified patterns. You can specify any number of patterns between the parentheses. If you specify more than one pattern, then you have to separate the patterns with the | operator.

Pattern: `car?(t)`
Only Matches: `car, cart`

Pattern: `car?([ted])`
Only Matches: `car, cart, care, card`

Pattern: `care?(ful|less|free)`
Only Matches: `care, careful, careless, carefree`

Pattern: `car?([a-z]|bohydrate|ob)`
Matches: the words **car, carbohydrate**, and **carob**, plus any four-letter lowercase word whose first three letters are **car**
Possible Matches: `car, cara, carb, carc, carz, carbohydrate, carob`
Does Not Match: `carA, car3, carzbohydrate, carobs`

Pattern: `car?(?|??)`
Matches: any three-, four-, or five-character string whose first three characters are **car**
Possible Matches: `car, card, carob, car54, car2z`
Does Not Match: `carbon, cave`

! BEWARE: White Space Within Patterns !

If you specify any white space within a pattern, the KornShell will treat the white space literally; in other words, the KornShell will treat the white space as part of the pattern. This can be a problem for many users who sprinkle white space liberally in order to make scripts more readable. However, you shouldn't put white space into a pattern unless you really mean it to be part of the pattern. For example, consider the following patterns:

Pattern `care?(ful | less| free)`
Only Matches: `care, careful , care less, care free`
Does Not Match: `careful, careless, carefree`

@(pattern1 | pattern2... | patternN)

Matches exactly one of the specified patterns. This pattern is identical to the pattern on the previous page except that this pattern does not match the null string*, but the previous pattern does.

Pattern: `car@(t)`
Only Match: `cart`
Does Not Match: `car`
(This pattern is functionally identical to **car[t]**.)

Pattern: `car@([ted])`
Only Matches: `cart, care, card`
Does Not Match: `car`

Pattern: `care@(ful|less|free)`
Only Matches: `careful, careless, carefree`
Does Not Match: `care`

Pattern: `@(orange|lemon|lime|grapefruit)`
Only Matches: `orange, lemon, lime, grapefruit`
(This pattern is similar to an enumerated data type declaration in C or Pascal.)

Pattern: `car@(?|??)`
Matches: any four- or five-character string whose first three characters are **car**
Possible Matches: `card, carob, car54`

---

* unless you explicitly list the null string `""` as one of the patterns.

*(pattern1|pattern2...|patternN)

Matches zero or more of the specified patterns.

Pattern: `car*(t)`
Matches: **car** or a string starting with **car** followed by one or more **t**'s
Possible Matches: `car, cart, cartt, carttt, cartttt`
Does Not Match: `caret, carttt3t`

Pattern: `car*([ted])`
Matches: **car** or a string starting with **car** followed by any combination of **t**'s, **e**'s, and **d**'s
Possible Matches: `car, cart, care, card, carte, carted, caret, careteeted`
Does Not Match: `t, e, te, carets`

Pattern: `*([a-z])`
Matches: the null string or any string containing only lowercase letters
Possible Matches: `zoo, keeper, tiger`
Does Not Match: `3, qb7, Kyoto`

Pattern: `*([0-9])`
Matches: the null string or any unsigned integer
Possible Matches: `5, 500, 6329531`
Does Not Match: `5.2, -500, +6329531`

Pattern: `care*(ful|less|ly)`
Only Matches: `care, careful, careless, carefully, carelessly`

Pattern: `?([+-])*([0-9]).*([0-9])`
Matches: the null string or a floating-point number that contains a decimal point
Possible Matches: `+523.632, -7.2`
Does Not Match: `5.23e2, -7`

Pattern: `*(truly|very|large| |,)`
Matches: the null string, or any combination of the words **truly**, **very**, and **large**, possibly separated by commas
Possible Matches:
`very large`
`truly very large`
`very, very, large`
Does Not Match:
`Very large`
`large: very large`

+ (*pattern1* | *pattern2...* | *patternN*)

Matches one or more of the specified patterns in any order. This pattern is identical to the pattern on the previous page except that this pattern does not match the null string*.

Pattern: `car+(t)`
Matches: any string beginning with **car** and followed by one or more **t**'s
Possible Matches: `cart, cartt, carttt, cartttt`
Does Not Match: `car, caret, carrot`

Pattern: `car+([ted])`
Matches: a string starting with **car** and followed by any combination of **t**'s and **e**'s
Possible Matches: `cart, care, card, carte, carted, caret, careteeted`
Does Not Match: `car, t, e, te, carets`

Pattern: `+([a-z])`
Matches: any string containing only lowercase letters
Possible Matches: `zoo, keeper, tiger`
Does Not Match: `"", 3, qb7, Kyoto`

Pattern: `care+(ful|less|ly)`
Only Matches: `careful, careless, carefully, carelessly`
Does Not Match: `care`

Pattern: `chapter+([0-9])`
Matches: any string beginning with **chapter** and ending with an integer
Possible Matches: `chapter5, chapter11, chapter108`
Does Not Match: `chapter, chapters, chapter2.bak, 1chapter`

---

* unless you explicitly list the null string `""` as one of the patterns.

!(*pattern1*|*pattern2...*|*patternN*)

Matches anything *except* one of the specified patterns. Some users find this pattern rather difficult to understand. An unconventional way to think about the **!** pattern is with the following equation:

!(*pattern1*|*pattern2...*|*patternN*) = * - @(*pattern1*|*pattern2...*|*patternN*)

Pattern: `car!(t)`
Matches: any string starting with **car**, except for **cart**
Possible Matches: `car, cars, car54, carambolaS, carrot`
Does Not Match: `cart`

Pattern: `!(*.bak)`
Matches: any string that does not end in **.bak**
Possible Matches: `car, 35, QB7`
Does Not Match: `car.bak, 35.bak, QB7.bak`

Pattern: `car!(*.bak|*.bu|*_1)`
Matches: any string starting with **car** that does not end in **.bak, .bu,** or **_1**
Possible Matches: `car, car54, carob`
Does Not Match: `car.bak, car54.bu, carob_1`

Simple Commands Containing Patterns

The UNIX command **ls** lists the names of all the objects in the current directory.

```
$ ls
APPLES    Nancy    Nantes    apples    bananas   net.bak
```

You can specify a pattern as an argument to the **ls** command. For example, the following command lists the names of all objects beginning with **N**:

```
$ ls N*
Nancy    Nantes
```

Here is how the KornShell performs the preceding command. First, the KornShell expands (*globs*) the pattern into a list of filenames. Then, the **ls** command runs using the list of filenames as input. In other words, although you've entered **ls N***, the **ls** command actually executes the following:

```
$ ls Nancy Nantes
```

Here are a few more **ls** commands containing patterns:

```
$ ls [Nn]*                     # list objects beginning with N or n
Nancy    Nantes    net.bak

$ ls *n*                       # list objects containing n
Nancy    Nantes    bananas   net.bak

$ ls [a-z]*                    # list objects starting with a lowercase letter
apples   bananas   net.bak

$ ls +([a-z])                  # list objects consisting of lowercase letters only
apples   bananas

$ ls *.bak                     # list objects that end in .bak
net.bak

$ ls !(*.bak)                  # list objects that do not end in .bak
APPLES    Nancy    Nantes    apples    bananas

$ ls *(apples|bananas|carambolas) # list objects that have one of these names
apples   bananas

$ print *n*                    # list objects containing n
Nancy    Nantes    bananas   net.bak
```

Table 3. KornShell Wildcards

<table>
<tr><th>Wildcard</th><th>Matches...</th><th>Matches null?</th></tr>
<tr><td>?</td><td>any one character</td><td>no</td></tr>
<tr><td>[char1char2...charN]</td><td>any one character from the specified list</td><td>no</td></tr>
<tr><td>[!char1char2...charN]</td><td>any one character other than one from the specified list</td><td>no</td></tr>
<tr><td>[char1–charN]</td><td>any character between char1 and charN inclusive</td><td>no</td></tr>
<tr><td>[!char1–charN]</td><td>any character other than between char1 and charN inclusive</td><td>no</td></tr>
<tr><td>*</td><td>any character or any group of characters</td><td>yes</td></tr>
<tr><td>?(pattern1|pattern2...|patternN)</td><td>zero or one of the specified patterns</td><td>yes</td></tr>
<tr><td>@(pattern1|pattern2...|patternN)</td><td>exactly one of the specified patterns</td><td>no</td></tr>
<tr><td>*(pattern1|pattern2...|patternN)</td><td>zero, one, or more of the specified patterns</td><td>yes</td></tr>
<tr><td>+(pattern1|pattern2...|patternN)</td><td>one or more of the specified patterns</td><td>no</td></tr>
<tr><td>!(pattern1|pattern2...|patternN)</td><td>any pattern except one of the specified patterns</td><td>yes</td></tr>
</table>

Chapter 6
Conditions

This chapter teaches you how to evaluate conditions.

If You're New to Programming...

A condition serves the same purpose in computer languages as in human languages. For example, here is a condition expressed in English:

```
"If you are age 62 or older, then the movie costs $3.00; otherwise,
the movie costs $6.00."
```

and here is the same condition expressed in the KornShell language:

```
if ((age >= 62))
then
   movie_cost='$3.00'
else
   movie_cost='$6.00'
fi
```

The only peculiar word in the KornShell syntax is **fi** (**if** spelled backwards). When speaking English, you mark the end of a declaration by lowering your tone. When writing English, you mark the end of a sentence with a period. Similarly, when writing in the KornShell, you mark the end of an **if** statement with **fi**.

The KornShell supports two different statements, **if** and **case**, for evaluating conditions. Although their syntax differs greatly, they both do roughly the same kinds of evaluations. Since they serve the same purpose, how do you choose which statement to use? It's usually a matter of style. Many programmers prefer **case** when evaluating a variable that has many possible values, but prefer **if** when evaluating a variable that has few possible values.

If You're an Experienced Programmer...

Every major high-level computer language supports some way to evaluate conditions. The keywords and syntax may vary, but there is always some way to branch depending on the outcome of a test.

The KornShell supports two statements, **if** and **case**, for evaluating conditions. Syntactically, **if** and **case** are very similar to condition-evaluating statements found in many high-level languages, including C and Pascal. However, despite these similarities in syntax, the KornShell can evaluate conditions more flexibly than either C or Pascal. That's because **if** and **case** in the KornShell can compare the value of a variable to a pattern.

In addition, you can use the **if** statement to run tests on objects in order to answer questions such as:

- Does a particular object exist?
- What kind of object is this? For example, is the object a directory, a file, or perhaps a link?
- Do you have permission to execute this object?

Tests on Numbers and Strings

The KornShell provides six different kinds of numerical comparisons (shown in Table 4) and eight different kinds of string comparisons (shown in Table 5). The comparisons are also known as *tests*.

Place numerical tests inside a pair of double parentheses ((...)) and place string tests inside a pair of double square brackets **[[...]]**. But what is the difference between a numerical test and a string test?

A numerical test compares two numerical values. The confusing part is that a variable with the string data type can hold a numerical value. Therefore, if you specify **$*variable*** inside a numerical test, it isn't mandatory that *variable* have the integer data type. However, it is mandatory that **$*variable*** evaluate to an integer value.

A string test compares two string values. If you specify **$*variable*** inside a string test, *variable* cannot have been declared as an integer data type.

Every test returns either true or false. For example, the following numerical test will return true if the value of **x** is equal to 6 and false otherwise:

```
((x == 6))                    # == operator inside ((...))
```

Now consider the following string comparison that returns true if **s1** and **s2** are equal and false otherwise:

```
[[ $s1 = $s2 ]]               # = operator inside [[...]]
```

Let's focus on white space for a moment. Within a pair of double parentheses ((...)), you can use as much or as little white space as you desire. For example, the following numerical tests are all syntactically correct:

```
((x == 6))                    # right
(( x==6 ))                    # right
(( x == 6 ))                  # right
```

However, inside a pair of double square brackets **[[...]]**, you *must* specify white space between every component. For example, compare the right and wrong ways to compare strings **s1** and **s2**:

```
[[ $s1 = $s2 ]]               # right
[[$s1 = $s2]]                 # wrong, need white space around [ and ]
[[ $s1=$s2 ]]                 # wrong, need white space around operator
```

Another syntactic point worth mentioning is that, inside ((...)), you don't need to place dollar signs in front of variable names.

Within **[[...]]**, you generally don't need to put quotes around the string arguments. You need to do this only when the KornShell might mistakenly interpret part of a string as a wildcard.

Table 4. Tests on Numbers

Test	Returns true if...
((*number1* == *number2*))	*number1* equals *number2*
((*number1* != *number2*))	*number1* does not equal *number2*
((*number1* < *number2*))	*number1* is less than *number2*
((*number1* > *number2*))	*number1* is greater than *number2*
((*number1* <= *number2*))	*number1* is less than or equal to *number2*
((*number1* >= *number2*))	*number1* is greater than or equal to *number2*

Table 5. Tests on Strings

Test	Returns true if...
[[*string1* = *string2*]]	*string1* equals *string2*
[[*string* = *pattern*]]	*string* matches *pattern*
[[*string1* != *string2*]]	*string1* does not equal *string2*
[[*string* != *pattern*]]	*string* does not match *pattern*
[[*string1* < *string2*]]	*string1* precedes *string2* in lexical order
[[*string1* > *string2*]]	*string1* follows *string2* in lexical order
[[**-z** *string*]]	*string's* length is zero; that is, *string* holds null value
[[**-n** *string*]]	*string's* length is nonzero; that is, *string* does not hold null value

Comparing Numbers with if

The KornShell supports lots of different syntaxes for comparing numbers. All the syntaxes accomplish pretty much the same thing; however, some syntaxes are more equal than others. This book uses Syntax #1 only, but we do present the others so that if you do encounter them in older KornShell and Bourne shell scripts they won't look completely alien to you.

```
USAGE="usage: if_num.ksh"  # demonstrates if/then with numbers

 print -n "Enter two numbers: "
 read x y
 if ((x == y))              # Syntax 1; use this one
 then
   print "You entered the same number twice."
 fi
 if test $x -eq $y          # Syntax 2; -eq is an old version of ==
 then
   print "You entered the same number twice."
 fi
 if let "$x == $y"          # Syntax 3
 then
   print "You entered the same number twice."
 fi
 if [ $x -eq $y ]           # Syntax 4
 then
   print "You entered the same number twice."
 fi
 if [[ $x -eq $y ]]         # Syntax 5
 then
   print "You entered the same number twice."
 fi
```

Executing This Script

```
$ if_num.ksh  # no match
Enter two numbers: 5 7

$ if_num.ksh  # a match
Enter two numbers: 5 5
You entered the same number twice.
You entered the same number twice.
You entered the same number twice.
You entered the same number twice.
You entered the same number twice.
```

! BEWARE: Common Mistakes Using if with Numbers !

Beginning KornShell programmers often have a tough time mastering the syntax of numerical comparisons. We now examine a few common mistakes.

If you are accustomed to programming in the C language, the temptation to exclude the keyword **then** will be very strong. Resist that temptation; **then** is mandatory. If you omit **then**, the KornShell will probably issue the following error message when you run the script:

```
syntax error: `fi´ unexpected
```

Don't mistake the KornShell's double equal sign operator == for the single equal sign operator =. The == operator tells the KornShell to compare two numbers. The = operator tells the KornShell to assign the value on the right to the variable on the left. For example, compare these two statements:

```
if ((x = y))     # assign value of y to x
if ((x == y))    # compare value of y to value of x
```

Another common mistake is to type a single pair of parentheses around the condition instead of a double pair of parentheses; for example:

```
if ((x == y))    # right
if (x == y)      # wrong, causes the error message, "x: not found"
```

Compound Statements

The following script demonstrates how to associate multiple commands with a condition. In the **if_numbers** example earlier in this chapter, we specified only one command (a **print** statement) with **then**. However, you can put multiple lines of code in between **then** and **fi**. Unlike some high-level languages (like C or Pascal), you do not mark the boundaries of such compound statements with BEGIN statements and END statements or { } pairs.

```
USAGE="usage: compound.ksh"  # multiple commands after then
 print -n "Enter a year: "
 read year

# Associating one command with a condition:
 if (( (year % 2) == 0 ))
 then
   print "$year is even."
 fi

# Associating multiple commands with a condition:
 if (( (year % 4) == 0 ))
 then
   print "$year is divisible by four."
   print "Perhaps it is a leap year."
   print "Perhaps it is an Olympic year."
 fi

# Associating zero commands with a condition.
# The colon : is called the null statement.  In the following context,
# the null statement acts as a placeholder.
 if (( (year % 47) == 0 ))
 then
   :    # We'll add some commands later.
 fi
# If we had omitted the colon and just left a blank line, then the
# KornShell would have issued an error message.
```

Executing This Script

```
$ compound.ksh
Enter a year: 1992
1992 is even.
1992 is divisible by four.
Perhaps it is a leap year.
Perhaps it is an Olympic year.
```

else and elif

In the previous **if/then** example, the KornShell executed statements only when the test was true. By comparison, this next script shows you how to execute one set of commands when the test is true and another set when the test is false.

```
USAGE="usage: if_else.ksh"  # demonstrates else and elif

 print -n "Enter two integers: "
 read  n1 n2

# This statement does only one test.
 if ((n1 < 0))          # here is the test
 then                   # the test was true
   print "The first integer is negative."
 else                   # the test was false
   print "The first integer is non-negative."
 fi

# This statement does two tests.
 if ((n2 < 0))          # here is the first test
 then                   # the first test was true
   print "The second integer is negative."
 elif ((n2 == 0))       # here is the second test
 then                   # the second test was true
   print "The second integer is zero."
 else                   # the first and second tests were both false
   print "The second integer is positive."
 fi
```

Executing This Script

```
$ if_else.ksh
Enter two integers: 5 -7
The first integer is non-negative.
The second integer is negative.
```

```
$ if_else.ksh
Enter two integers: -5 7
The first integer is negative.
The second integer is positive.
```

Comparing Strings with if

The KornShell supports three different **if** syntaxes for comparing strings. When writing new scripts, use Syntax 1 because it is more forgiving than Syntax 2 or Syntax 3. We show Syntax 2 and Syntax 3 purely for historical reasons; you may run into them in older scripts. In addition, older implementations of the KornShell do not support Syntax 1, so you may be forced to use Syntax 2 or 3 after all.

```
USAGE="usage: if_str.ksh" # using if to compare strings

 print -n "Enter string1: "
 read str1
 print -n "Enter string2: "
 read str2
 print

 if [[ $str1 = $str2 ]]          # Syntax 1; use this syntax
 then
   print "The two strings are identical using [[...]]."
 fi

 if [ "$str1" = "$str2" ]        # Syntax 2
 then
   print "The two strings are identical using [...]."
 fi

 if test "$str1" = "$str2"       # Syntax 3
 then
   print "The two strings are identical using test."
 fi
```

Executing This Script

```
$ if_str.ksh
Enter string1: The dog in the fog
Enter string2: The dog in the fog

The two strings are identical using [[...]].
The two strings are identical using [...].
The two strings are identical using test.
```

Comparing Alphabetical Order with < and >

The < and > operators perform triple duty in the KornShell. If you specify < or > within ((...)), the KornShell does a numerical comparison. However, if you specify < or > within [[...]], the KornShell does a *lexical* comparison of two strings. (The third use of < and >, input and output redirection, is described in Chapter 12.) A string's lexical value is the ASCII value of each character in the string.

```
USAGE="usage: alphaord.ksh"  # using < or > to compare strings

 print -n "Enter a string: "
 read s1
 print -n "Enter another string: "
 read s2

# Compare the lexical order of two strings.  The comparison will be
# case-sensitive.
 if [[ $s1 < $s2 ]]
 then
   print "$s1 would appear before $s2 in an encyclopedia."
 elif [[ $s1 = $s2 ]]
 then
   print "$s1 and $s2 are the same string."
 else
   print "$s2 would appear before $s1 in an encyclopedia."
 fi
```

Executing This Script

```
$ alphaord.ksh
Enter a string: novas
Enter another string: supernovas
novas would appear before supernovas in an encyclopedia.

$ alphaord.ksh
Enter a string: solar system
Enter another string: astronomy
astronomy would appear before solar system in an encyclopedia.
```

Loosely speaking, if you're comparing two strings that contain only letters, then lexical order corresponds to alphabetical order. (Though do read "BEWARE: Common Mistakes Comparing Strings" later in this chapter for an interesting exception.)

Comparing a String to a Pattern with if

The following script shows how you can compare a string to a pattern.

```
USAGE="usage: if_pat.ksh"    # comparing a string to a pattern

 print -n "Enter a string: "
 read s

 if [[ $s = c* ]]     # true if $s starts with an 'c'
 then
   print "$s starts with the letter 'c'."
 fi

 if [[ $s != *n ]]    # true if $s does not end with an 'n'
 then
   print "$s does not end with the letter 'n'."
 fi

# The following condition will be true if $s is one of the listed
# fruits.  See Chapter 5 if the @ pattern confuses you.
 if [[ $s = @(orange|lemon|lime|grapefruit|carambola) ]]
 then
   print "$s is a citrus fruit."
 else
   print "$s is not a citrus fruit."
 fi
```

Executing This Script

```
$ if_pat.ksh
Enter a string: carambola
carambola starts with the letter 'c'.
carambola does not end with the letter 'n'.
carambola is a citrus fruit.
```

! BEWARE: Common Mistakes Comparing Strings !

Since you can compare two numbers with a statement like this:

```
if ((x == y))           # right
```

you might expect that you could compare two strings in a similar fashion; however, you cannot do this:

```
if (($str1 == $str2)) # wrong
```

While we're on the subject of nasty tricks that the KornShell can play on you, please study the following two lines closely:

```
if [[ $str1 = $str2 ]] # right; need white space around [[ and ]]
if [[$str1 = $str2]]   # wrong; white space is missing
```

You can compare a string to a pattern, but you cannot compare a pattern to another pattern. Also, if you are comparing a string to a pattern, note that you must specify the string on the left side of the equal sign and the pattern on the right. For example, compare these two evaluations:

```
if [[ $str = *.bak ]]  # right
if [[ *.bak = $str ]]  # wrong
```

Also, you may be comparing a string to a pattern and you don't realize it! This happens when the string on the right contains a wildcard. If you want the KornShell to expand the wildcard into a pattern, then you're fine. On the other hand, if you want the KornShell to interpret the wildcard character literally, place the string inside a pair of double quotes; for example:

```
if [[ $str = What is your name? ]]    # ? is a wildcard
if [[ $str = "What is your name?" ]]  # ? is just a "?"
```

The < and > operators also impose their share of harsh justice on the unwary. The shell script called **alphaord.ksh** probably left you with the impression that the < operator was a sure-fire way to check alphabetical order. In fact, the < operator works well in comparing two uppercase strings or two lowercase strings, but may fool you when comparing an uppercase string to a lowercase string. That's because the < operator ranks all uppercase strings ahead of lowercase strings. For example, the **alphaord.ksh** script would tell you that "ZZZ" would appear before "aaa" in a dictionary. Fortunately, the KornShell provides a workaround to this problem. See Chapter 13 for a description of the **-u** and **-l** options to **typeset**.

Boolean AND, Boolean OR

It is sometimes useful to combine tests. For example, we might want to say that a condition is true only if two subconditions are true. We can combine tests with the *Boolean* AND operator **&&** and the Boolean OR operator **||**. By the way, another name for a Boolean AND is *logical* AND.

A Boolean AND operation takes two operands as input. If both operands (tests) are true, then the AND operation is true; otherwise, the AND operation is false.

A Boolean OR operation also takes two operands as input but is less demanding than AND. An OR operation is true if one or both of the operands is true. An OR operation is false only if both operands are false.

```
USAGE="usage: boolean1.ksh"  # demonstrates && and ||

 print -n "Enter your age -- "
 read  age

 if ((age < 6)) || ((age > 64))          # || is boolean OR
 then
   print "We give a discount to children and senior citizens."
   print "Ticket price is \$2.50"
 elif  ((age >= 13)) && ((age <= 19))  # && is boolean AND
 then
   print "You are a teenager.  We charge double for teenagers."
   print "Ticket price is \$10.00"
# You can also put boolean operators within ((...)).
 elif ((age >= 40 && age <= 43))
 then
   print "These are difficult years.  We won't charge you."
 else
   print "Ticket price is \$5.00"
 fi
```

Executing This Script

```
$ boolean1.ksh
Enter your age -- 15
You are a teenager.  We charge double for teenagers.
Ticket price is $10.00
```

The case Statement

Here is a simple **case** example. Notice that you can associate any number of statements with each possible value. Just remember to put a double semicolon (;;) after the last statement in each group.

```
USAGE="usage: case1.ksh"  # multiple statements per condition
 print -n "How do you feel? (wonderful, ok, not good): "
 read a_feeling

# Compare value of a_feeling to three possible values: "wonderful",
# "ok", and "not good".  If $a_feeling matches one of these values,
# then the KornShell will execute the statements between ) and ;;
 case $a_feeling in
    "wonderful") print "I'm happy."    # if $a_feeling = "wonderful"...
                 print "Really glad." # ...then execute this statement
                 mood_quotient=10;;    # ...and this one

    "ok")        print "That's good." # if $a_feeling = "ok"...
                 mood_quotient=5;;     # ...then execute this statement

    "not good")  mood_quotient=1;;     # if $a_feeling = "not good"...
                                       # ...then execute mood_quotient=1
 esac  # esac ("case" spelled backwards) marks the end of a case
       # statement just as fi marks the end of an if statement

 print "Your mood quotient is $mood_quotient."
```

Executing This Script

```
$ case1.ksh
How do you feel? (wonderful, ok, not good): wonderful
I'm happy.
Really glad.
Your mood quotient is 10.

$ case1.ksh
How do you feel? (wonderful, ok, not good): not good
Your mood quotient is 1.
```

The problem with this script is that the user might not type in “wonderful”, “ok”, or “not good”; for example:

```
$ case1.ksh
How do you feel? (wonderful, ok, not good): fair
Your mood quotient is .
```

Unexpected Values in a case Statement

Sometimes, a user will enter a value that does not match the expected input. You can, however, catch this unexpected input by specifying a simple * as the last possible value in a **case** statement. Remember that a single * matches any possible string (even the null string).

If you're an experienced C programmer, the final * may remind you of **case default** in a C **switch/case** statement.

```
USAGE="usage: case2.ksh"  # accounting for unexpected case values

 print -n "How do you feel? (wonderful, ok, not good) -- "
 read a_feeling

# If a_feeling is any value other than wonderful, ok, or not good,
# then a_feeling matches *.
 case $a_feeling in
    "wonderful") print "I'm glad for you.";;
    "ok")        print "That's good.";;
    "not good")  print "I'm sorry to hear that.";;
    *)           print "I wasn't expecting that answer.";;
 esac
```

Executing This Script

```
$ case2.ksh
How do you feel? (wonderful, ok, not good) -- pas mal
I wasn't expecting that answer.
```

Wildcards in a case Statement

Of course, the noble * isn't the only wildcard you can use in a **case** statement. The following script demonstrates other wildcards within a **case** statement.

```
USAGE="usage: casewild.ksh"  # demonstrates wildcards

 print -n "Do you want some advice? "
 read advice

 case $advice in
   [Yy][Ee][Ss]) print "Plastics!";;
   [Mm]*)        print "Be a little more decisive.";;
   [Nn][Oo])     print "Your loss.";;
# The following pattern will match any integer.
   +([0-9]))     print "You have a future in math.";;
   *)            print "I can't help you.";;
 esac
```

Executing This Script

```
$ casewild.ksh
Do you want some advice (yes or no): YES
Plastics!

$ casewild.ksh
Do you want some advice (yes or no): yes
Plastics!

$ casewild.ksh
Do you want some advice (yes or no): Yes
Plastics!

$ casewild.ksh
Do you want some advice (yes or no): 542
You have a future in math.
```

Multiple Patterns in a case Statement

You can compare multiple constants or patterns by separating them with a vertical bar |.

```
USAGE="usage: casempat.ksh"    # multiple patterns in a case statement

 print -n "How do you feel? "
 read a_feeling

 case $a_feeling in
   "wonderful"|"great"|"excellent"|"marvelous"|"superb"|"happy")
               print "I'm glad for you."
               print "Really glad."
               mood_quotient=10;;
   "good"|"pretty good"|"ok"|"I can't complain")
               print "That's good."
               mood_quotient=5;;
   "not good"|"rotten"|"bad"|"horrible"|"I'm still living")
               mood_quotient=1;;
   *)          mood_quotient="undefined";;
 esac

 print "Your mood quotient was $mood_quotient."
```

Executing This Script

```
$ casempat.ksh
How do you feel? marvelous
I'm glad for you.
Really glad.
Your mood quotient was 10.

$ casempat.ksh
How do you feel? I'm still living
Your mood quotient was 1.

$ casempat.ksh
How do you feel? like sushi
Your mood quotient was undefined.
```

! BEWARE: Common Mistakes in case !

Here are a few things to look out for inside **case** statements.

Most programmers compulsively match an open parenthesis "(" with a closing parenthesis ")." The KornShell **case** statement is a bit of a shocker because the) does *not* mark the end of something opened with (. For example, compare the following:

```
 case $a_feeling in
#   ("wonderful")  mood_quotient=8;;     # wrong
     "wonderful")  mood_quotient=8;;     # right
 esac
```

Whenever you specify multiple constants separated by vertical bars, you must remember to enclose multiple word constants inside single or double quotes. (See Chapter 2 for the difference between single and double quotes.) For example, compare the following two **case** statements:

```
 case $a_feeling in
#   pretty good|totally hip)    mood_quotient=8;;    # wrong
   "pretty good"|"totally hip") mood_quotient=8;;    # right
 esac
```

If you forget the quotes, the KornShell will probably issue a syntax error.

If your **case** statement contains patterns, remember that the order in which you specify the patterns may affect the behavior of your script. You must exercise care because more than one pattern in your **case** statement may match the value of the variable. If multiple patterns do match, the **case** statement picks the first match only. For example, compare the following two **case** statements:

```
# first
 case $a_feeling in
   "wonderful") mood_quotient=10;;
   w*)          mood_quotient=7;;
 esac

# second
 case $a_feeling in
   w*)          mood_quotient=7;;
   "wonderful") mood_quotient=10;;   # never gets here
 esac
```

Suppose that **a_feeling** contains "wonderful." The first **case** statement would assign the value 10 to **mood_quotient** and the second **case** statement would assign the value 7 to **mood_quotient**.

Tests on Objects

It has become fashionable to speak of files, directories, links, and other nouns of computer science as *objects*. The KornShell provides an easy way to determine an object's characteristics. Table 6 through Table 9 list the 20 tests that you can perform on objects. (A lot of these tests have meaning only in the UNIX operating system; see a UNIX reference book for information.) Place these tests inside a pair of double square brackets (and remember to leave some white space after **[[** and before **]]**); for example:

```
[[ -f $myfile ]]              # is $myfile a regular file?
[[ -x /usr/users/judyt ]]     # is /usr/users/judyt executable?
```

Each test returns either true or false. For example, the **-d** test returns true if *object* is a directory and false otherwise.

If you are testing only one object and that one object does not exist, then the test always returns false.

What Kind of Object Is This?

There are times when it would be helpful to know what kind of object is stored at a particular pathname. Table 6 and Table 7 list the available KornShell tests.

Table 6. Tests on Object Type

Test	**Returns true if object...**
-a *object*	exists; any type of object is fine, just as long as the KornShell can see it
-f *object*	is a regular file (as opposed to a directory, character special file, block special file, named pipe, or socket); note that if *object* is a symbolic link, **-f** *object* returns true
-d *object*	is a directory
-c *object*	is a character special file
-b *object*	is a block special file
-p *object*	is a named pipe
-S *object*	is a socket; don't confuse this test with the **-s** test (in Table 7)
-L *object*	is a symbolic (soft) link to another object

Table 7. Miscellaneous Tests

Test	**Returns true if...**
-k *object*	*object's* "sticky bit" is set
-s *object*	*object* isn't empty; in other words, if *object* contains nothing (has a length of zero bytes), then this test returns false

Here's a script that uses some of those tests:

```
USAGE="usage: obj_type.ksh"   # what kind of object is this?

 print -n "Enter the pathname of an object: "
 read pathname

# The ! operator means "not"; see next page for more details.
 if [[ ! -a $pathname ]] # Does this object not exist?
 then
  print "There is no object at this pathname."
 elif [[ -L $pathname ]] # Is this object a symbolic link?
 then
  print "$pathname is a symbolic link."
 elif [[ -f $pathname ]] # Is this object a regular file?
 then
  print "$pathname is a file"
 elif [[ -d $pathname ]] # Is this object a directory?
 then
  print "$pathname is a directory"
 else
# Object must be something offbeat, like a socket.
  print "$pathname is not a file, directory, or symbolic link."
 fi
```

Executing This Script

```
$ obj_type.ksh
Enter the pathname of an object: gorp
There is no object at this pathname.

$ obj_type.ksh
Enter the pathname of an object: paint
paint is a symbolic link.
```

Boolean NOT

Use the NOT operator **!** to ask a negative question. For example, you can use **-f** to ask the KornShell if a certain file exists, or you can use **! -f** to ask if a certain file does not exist. You can use the NOT operator only within **((...))** or within **[[...]]**.

```
USAGE="usage: bool_not.ksh"  # demonstrates the NOT operator !

# If a certain directory (~/fun) does not exist, then create it.
# ~ means the HOME directory, so ~/fun means the directory named
# fun underneath your HOME directory
 if [[ ! -d ~/fun ]]
 then
   print "Directory ~/fun does not exist.  Now creating it."
   mkdir ~/fun  # mkdir is the UNIX command to create a directory
   print
 fi

# If the allison file exists, but the kelton file does not,
# then pause for 2 seconds.
 if [[ -f /tmp/allison  &&  ! -f /tmp/kelton ]]
 then
   print "We must now pause for 2 seconds."
   sleep 2   # UNIX command to pause script for 2 seconds
   print "Thank you."
 fi
```

Executing This Script

Before running this script, create a file at pathname **/tmp/allison**. The contents of **/tmp/allison** are irrelevant.

```
$ bool_not.ksh
Directory ~/fun does not exist.  Now creating it.

We must now pause for 2 seconds.
Thank you.
```

How Is This Object Protected?

Most operating systems support some method for the creator of an object to protect that object against undesired use. That's a fancy way of saying that users can tell other users "hands off my stuff." On the UNIX operating system, the owner of an object can specify read, write, and execute permissions. If you are working on a UNIX system, you'll probably use the **chmod** utility to alter these permissions. For information on **chmod**, type the following command:

```
$ man chmod
```

or, better yet, read about **chmod** in a good UNIX tutorial.

Table 8 lists all the KornShell tests of object permissions.

Table 8. Object Permissions

Test	**Returns true if...**
-r *object*	I may read this *object*
-w *object*	I may write to (modify) this object
-x *object*	*object* is a file, then I may execute it; if *object* is a directory, then I may search through it
-O *object*	I own *object*; in the UNIX operating system, only the owner of an object can change its protections
-G *object*	the group to which I belong owns *object*
-u *object*	*object's* set-user-id bit is set
-g *object*	*object's* set-group-id bit is set

The following script (on the next page) uses some of these tests to examine object permissions.

```
USAGE="usage: obj_perm.ksh"    # check object permissions

 print -n "Enter the pathname of a file: "
 read pathname

 if [[ -r $pathname ]]    # -r checks for read permission
 then
   print "You can read it"
 else
   print "You cannot read it."
 fi

 if [[ -w $pathname ]]    # -w checks for write permission
 then
   print "You can write to it."
 else
   print "You cannot write to it."
 fi

 if [[ -x $pathname ]]    # -x checks for execute permission
 then
   print "You can execute it."
 else
   print "You cannot execute it."
 fi
```

Executing This Script

```
$ obj_perm.ksh
Enter the pathname of a file: /usr/users/my_plans
You can read it.
You cannot write to it.
You cannot execute it.
```

Use the UNIX command **chmod** to change permissions.

Comparing the Date of Last Modification

The tests in Table 9 compare two objects. For example, the **–ot** test returns true if a particular object is "older than" another object. An object's age, in this context anyway, refers to the last time a user modified it. So, a file last modified in February is older than a file last modified in March.

Table 9. Comparing Two Objects

Test	Returns true if...
object1 **–nt** *object2*	*object1* is newer than *object2*
object1 **–ot** *object2*	*object1* is older than *object2*
object1 **–ef** *object2*	*object1* is another name for *object2*; **–ef** stands for equivalent file

Here are the rules if one or both of those objects don't exist:

- If neither *object1* nor *object2* exists, the test is automatically false.
- If one of the objects does not exist but the other does, the KornShell considers the existing object to be newer than the nonexistent one.

```
USAGE="usage: file_age.ksh"  # demonstrates -ot test
# Suppose program.c is a C program and that a.out is the executable
# version of program.c.   This script compiles program.c only if it
# has been modified some time after a.out was modified.

 if [[ a.out -ot program.c ]]
 then    # a.out is older than program.c, or a.out does not exist
   print "Must compile program.c"
   cc program.c  # cc is the UNIX command to compile a C program
 else    # a.out is not older than program.c
   print "No need to compile program.c; a.out is up-to-date."
 fi
```

This script is overly simplistic. It might be necessary to compile **program.c** even if **a.out** were younger. For example, **program.c** might contain some #include files which changed after compilation.

Executing This Script

```
$ file_age.ksh
No need to compile program.c; a.out is up-to-date.
```

Did the script work properly? Let's find out when **a.out** and **program.c** were last modified.

```
$ ls -l a.out program.c       # UNIX command for object information
-rwxrwxrwx  1 rosenberg    3529 Jan 19 11:11 a.out
-rwxrwxrwx  1 rosenberg     209 Jan 19 11:10 program.c
```

It looks as if **program.c** is older (by one minute) than **a.out**.

Mixing Tests

This script uses Boolean operators **&&** and **||** to combine five simple tests into one complex test. The tests check the script user's age and maturity to judge whether the user may read a particular file. Naturally, the file itself has to be available and readable, so the script also performs **-f** and **-r** tests.

```
USAGE="usage: mixtests.ksh"   # combining a variety of tests
 print -n "Enter your age: "
 read age
 print -n "Are you mature (yes or no): "
 read mature

# Perform five tests.  Use pairs of single parentheses (...) to group
# the operations into the correct order.  Notice that this complex
# condition actually spans the next two lines.
if ( (( age >= 18)) || ( ((age >= 16)) && [[ $mature = [Yy]* ]] ) ) &&
   [[ (-f lawrence) && (-r lawrence) ]]
 then
   print "You may read this classic."
   print
   cat lawrence  # cat is the UNIX command to display a file
 else
   print "I'm sorry, but you may not read this classic."
 fi
```

Executing This Script

Before running this script, use a text editor to create a short text file named **lawrence** and put some text inside it. Here's what happened when I ran the script:

```
$ mixtests.ksh
Enter your age: 17
Are you mature (yes or no): no
I'm sorry, but you may not read this classic.

$ mixtests.ksh
Enter your age: 16
Are you mature (yes or no): yes
You may read this classic.

                         Lady Chatterley's Louvers

    Young Lady Chatterley was torn between her tempestuous desire to
find quality vinyl replacement windows and her overwhelming passion
to stay within the ancestral family budget.
```

---

if execute one or more commands if a condition is true.

Syntax:

if/then

if *condition*
then
    command1
    ...
    [*commandN*]
fi

if/then/else

if *condition*
then
    command1
    ...
    [*commandN*]
else
    command1
    ...
    [*commandN*]
fi

if/then/elif/else

if *condition1*
then
    command1
    ...
    [*command*N]
elif *condition2*
then
    command1
    ...
    [*commandN*]
else
    command1
    ...
    [*commandN*]
fi

Where:

condition is usually a numerical comparison, string comparison, or object test; however, *condition* can also be the name of any user program, operating system command, KornShell script, or KornShell statement (except for **if**, **then**, **elif**, or **else**). In short, *condition* can be anything that evaluates to true or false. Every program, operating system command, and KornShell statement returns an exit status. The error status is a number symbolizing the success or failure of the command. An error status of zero symbolizes success (or true) and a nonzero exit status symbolizes failure (or false).

command is the name of any user program, operating system command, KornShell script, or KornShell statement (except for **fi**). For example, a "command" could be a user-written program like **a.out**, a UNIX utility like **sort**, or a KornShell **print** statement. In fact, a command could be anything that is legal outside of an **if** statement. In addition, *command* can also be a colon (:) by itself, indicating that no commands will be executed.

Quick Summary:

The **if** statement evaluates a *condition*. If the *condition* is true, something happens; if the *condition* is false, something else happens. You can choose among several formats of the **if** statement depending on how many conditions you wish to evaluate.

In the simplest format (the **if/then** syntax), if the *condition* is true, the KornShell executes the *commands* between **then** and **fi**. If the *condition* is false, the KornShell ignores all the *commands* between **then** and **fi**.

In the **if/then/else** syntax, if the *condition* is true, the KornShell executes the *commands* between **then** and **else**. If the *condition* is false, the KornShell executes the *commands* between **else** and **fi**.

The **if/then/elif/else** syntax supports multiple conditions. The KornShell evaluates *condition1* first, then *condition2*, and so on. (There is no practical limit to the number of **elif** statements in an **if**.) As soon as the KornShell finds a true *condition*, it executes the associated *commands* and then ignores all remaining conditions. In other words, although several *conditions* may be true, only the first true *condition* matters. If none of the *conditions* are true, the KornShell executes the commands between **else** and **if**.

---

case compare the value of an argument to one or more patterns and then execute commands associated with the matching pattern.

Syntax:

case *value* **in**
pattern1) *command1*
...
commandN;;
pattern2) *command1*
...
commandN;;
...
patternN) *command1*
...
commandN;;
esac

Where:

value is any value. Typically, you specify the value of a variable.

pattern is any constant, pattern, or group of patterns. A *constant* could be any integer (like 18) or string value (like "marvelous"). A *pattern* could be any pattern described in Chapter 5. You are allowed to specify multiple patterns. If you do, you need to use the | symbol to separate them.

command is the name of any program, shell script, or KornShell statement (except for **esac**). For example, a "command" could be a user-written program like **a.out**, a UNIX command like **sort**, or a KornShell **print** statement. In fact, a command could be anything that is legal outside of a **case** statement. You can specify any number of *commands* or no commands at all. Just remember to place two semicolons (;;) after the last command.

Quick Summary:

In a **case** statement, you specify a *value* and one or more *patterns*. The KornShell first compares *value* to *pattern1*. If *value* matches *pattern1*, then the KornShell executes the commands associated with *pattern1* and then skips over the remainder of the **case** statement. If *value* does not match *pattern1*, the KornShell ignores the commands associated with *pattern1* and compares *value* to *pattern2*. If *value* matches *pattern2*, the KornShell executes the commands associated with *pattern2* and then skips the rest of the **case** statement. If *value* does not match *pattern2*, the KornShell ignores the commands and compares *value* to *pattern3* and so on through *patternN*. It is possible that *value* will not match any *patterns*. **esac** marks the end of a **case** statement.

Chapter 7
Loops

This chapter teaches you how to create loops.

If You're New to Programming...

A loop executes the same group of commands or KornShell statements many times. By creating a loop, you can reduce the length of your KornShell script. If you're new to programming, you may well ask why you'd want to execute the same group of commands over and over again. The answer is that although the commands themselves remain constant, input to the commands can change on every loop iteration.

For example, suppose you create a group of commands that counts the number of vowels in a word. Further suppose that you intend to count the number of vowels in four input words. If you don't create a loop, the structure of your script will be something like the following:

```
input word #1
count number of vowels in word #1

input word #2
count number of vowels in word #2

input word #3
count number of vowels in word #3

input word #4
count number of vowels in word #4
```

By writing the same script with a loop, you simplify the structure to this:

```
loop 4 times
   input a word
   count number of vowels in word
end loop
```

The KornShell supports three statements for looping: **while**, **until**, and **for**.

The **while** loop continues looping while a specified condition is true. That is, when you specify a **while** loop, you also specify a condition. The loop continues as long as that condition stays true. When the condition becomes false, the script stops looping. For example, the condition might be something like ((x != 5)). Therefore, the loop continues as long as **x** doesn't equal 5. The loop could conceivably run for thousands or even millions of iterations before **x** becomes 5. On the other hand, if **x** equals 5 before the loop begins, the loop won't execute even once.

The **until** loop is the reverse of a **while** loop. The **until** loop continues looping while a specified condition is false. You will probably find it easier to use **while** loops instead of **until** loops.

When you write a **for** statement, you usually specify a list of values. The list could be a bunch of numbers, a bunch of strings, a bunch of filenames, or any combination of these things. For example, the list might be a simple shopping list: apples, rice, corn. During the first **for** loop iteration, the KornShell assigns the first element in the list (apples) to a specified variable. During the second iteration, the KornShell assigns the second element in the list (rice) to the specified variable. During the third iteration, the KornShell assigns the third element in the list (corn) to the specified variable. After the third iteration, the list ends, so the loop ends. The **for** loop is particularly versatile because you can use wildcards to generate lists of filenames.

If You're an Experienced Programmer...

The KornShell supports three statements for looping:

- **while**
- **until**
- **for**

The **while** and **until** loops are very similar. A **while** loop executes as long as a specified condition is true; an **until** loop executes as long as a specified condition is false. (See Chapter 6 for a discussion of conditions.) A typical terminating condition for a **while** or **until** loop might be a counter variable reaching a certain level, a certain word being inputted, or the end of input data.

Many languages support **for** loops; however, the KornShell **for** loop is rather unusual. In the KornShell, you use the **for** loop to establish a list of values for a variable. Each time through the loop, the KornShell will assign a new value from the list to the variable. For example, if the list is ten items long, then the loop will execute ten times, each time assigning a new value to the specified variable.

In addition to **for**, **while**, and **until**, the KornShell also supports two statements that have meaning only within a loop—**break** and **continue**. Use **break** to jump out of a loop; use **continue** to skip to the next iteration of the loop. If you're used to the C language, you should recognize that the **break** and **continue** of the KornShell work as in C.

A Simple while, until, and for Loop

On these two pages, we compare the three looping statements of the KornShell. The three scripts produce identical output; however, each script uses a different looping statement to accomplish the task.

The following script demonstrates a **while** loop. Each time through the loop, the script prints the value of a loop counter. The loop executes as long as the value of **n** is less than or equal to 4.

```
USAGE="usage: while_ex.ksh"  # demonstrates while loop

 integer n=1  # declare n as an integer; initialize it to 1

# Loop while condition is true.
 while ((n <= 4))
 do
    print "$n"
    ((n = n + 1))  # increment the loop counter
 done
# This loop executes four times.
```

Executing This Script

```
$ while_ex.ksh
1
2
3
4
```

In the next script, we've replaced **while** with **until**.

```
USAGE="usage: until_ex.ksh"  # a simple until loop

 integer n=1  # declare n as an integer and initialize loop counter

# Loop until condition becomes true.
 until ((n > 4))
 do
    print "$n"
    ((n = n + 1))
 done
# This loop executes four times.
```

Executing This Script

```
$ until_ex.ksh
1
2
3
4
```

The **for** loop specifies a list of values for a variable. The first time through the loop, the variable will have the value of the first element in the list. The next time through the list, the variable will have the value of the second element in the list, and so on.

For example, the following **for** loop executes four times because the list consists of four elements: **1**, **2**, **3**, and **4**. The first time through the loop, the **for** statement assigns the value **1** to variable **n**. The second time through the loop, the **for** statement assigns the value **2** to variable **n**.

```
USAGE="usage: for_ex.ksh"      # for loop

# Loop as long as there is another element in the list.  By the way,
# the word "in" is a keyword that separates the name of the variable
# from the list of elements.
 for n in 1 2 3 4     # a list with four elements
 do
   print "$n"
 done
# This loop executes four times.
```

Executing This Script

```
$ for_ex.ksh
1
2
3
4
```

Lists in for Loops

We don't want to give you the impression that a **for** loop list has to consist of an ordered sequence of numbers. The following script demonstrates numerical lists, string lists, and mixed lists.

```
USAGE="usage: for_list.ksh"  # lists in for loops
 integer number        # declare number as an integer
 integer square        # declare square as an integer

 for number in 1 50 100                        # a list of three numbers
 do
   ((square = number * number))
 print "$number $square"
 done
 print

 for city in Boston Kyoto Copenhagen            # a list of three words
 do
   print "$city"
 done
 print

# If a list entry contains white space (spaces or tabs), enclose the
# entry inside a pair of double quotes.
 for bizarre in Miami 7 "San Fran" 9     # a list of numbers and words
 do
   print $bizarre
 done
```

Executing This Script

```
$ for_list.ksh
1 1
50 2500
100 10000

Boston
Kyoto
Copenhagen

Miami
7
San Fran
9
```

! BEWARE: for Loop Confusion !

The **for** loop is common to many languages. Because it is so common, many beginning KornShell programmers expect the KornShell's **for** statement to work the same way as **for** statements in other languages. However, the KornShell **for** statement is somewhat different.

When using a **for** loop in a high–level language, you usually specify the loop's starting and ending conditions, plus some sort of iterative command. Compare that to the KornShell's **for** loop in which the programmer constructs a list of values.

For example, suppose you wanted to create a loop with a starting value of 100, an ending value of 1,000,000, and an incrementing value of 10. In most high–level languages, a **for** loop could easily accomplish this. Here is how it might look in the C language:

```
for (count = 100; count <= 1000000; count+=10)
    {
     ...
    }
```

It would be excruciatingly tedious to accomplish this with a KornShell **for** loop; although you could use a KornShell **while** loop as follows:

```
count=100
while ((count <= 1000000))
do
    ...
    ((count = count + 10))
done
```

Using while to Average Five Integers

The following script uses a **while** loop to average exactly five input integers.

```
USAGE="usage: average.ksh"  # averaging five integers

# Declare loop_counter and running_total as integers and set the
# starting value of each to zero.
 integer loop_counter=0
 integer running_total=0

 while ((loop_counter < 5)) # the loop termination condition
 do
   print -n "Enter a test score: "
   read test_score
   ((running_total = running_total + test_score)) # sum input values
   ((loop_counter = loop_counter + 1))       # increment loop_counter
 done

# Get average by dividing the running_total by five.
# Note that the average will never be rounded up, only down.
 ((average = running_total / 5))

 print "\nThe average is $average"
```

Executing This Script

```
$ average.ksh
Enter a test score: 4
Enter a test score: 7
Enter a test score: 2
Enter a test score: 5
Enter a test score: 3

The average is 4
```

Using break to Leave a Loop

This script finds the average of up to four integers. Ordinarily, you establish the loop termination condition at the beginning of a loop. Use a **break** statement to establish a second loop termination condition in the middle of a loop.

```
USAGE="usage: break1.ksh"  # demonstrates break
 integer loop_counter=0
 integer running_total=0
 while ((loop_counter < 4)) # a loop termination condition
 do
   print -n "Enter a test score (or -99 if finished): "
   read test_score
   if ((test_score == -99)) # a second loop termination condition
   then
     break    # stop looping
   fi
   ((running_total = running_total + test_score)) # sum input values
   ((loop_counter = loop_counter + 1))            # count input values
 done

# The break statement skips over remainder of loop, so that script
# next executes the following line:
 if ((loop_counter != 0))
 then  # calculate the average
   print "The average is $((running_total / loop_counter))"
 else
   print "No data to average."      # avoid dividing by zero
 fi
```

Executing This Script

```
$ break1.ksh
Enter a test score (or -99 if finished): 4
Enter a test score (or -99 if finished): 7
Enter a test score (or -99 if finished): 2
Enter a test score (or -99 if finished): 5
The average is 4

$ break1.ksh
Enter a test score (or -99 if finished): 4
Enter a test score (or -99 if finished): 8
Enter a test score (or -99 if finished): -99
The average is 6
```

Using continue to Skip Part of One Loop Iteration

Use **continue** to skip a portion of one loop iteration. In essence, **continue** tells the KornShell to ignore the remainder of the loop and return to the beginning of the loop. The following script finds the average of five test scores but ignores "suspicious" scores.

```
USAGE="usage: cont1.ksh"  # demonstrates continue statement

 integer loop_counter=0
 integer running_total=0
 while ((loop_counter < 5)) # loop termination condition
 do
   print -n "Enter a test score: "
   read test_score
# Ignore input values less than 0 or greater than 100.
   if (( (test_score < 0) || (test_score > 100) ))
   then
     print "This value looks suspicious; ignoring it."
     continue  # skip the rest of this loop iteration
   fi
   ((running_total = running_total + test_score))
   ((loop_counter = loop_counter + 1))
 done

 print "The average is $((running_total / loop_counter))"
```

Executing This Script

```
$ cont1.ksh
Enter a test score: 90
Enter a test score: 87
Enter a test score: 94
Enter a test score: 130
This value looks suspicious; ignoring it.
Enter a test score: 93
Enter a test score: -5
This value looks suspicious; ignoring it.
Enter a test score: 88
The average is 90
```

Using : to Create an Always True Loop

The colon, when used as a condition, means "always true." Therefore, using it establishes a potentially infinite loop. Since it is unlikely that you would desire an infinite loop, you must provide some loop termination condition inside the body of the loop, that is, somewhere between **do** and **done.** Then, when the termination condition becomes true, you can issue a **break** statement (to leave the loop) or an **exit** statement (to leave the script altogether).

Incidentally, the **while :** KornShell statement* serves the same purpose as the **while (1)** statement in C or the **while true** statement in Pascal.

```
USAGE="usage: trueloop.ksh"   # using the colon to mean "always true"
integer grand_total=0    # initialize grand_total
# This while loop sums any number of input integers.
 while :   # potentially infinite loop
 do
   print "\nThe sum of all input values is $grand_total"
   print -n "Enter an integer, or enter -99 to quit: "
   read number
   if ((number == -99))   # loop termination condition
   then
     break    # jump out of the loop
   else
     ((grand_total = grand_total + number))
   fi
 done
```

Executing This Script

```
$ trueloop.ksh

The sum of all input values is 0
Enter an integer, or enter -99 to quit: 5

The sum of all input values is 5
Enter an integer, or enter -99 to quit: 100

The sum of all input values is 105
Enter an integer, or enter -99 to quit: -99
```

* Actually, **the colon :** is the null statement. The error status of the null statement is always 0. Since 0 corresponds to "true," the null statement always evaluates to a true condition.

! BEWARE: Philosophical Disagreements with C !

C language programmers should be aware that the KornShell and the C programming language view truth differently. In the C programming language, zero means false, and any nonzero number means true. In the KornShell, zero means true, and any nonzero number means false.

However, there is more to say about this philosophical difference. Consider the following KornShell script:

```
USAGE="usage: ala_c.ksh"  # what is truth?
 integer n=3
 while ((n))  # loop as long as the condition is true
 do
   print $n
   ((n = n - 1))
 done
```

Executing this script produces the following output:

```
$ ala_c.ksh
3
2
1
```

How in the world did this script work? After all, the KornShell interprets a nonzero value as false. Since **n** equals 3 (false) at the start of the loop, why did the loop execute at all?

I'm afraid that the answer is rather complicated, but here goes. In the C language, the expression:

```
(n)
```

evaluates to the value of variable **n**. However, in the KornShell, the expression

```
((n))
```

evaluates to the logical negation of **n**. In other words, if **n** is nonzero (false), the KornShell evaluates `((n))` to the logical negation of **n**, which is true. On the other hand, if **n** is zero (true), then the KornShell evalutes `((n))` to the opposite of true, which is false.

Are you still with me? Let's try it again. As long as **n** is not equal to zero, the expression `((n))` will have an exit status of true. When **n** becomes zero, the expression `((0))` will have an exit status of false.

A List of Filenames in a for Loop

In the following **for** loop, the list consists of three explicit pathnames.

```
USAGE="usage: for_cnst.ksh"  # list of filenames in a for loop

# Generate a list of three explicit object names:
 for object in tiger.c /usr/users/lion.c panther
 do
   if [[ ! -a $object ]]
   then
     print "$object does not exist."
   elif [[ -f $object ]]
   then
     print "$object exists and is a regular file."
     print "$object contains the following text:\n"
     cat $object # cat is the UNIX command to display a file's contents
     print
   else
     print "$object exists but is not a regular file."
   fi
 done
```

Executing This Script

Before running this script, create a file named **tiger.c** and a directory named **panther**. Put some text into **tiger.c**; any text will do. Here's what happened when I ran the script:

```
$ for_cnst.ksh
tiger.c exists and is a regular file.
tiger.c contains the following text:

main()  /* main routine of tiger */
{
  printf("Tiger, tiger, burning bright.\n");
}

/usr/users/lion.c does not exist.
panther exists but is not a regular file.
```

There is one slight flaw with the previous script. If **$object** is a regular file but isn't a text file, then **–f $object** still returns true. For example, if **$object** is an executable binary file, then **–f $object** returns true and the script proceeds to execute **cat $object**. However, because **$object** isn't a text file, **cat $object** will display all sorts of gibberish.

Patterns in a for Loop

The previous example contained an explicit list of object names, but what do you do if you want to create a list of all the object names in the current directory? The answer is simple: use wildcards. For example, the following **for** loop generates a list of all the objects in the current directory:

```
for x in *
```

The * wildcard is so powerful that it will match every object, including subdirectories and sockets. Use object tests to restrict the kinds of objects you wish to match.

```
USAGE="usage: for_pat.ksh"   # patterns in a for loop list

print "Here is a list of every object in the current directory:"
for object in *
do
  print "\t$object"
done

print "\nHere is a list of every regular file"
print "in the current directory:"
for object in *    # generate list of every object
do
  if [[ -f $object ]]   # only print regular files
  then
    print "\t$object"
  fi
done

print "\nHere is a list of every modifiable C and assembly language"
print "source file in the current directory:"
for object in *.c *.s
do
  if [[ (-f $object) && (-w $object) ]]
  then
    print "\t$object"
  fi
done
```

Executing This Script

Before running the script, we'll issue an **ls -l** command to find out what's inside the current directory:

```
$ ls -l          # UNIX command to display contents of current directory
total 11
-rwxrwxrwx  1 rosenberg    1300 Feb  5 09:39 a.out
-rwxrwxrwx  1 rosenberg     413 Feb  5 09:42 debbie.s
-rwxrwxrwx  1 rosenberg     578 Feb  5 09:41 ev.c
-rwxrwxrwx  1 rosenberg     623 Feb  5 09:39 ev.o
-rwxrwxrwx  1 rosenberg     608 Feb  5 09:42 for_pat
drwxrwxrwx  1 rosenberg    1024 Feb  5 09:43 libraries
-rwxrwxrwx  1 rosenberg     752 Feb  5 09:41 lou.c
-rwxrwxrwx  1 rosenberg     623 Feb  5 09:39 lou.o
-rwxrwxrwx  1 rosenberg     175 Feb  5 09:42 sarah.s
drwxrwxrwx  1 rosenberg    1024 Feb  5 09:43 under

$ for_pat.ksh # run the script
Here is a list of every object in the current directory:
            a.out
            debbie.s
            ev.c
            ev.o
            for_pat
            libraries
            lou.c
            lou.o
            sarah.s
            under

Here is a list of every regular file
in the current directory:
            a.out
            debbie.s
            ev.c
            ev.o
            for_pat
            lou.c
            lou.o
            sarah.s

Here is a list of every modifiable C and assembly language
source file in the current directory:
            ev.c
            lou.c
            debbie.s
            sarah.s
```

Searching for Objects in Subdirectories

Often, you will want to search not only the current directory, but its subdirectories as well. For UNIX systems, ***** matches all objects in the current directory; ***/*** matches all objects one level underneath the current directory; ***/*/*** matches all objects two levels underneath the current directory; and so on. For systems other than the UNIX operating system, the pattern you use depends on the operator(s) that the system uses to delimit directories in pathnames.

If you want to match *all* the objects underneath a certain directory (as opposed to matching directories down to a certain depth), you can:

- Use the UNIX command **find.**
- Use the UNIX command **ls -R.**
- Write a recursive KornShell function. (See Chapter 16 for an example.)

The following script introduces a KornShell reserved variable named **PWD**. This variable holds the name of the current directory.

```
USAGE="usage: dive.ksh"  # scanning a directory and its subdirectories

 print "These objects are two levels underneath $PWD:"
 for object in */*
 do
   print "\t$object"
 done

 print "$PWD and the directories two levels below it contain"
 print "the following objects: "
 for object in *  */*  */*/*
 do
   print "\t$object"
 done

 print "$PWD and the next two levels below it contain"
 print "the following directories: "
 for object in *  */*  */*/*
 do
   if [[ -d $object ]]
   then
      print "\t$object"
   fi
 done
```

Executing This Script

```
$ dive.ksh      # assume that current directory is /miranda/fruit
These objects are two levels underneath /miranda/fruit:
            apple/green
            apple/red
            grapefruit/pink
            grapefruit/yellow
/miranda/fruit and the directories two levels below it contain
the following objects:
            apple
            dive.ksh
            farm_income
            grapefruit
            machinery
            apple/green
            apple/red
            grapefruit/pink
            grapefruit/yellow
            apple/green/granny_smith
            apple/red/mac
/miranda/fruit and the next two levels below it contain
the following directories:
            apple
            grapefruit
            apple/green
            apple/red
            grapefruit/pink
            grapefruit/yellow
```

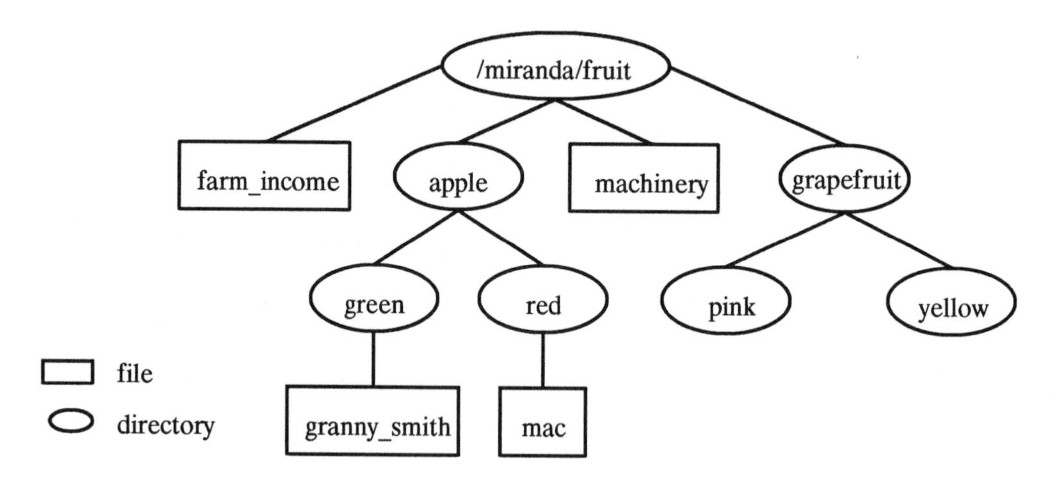

Figure 1. Organization of directory **/miranda/fruit**

! BEWARE: Nonexistent Patterns !

Suppose that no filename matches the pattern in a **for** loop. For example, consider the following loop:

```
for file in st*
do
  wc -l $file   # UNIX command that counts lines in a file
done
```

If no file matches the pattern **st***, does the KornShell issue an error? Yes and no. Let's examine this situation carefully.

The KornShell attempts to expand the pattern **st***; however, no filename matches this pattern. Since **st*** cannot be expanded, the KornShell sets the loop list to the literal value **st***. In other words, the list will consist of only one value, **st***. So far, none of the preceding activity causes the KornShell to issue an error. However, the command **wc –l** will attempt to count the lines in a file named **st***. Since no file by that name exists, the **wc –l** command will issue an error like the following:

```
st*: No such file or directory
```

Here is a better way to write the same script:

```
for file in st*
do
  if [[ -f $file ]]
  then
    wc -l $file
  fi
done
```

A Loop within a Loop

The KornShell permits you to create *nested loops*; in other words, you may put a loop inside another loop. For example, in the following script, we put a **for** loop inside a **while** loop. The script tests each integer from 11 to 99 to determine whether it is prime or composite.

```
USAGE="usage: nested.ksh"  # demonstrates nested loops

# The outer loop generates integers from 11 to 99
integer n=11
 while ((n <= 99))     # here's the start of the outer loop
 do
   answer=prime
  # The inner loop tests each value of n to determine whether n is
  # prime or composite.  The values of d (2, 3, 5, and 7) are the prime
  # factors of integers less than 100.
   for d in 2 3 5 7   # here's the start of the inner loop
   do
     ((remainder = n % d))
    # If a number is evenly divisible by a prime factor,
    # then it is composite.
     if ((remainder == 0))
     then
       answer=composite
       break
     fi
   done  # end of inner loop

   print "$n is $answer"
   ((n = n + 1))
 done  # end of outer loop
```

Executing This Script

```
$ nested.ksh
11 is prime
12 is composite
13 is prime
  .
  . # omitting the next 83 lines of output
  .
97 is prime
98 is composite
99 is composite
```

The break Statement within a Nested Loop

The following script demonstrates a **break** statement within a nested loop. You can optionally specify an integer argument, *n*, to **break**. If you do, the KornShell will jump out of the *n* loops enclosing **break.**

```
USAGE="usage: break2.ksh"  # using break within a nested loop
 print "Here are pairs of numbers with products less than 50: "
 for x in 1 2 3
 do
   print -n "\n\t$x times "
   for y in 10 20 30
   do
     if (( (x * y) >= 50 ))
     then
       break    # use break to jump out of inner loop
     fi
     print -n "$y, "
   done
 done

 print "\n\tAll done."
```

Executing This Script

```
$ break2.ksh       # run this script
Here are pairs of numbers with products less than 50:

            1 times 10, 20, 30,
            2 times 10, 20,
            3 times 10,
            All done.
```

Now make a small change to the program. Change the **break** statement to **break 2**. Now, the KornShell will break out of the current loop *and* the loop enclosing it.

```
$ break2.ksh       # run it again, this time with break 2 instead of break.
Here are pairs of numbers with products less than 50:

            1 times 10, 20, 30,
            2 times 10, 20,
            All done.
```

---

while loop as long as the specified condition is true.
until loop as long as the specified condition is false.

Syntax:

while *condition*
do
    command1
    ...
    commandN
done
	until *condition*
	do
	    command1
	    ...
	    commandN
	done

Where:

condition is usually a numerical comparison, string comparison, or object test; however, *condition* can also be the name of any user program, operating system command, KornShell script, or KornShell statement (except for **while, do**, or **done**). In short, *condition* can be anything that evaluates to true or false. Every program, operating system command, and KornShell statement returns an error status. The error status is a number symbolizing the success or failure of the command. An error status of zero symbolizes true and a nonzero error status symbolizes false. See "BEWARE: Philosophical Disagreements with C" earlier in this chapter.

command is the name of any user program, operating system command, KornShell script, or KornShell statement (except for **done**). For example, a "command" could be a user-written program like **a.out**, a UNIX utility like **sort**, or a KornShell **print** statement. In fact, a command could be anything that is legal outside of an **if** statement. In addition, *command* can also be a colon (:) by itself, indicating that no commands will be executed.

Quick Summary:

The **while** statement establishes a loop. The loop consists of all the commands between **do** and **done**. The KornShell executes the loop as long as the condition is true.

The **until** statement is identical to **while** except that **until** executes the loop as long as the condition is false. In other words, as soon as the condition becomes true, the **until** loop stops executing.

for — loop through all elements of a list.

Syntax:

```
for variable in list
do
    command1
    ...
    commandN
done
```

```
for variable
do
    command1
    ...
    commandN
done
```

Where:

variable — is any variable name.

list — is a list of strings or numbers. (Remember that the KornShell regards just about everything as a string). If the list contains any KornShell wildcards, the KornShell expands the wildcards into filenames before beginning the loop.

command — is the name of any user program, operating system command, KornShell script, or KornShell statement (except for **done**). For example, a "command" could be a user-written program like **a.out**, a UNIX utility like **sort**, or a KornShell **print** statement. In fact, a command could be anything that is legal outside of an **if** statement. In addition, *command* can also be a single colon (:) by itself, indicating that no commands will be executed.

Quick Summary:

The **for** statement establishes a loop. The body of the loop consists of all the *commands* between **do** and **done**. The KornShell executes the body of the loop one time for every element in *list*. During the first iteration of the loop, the KornShell assigns the first element in *list* to *identifer*. During the second iteration, the KornShell assigns the second element in *list* to *identifier*, and so on.

If you specify **for** *variable* without specifying **in** *list*, then the list of elements consists of the entire set of positional parameters. See Chapter 9 for details on this syntax.

---

break jump out of the current loop (or loops).
continue skip to the next iteration of the current loop (or loops).

Syntax:

break *number*

continue *number*

Where:

number	is an optional integer corresponding to the number of levels of nesting to jump out of (**break**) or to skip iterations of (**continue**). The default value of *number* is 1.

Quick Summary:

Use a **break** statement to stop execution of the current loop and resume execution immediately after the end of the loop. In other words, use a **break** statement to jump out of a loop.

Use a **continue** statement to stop execution of the current loop iteration and resume execution at the top of the loop. In other words, use a **continue** statement to skip part of the loop for one cycle.

The optional *number* only has meaning when the current loop is enclosed (nested) inside another loop. In that case, you can specify the *number* of enclosing loops to which the **break** or **continue** applies. For example, suppose that the current loop is enclosed by two other loops. A **break** (or **break 1**) statement will cause a jump out of the current loop only; a **break 2** statement will exit from the current loop and the loop enclosing it; a **break 3** statement will exit from the current loop and both loops enclosing it.

Incidentally, you may specify a *number* greater than the number of enclosing loops. That is, if you are inside a single loop, specifying **continue 9** (or **break 9**) will not cause a KornShell error. Instead, the KornShell will apply the **continue** or **break** to all enclosing loops.

Beginning programmers often confuse **exit**, **break**, and **continue**. All three change the flow of control, but let's see how their use differs:

- Use **exit** to leave a KornShell script altogether.
- Use **break** to leave a loop but stay within the KornShell script.
- Use **continue** to leave the current iteration of the loop but stay within the loop.

Chapter 8

Creating Menus

Use the **select** statement to create simple, but very useful, menu–driven interfaces.

By "menu–driven interface," I'm not referring to the modern, mouse–oriented, point–and–click interface in the style of an Apple Macintosh. That kind of programming effort takes time, effort, and know–how! Plus, your users have to have some kind of newfangled monitor that can display those fancy graphics! Do you think real users like that sort of cuddly interface?

Don't answer that last question. Let me get to the point: the **select** statement lets you create menus that ask the user to enter number 1 if they want to do something, number 2 if they want to do something else, number 3 if they want to do a third thing, and so on. You can laugh if you want at its quaint, old–fashioned ways, but this really is a useful feature. In fact, you can use **select** to provide portable, hardware–independent menus.*

I like to use **select** to insulate users from the brutalities of UNIX command syntax. For example, can you remember the options that accompany the UNIX **ps** command? I can't. That's why I like to place the options inside a **select** loop and give myself useful prompts.

---

* Actually, a clever programmer could use **select** to generate menu entries and then display the entries on a graphical user interface, but I won't cover that.

A Simple select Example

The following script generates a two-entry menu. After displaying the two entries, the script prompts the user for input. The prompt is stored inside a variable named **PS3**. No matter what the user enters, the script responds with a polite "Thank you." In other words, the script makes no attempt to process the user's choice.

```
USAGE="usage: select1.ksh"  # a simple select statement

 print "To stop the script, type the character(s) that signify "
 print "end-of-file for your operating system.  If you are using "
 print "the UNIX operating system, end-of-file is usually <CONTROL>d."

 PS3="Enter your choice: "   # PS3 is the prompt

 select menu_list in English francais   # list consists of two entries
 do
   print "Thank you.\n"     # a case statement usually goes here
 done
```

Executing This Script

```
$ select1.ksh
To stop the script, type the character(s) that signify
end-of-file for your operating system.  If you are using
the UNIX operating system, end-of-file is usually <CONTROL>d.
1) English
2) francais
Enter your choice: 1
Thank you.

Enter your choice: 2
Thank you.

Enter your choice: <CONTROL>d *** EOF ***
```

(My system happens to print *****EOF***** when I type the end-of-file character; your system might not.)

A select with a case

This script is similar to the previous one except that this one contains a **case** statement to process user input. In this script, the **case** statement takes an action depending on the user's input.

```
USAGE="usage: select2.ksh"  # select statement containing case

 print "To stop the script, type the character(s) that signify "
 print "end-of-file for your operating system.  If you are using the "
 print "UNIX operating system, end-of-file is usually <CONTROL>d."

 PS3="Enter your choice: "    # PS3 is the prompt

 select menu_list in English francais  # list consists of two entries
 do
   case $menu_list in
     English) print "Thank you";;
     francais) print "Merci.";;
   esac
 done
```

Executing This Script

```
$ select2.ksh
To stop the script, type the character(s) that signify
end-of-file for your operating system.  If you are using the
UNIX operating system, end-of-file is usually <CONTROL>d.
1) English
2) francais
Enter your choice: 1
Thank you
Enter your choice: 2
Merci.
Enter your choice: <CONTROL>d *** EOF ***
```

Unexpected User Input

Even though you're spoon-feeding the user, the user might still blow it. What happens if the user doesn't enter one of the menu choices?

```
USAGE="usage: select3.ksh"  # unexpected user input
 print "To stop the script, type the character(s) that signify "
 print "end-of-file for your operating system.  If you are using the "
 print "UNIX operating system, end-of-file is usually <CONTROL>d."

 PS3="Enter your choice: "    # PS3 is the prompt

 select menu_list in English francais  # list consists of two entries
 do
   case $menu_list in
      English) print "Thank you.";;
      francais) print "Merci.";;
# Use a * pattern to catch any input values other than 1 or 2.
      *) print "You can only enter 1 or 2.";;
   esac
 done
```

Executing This Script

```
$ select3.ksh
To stop the script, type the character(s) that signify
end-of-file for your operating system.  If you are using the
UNIX operating system, end-of-file is usually <CONTROL>d.
1) English
2) francais
Enter your choice: 1
Thank you.
Enter your choice: 5
You can only enter 1 or 2.
Enter your choice: <CONTROL>d *** EOF ***
```

Gracefully Exiting from Menus

The following script demonstrates how to exit gracefully from a **select** statement. In this one, the poor user won't have to type an end-of-file character to end the menu selection; instead, the user will merely select a particular menu entry.

```
USAGE="usage: select4.ksh"  # leaving a select statement

 PS3="Enter your choice: "    # PS3 is the prompt

# This menu contains three entries.
# If the user picks "I've had enough", the script ends.
 select menu_list in English francais "I've had enough"
 do
   case $menu_list in
     English) print "Thank you.";;
     francais) print "Merci.";;
     "I've had enough") break;;
     *) print "You can only enter 1, 2, or 3.";;
   esac
 done

 print "So long!"
```

Executing This Script

```
$ select4.ksh
1) English
2) francais
3) I've had enough
Enter your choice: 2
Merci.
Enter your choice: 3
So long!
```

Repeating the Menu Selections

The previous script lists the menu choices only once. The following script (which is almost identical to the previous script) allows the user to see the menu choices any time he or she wants. In fact, the only difference between this script and the last is in the value of **PS3**. This script tells the user to press <RETURN> to repeat the menu choices. In fact, whenever the user enters a blank line, the script will repeat the menu choices. The reason this works has to do with a bizarre variable named **REPLY**. I say "bizarre" because if you look at the script you won't see it. Nevertheless, it's there. (Trust me on this one.) Whatever the user types in as a response to **PS3** the KornShell automatically assigns to **REPLY**. The **select** statement always looks at the value of **REPLY**. If the value of **REPLY** is the null string (a blank line), **select** redisplays the menu choices.

```
USAGE="usage: select5.ksh"  # repeating menu entries

 PS3="Enter your choice (or press <RETURN> to repeat): "

# Create a potentially infinite loop.
 select menu_list in English francais "I've had enough"
 do
    case $menu_list in
        English) print "Thank you.";;
        francais) print "Merci.";;
        "I've had enough") break;;    # break ends the loop
        *) print "You can only enter 1, 2, or 3.";;
    esac
 done
```

Executing This Script

```
$ select5.ksh
1) English
2) francais
3) I've had enough
Enter your choice (or press <RETURN> to repeat): 2
Merci.
Enter your choice (or press <RETURN> to repeat): <RETURN>
1) English
2) francais
3) I've had enough
Enter your choice (or press <RETURN> to repeat): 3
```

Wildcards in Menu Entries

The **select** statement (like the **for** statement) allows you to use wildcards to generate a list of menu entries. Like **for**, the KornShell will expand any wildcards in a **select** statement to all appropriate object names. For example, the following **select** statement contains the pattern **chapter?** So, if there are six files that match this pattern, then the menu will contain six entries (plus the "stop script" entry).

```
USAGE="usage: select6.ksh"  # wildcards in menus

 PS3="Status of which chapter: "    # PS3 is the prompt

 select menu_list in chapter? "stop script"
 do
   case $menu_list in
       chapter1)  print "Half completed.";;
       chapter2)  print "Nearing Completion.";;
       chapter3)  print "Nearing Completion.";;
       chapter4)  print "Completed.";;
       chapter5)  print "Nearing Completion.";;
       chapter6)  print "Half completed.";;
       "stop script") exit;;
       *)         print "Improper choice.";;
   esac
 done
```

Executing This Script

Before running this script, create six files. It makes no difference what you put inside the six files; in fact, each of the files could be empty. Name the files **chapter1**, **chapter2**, **chapter3**, **chapter4**, **chapter5**, and **chapter6**.

```
$ select6.ksh
1) chapter1
2) chapter2
3) chapter3
4) chapter4
5) chapter5
6) chapter6
7) stop script
Status of which chapter: 4
Completed.
Status of which chapter: 1
Half completed.
Status of which chapter: 7
```

Wildcards in case Statements

The last script was useful, but the following script goes it one better.

```
USAGE="usage: select7.ksh"  # more wildcards in menus

 PS3="Status of which chapter: "    # PS3 is the prompt

 select menu_list in chapter* "stop script"
 do
   case $menu_list in
       chapter[16]) print "Half completed.";;
       chapter[235]) print "Nearing Completion.";;
       chapter[4])  print "Completed.";;
       "stop script") exit;;
       *)            print "Improper choice.";;
   esac
 done
```

Executing This Script

If you created six files in order to run the **select6.ksh** example (that appeared on the previous page), then you're ready to run **select7.ksh**. If you didn't create those files, you had better do so now. (Read the description on the previous page.)

```
$ select7.ksh
1) chapter1
2) chapter2
3) chapter3
4) chapter4
5) chapter5
6) chapter6
7) stop script
Status of which chapter: 4
Completed.
Status of which chapter: 1
Half completed.
Status of which chapter: 7
```

A Practical select Example

This script shows a practical use of **select**. This script hides the syntax of UNIX commands from the user. The user can select the kind of operation he or she wants to perform without knowing the name of the UNIX command that gets it done.

```
USAGE="usage: select8.ksh"      # using OS commands in menus
 PS3="Please enter a number: "  # here is the prompt
 select cmd in "list files" "delete a file" "copy file" "quit menu"
 do
   case $cmd in
      "list files")
         ls;;      # UNIX command to list contents of directory
      "delete a file")
         print "Which file do you want to delete?"
         read doomed_file
         rm $doomed_file;;  # UNIX command to delete files
      "copy file")
         print "What existing file do you want to copy?"
         read file_to_copy
         print "What do you want to call the copy?"
         read file_to_create
         cp $file_to_copy $file_to_create;;# UNIX command to copy files
      "quit menu")  # if user enters 4, leave the script
         exit;;
      *)  # if user enters an unexpected number, print error message
         print "You did not enter a number between 1 and 4.";;
   esac
 done
```

Executing This Script

```
$ select8.ksh
1) list files
2) delete a file
3) copy file
4) quit menu
Please enter a number: 1
a         chapter3    repeat_selections
ch.doc    chapter4    select_case
Please enter a number: 2
Which file do you want to delete?
chapter3
Please enter a number: 4
```

Menus Inside of Menus (Submenus)

The following script shows you how to create a menu within another menu—a submenu. That is, one of the menus leads to a second menu.

In case you aren't familiar with UNIX commands, the **ls** command lists the names of all objects in a directory, and **ls -l** lists detailed information about every object.

```
USAGE="usage: select9.ksh"   # menus within other menus

main_menu_prompt="Main Menu: enter 1, 2, or 3 (or <RETURN>): "
submenu_prompt="Submenu: please enter 1 or 2: "

   PS3="$main_menu_prompt"  # assign main menu prompt to PS3
   select cmd in "list files" "delete a file" "quit menu"
   do
      case $cmd in
         "list files")
            PS3="$submenu_prompt"   # assign submenu prompt to PS3
    # If user selects "list files", a submenu will appear.
            select option in "quick list" "detailed list"
            do
               case $option in
                 "quick list") ls
                               break;;     # leave submenu
                 "detailed list") ls -l
                                  break;;  # leave submenu
                 *) print "You must enter 1 or 2."
                    break;;
               esac
            done
            PS3=$main_menu_prompt;;  # change prompt back again

         "delete a file")
            print "Which file do you want to delete?"
            read doomed_file
            rm "$doomed_file";;    # UNIX command to delete files

         "quit menu")    # if user enters 4, leave the script
            exit;;
         *)       # if user enters a bad number, print an error message
            print "You did not enter a number between 1 and 4."
      esac
  done   # end of outer select
```

Executing This Script

```
$ select9.ksh
1) list files
2) delete a file
3) quit menu
Main Menu: enter 1, 2, or 3 (or <RETURN>): 1
1) quick list
2) detailed list
Submenu - please enter 1 or 2: 2
total 115
drwxrwxrwx  1 rosenberg    1024 Dec  2 10:24 a
-rwxrwxrwx  1 rosenberg   20492 Dec 11 10:35 ch.doc
-rwxrwxrwx  1 rosenberg   20219 Dec 11 10:32 ch.doc.bak
-rwxrwxrwx  1 rosenberg   20492 Dec 11 11:14 ch.doc.bu
-rwxrwxrwx  1 rosenberg    7939 Dec 11 10:31 ch.mm
-rwxrwxrwx  1 rosenberg    7275 Nov 20 09:23 ch.mm.bak
1) list files
2) delete a file
3) quit menu
Main Menu - please enter 1, 2, or 3: 3
```

select generate a menu.

Syntax:

select *variable* **in** *list*
do
    command1
    ...
    commandN
done

select *variable*
do
    command1
    ...
    commandN
done

Where:

variable is any variable name.

list is a list of strings, numbers, or filenames. If the list contains any KornShell wildcards, the KornShell expands the wildcards into filenames before beginning the loop.

command is the name of any user program, operating system command, KornShell script, or KornShell statement (except for **done**). However, *command* is typically a **case** statement.

Quick Summary:

The **select** and **for** statements share the same syntax. Both statements create loops; however, the primary purpose of the **select** statement is to create a looping menu. The elements of *list* form the menu's entries. So, if *list* consists of six elements, the menu will contain each of those six entries. The **select** statement places a number in front of each of the menu entries. In our example, the menu entries are numbered 1 through 6.

After displaying the menu entries, the KornShell automatically prompts the user to enter a menu entry. You control the text of the prompt by assigning a string to variable **PS3**. In other words, whatever text you assign to **PS3** will be the prompt that the user sees. The user then selects a menu entry by typing a number.

If you specify **for** *variable* without specifying **in** *list*, then the list of elements consists of the entire set of positional parameters. See Chapter 9 for details on this syntax.

Chapter 9
Command Line Arguments and Positional Parameters

This chapter describes command line arguments and positional parameters.

If You're New to Programming...

How do shell scripts get input data? Up until now, we've used the **read** statement to assign variables. That is, after invoking the script, we'd prompt the user for some information and then use **read** to record the user's input. So, the user sees the script like this:

```
$ myscript.ksh
Enter a string: Ignatov
Enter a number: 11
```

Another way of gathering data is to have the user specify it when invoking the script, something like this:

```
$ myscript.ksh Ignatov 11
```

That is, the user types the name of the script followed by one or more values. These values are called *command line arguments*. Then, the KornShell script must somehow interpret these values. Fortunately, this process is neither mysterious nor particularly difficult. In fact, the KornShell provides several programming constructs to help you analyze the command line arguments.

Another name for command line arguments is *positional parameters*. The set of positional parameters is a collection of values, each stored in a different cell and each accessible by number. That definition should remind you of arrays. In fact, the set of positional parameters is very much like an array. For example, you can use the **set** statement to define both positional parameters and arrays. However, you can also define positional parameters with command line arguments or with function calls (described in Chapter 10).

The KornShell automatically assigns a special name to each positional parameter. For example, the KornShell gives the name **$1** to the command line argument immediately following the script name. See Table 10 for a complete list of positional parameter names. The KornShell does support a powerful, if complicated, statement called **getopts** to help you analyze single-letter arguments known as *switches* or *options*. However, its purpose and syntax may be too convoluted for beginners.

If You're an Experienced Programmer...

Picking arguments off the command line can be a nuisance in many high-level programming languages. I've certainly thrown my hands in the air and screamed "argv!" on occasion. For this reason and others, many programmers use KornShell scripts as "front-ends" to their compiled programs. That is, they use the KornShell to swallow the command line whole and then feed a predigested version of it to the compiled program.

Broadly speaking, there are three classes of information that a user can specify on the KornShell command line:

- Simple arguments (like numbers, strings, pathnames, etc.)
- Single-letter options preceded by a minus sign (**-x**) or a plus sign (**+x**).
- I/O redirection operators (like > or <)

Another name for command line arguments is *positional parameters*. Actually, the positional parameters have a broader scope than command line arguments. In other words, command line arguments are just one way of setting the values of positional parameters. Another way is with the **set** statement. A third way is with function calls (described in Chapter 10).

The KornShell provides the following features to help you analyze command line arguments:

- A positional parameter shorthand
- A mechanism for setting the values of undefined positional parameters
- The **shift** statement, which does the command line equivalent of a "left shift" operation
- The **getopts** statement to parse single-character command line options
- The **set** statement, which can set positional parameters independently of command line arguments

Positional Parameters

Whenever you invoke a script, issue certain **set** statements, or make a function call, the KornShell assigns values to the *positional parameters*. Table 10 lists all the positional parameters and their meanings. For example, if you invoke a script named **judy** as follows:

```
$ judy hi ho
```

the KornShell assigns "judy" to **$0**, "hi" to **$1**, and "ho" to **$2**. Positional parameters larger than 9 must be encased in braces; for example, notice the right and wrong ways to specify the eleventh positional parameters:

```
print ${11} # right
print $11   # wrong, means $1 followed by the digit 1
```

Table 10. Positional Parameters

Positional parameter	Meaning
$0	if command line argument, name of script; if function call, name of function; if **set** statement, pathname of the KornShell itself
$1 **$2** **$3** . . . **${10}** **${N}**	name of first argument to script, function, or **set** name of second argument to script, function, or **set** name of third argument to script, function, or **set** . . . name of tenth argument to script, function, or **set** name of *n*th argument to script, function, or **set**
$#	number of currently set positional parameters
$@** or **$*	expands every positional parameter, one at a time

The KornShell imposes no limit on the number of positional parameters, but hardware and operating system constraints will effectively limit this number.

You can use the assignment operator (=) to assign the value of a positional parameter to other values, but you cannot use = to assign a value to a positional parameter; for example:

```
x=$1          # right
$1="hi"       # wrong
1="hi"        # wrong
```

Positional parameters **$*** and **$@** are identical; however, "$@" and "$@" are not identical. For full details, see Page 127; for now, here are the differences:

```
"$@" expands to "$1" "$2" ... "$n"
"$*" expands to "$1s$2s...$n" # where s is the first character
                              # assigned to the IFS variable
```

Assigning Positional Parameters with Command Line Arguments

This script demonstrates how to invoke a KornShell script and pass it arguments on the command line. The passed arguments will become positional parameters. That is, the KornShell will assign the first command line argument to positional parameter **$1**, the second command line argument to positional parameter **$2**, and the third command line argument to **$3**.

```
USAGE="usage: param1.ksh arg1 arg2 arg3" # assigning $1, $2, and $3

 print "The name of the shell script is $0"
 print "The first argument after the shell script name is $1"
 print "The second argument after the shell script name is $2"
 print "The third argument after the shell script name is $3"
 print

 print "Here are all the arguments:"
 print $*
```

Executing This Script

The usage line of this script tells us that in order to invoke this script properly, you need to specify the name of the script (**param1.ksh**) followed by three arguments. The usage line does not tell us what kind of arguments we have to specify, so any three arguments ought to be just fine.

```
$ param1.ksh dog fish 343
The name of the shell script is pos_param1
The first argument after the shell script name is dog
The second argument after the shell script name is fish
The third argument after the shell script name is 343

Here are all the arguments:
dog fish 343
```

Counting Positional Parameters

Use the **$#** operator to determine how many command line arguments there are. The following script expects exactly one argument; if the user invokes the script incorrectly, the script displays the usage line.

Notice that the usage line in the following script contains **$0** instead of the actual script filename. Remember that **$0** stands for the name of the script file itself. Using **$0** instead of an explicit filename ensures that the usage line will always match the actual filename.

```
USAGE="usage: $0 arg1"     # counting command line arguments

# This script expects to receive exactly one argument.
# If it doesn't, the script reports the proper usage.

# The symbol $# equals the number of arguments.
 if (($# > 1))
 then
   print "You passed too many arguments to $0."
   print "$USAGE"
 elif (($# == 1))
 then
   print "You invoked $0 correctly."
 else
   print "You forgot to specify an argument to $0."
   print "$USAGE"
 fi
```

Executing This Script

Assume that the preceding script is stored in a file named **counting_params**.

```
$ param2.ksh                   # invoke script with zero arguments
You forgot to specify an argument to param2.ksh.
usage: param2.ksh arg1

$ param2.ksh apricot           # invoke script with one argument
You invoked counting_params correctly.

$ param2.ksh apricot banana  # invoke script with two arguments
You passed too many arguments to param2.ksh.
usage: param2.ksh arg1
```

Command Line Arguments or Run Time Arguments

The following script is very forgiving. The user is supposed to pass an argument on the command line. However, if the user forgets, the script will prompt for a value. In other words, there is no wrong way to call this script.

```
USAGE="usage: param3.ksh [dir_pathname]"    # command line or run time

 if (($# > 0))
 then  # user has entered one or more command line arguments
    dir_name=$1
   # If user enters multiple arguments, the script ignores all
   # but the first argument.
 else  # user has entered zero command line arguments
   print -n "Enter the name of one directory: "
   read dir_name
 fi

 print "You specified the following directory: $dir_name"
 if [[ ! -d $dir_name ]]
 then
   print "Gee, I'm sorry, but $dir_name isn't a directory."
 fi
```

Executing This Script

```
$ param3.ksh                  # zero directories on command line
Enter the name of one directory: /usr/users/jan
You specified the following directory: /usr/users/jan

$ param3.ksh /usr/users/jan  # one directory on command line
You specified the following directory: /usr/users/jan

$ param3.ksh /usr/users/jan /usr/users/jan/songs  # two directories on command line
You specified the following directory: /usr/users/jan
```

Default Values of Positional Parameters

The following script is a subtle variant of the preceding one. In the following script, the user may specify a directory name on the command line. However, if the user does not, the script automatically assigns a *default* directory name. In this case, the default directory name is **/usr/users/eddy**.

```
USAGE="usage: param4.ksh [pathname_of_directory]"  # default values

# If user specifies at least one command line argument, then the value
# of dir_name will be $1.  If user specifies zero command line
# arguments, then the value of dir_name will be /usr/users/eddy.

  dir_name=${1:-/usr/users/eddy}

  print "Checking the following directory: $dir_name"
  if [[ ! -d $dir_name ]]
  then
    print "Gee, I'm sorry, but $dir_name isn't a directory."
  fi
```

Executing This Script

```
$ param4.ksh # don't specify a directory on the command line; use default
Checking the following directory: /usr/users/eddy
Gee, I'm sorry, but /usr/users/eddy isn't a directory.

$ param4.ksh /usr/users/adrienne  # specify a directory on the command line
Checking the following directory: /usr/users/adrienne
```

The **${1:–$/usr/users/eddy}** expression belongs to a class of expressions called parameter expansion modifiers that are explained in Chapter 13.

Using set to Specify Positional Parameters

The **set** statement performs a variety of feats. For now, let's concentrate on its ability to set, unset, or sort positional parameters. In other words, you don't have to insist that the user type arguments on the command line in order to get all the features of positional parameters.

```
USAGE="usage: set1.ksh"    # the set statement
 set Ignatov Brunn Gatto Rastelli  # assign $1, $2, $3, and $4
 print "Here is a list of $# great jugglers: "
 for jugglers in "$@"
 do
    print "\t$jugglers"
 done

 set -s       # sort all the positional parameters in lexical order
 print "\nHere is the same list, sorted alphabetically: "
 for jugglers in "$@"
 do
    print "\t$jugglers"
 done

 set --       # set -- "unsets" all positional parameters
 print "\nWhere have all the jugglers gone? Long time passing: "
 for jugglers in "$@"
 do
    print "\t$jugglers"
 done
```

Executing This Script

```
$ set1.ksh
Here is a list of 4 great jugglers:
            Ignatov
            Brunn
            Gatto
            Rastelli

Here is the same list, sorted alphabetically:
            Brunn
            Gatto
            Ignatov
            Rastelli

Where have all the jugglers gone? Long time passing:    # empty list
```

Processing Positional Parameters with shift

The **shift** statement eliminates the leftmost argument(s). That is, **shift** slides all the positional parameters to the left by one or more positions. Incidentally, shifting too far causes a KornShell error. For example, if there are only four positional parameters, the statement **shift 5** will cause an error.

```
USAGE="usage: shift_ex.ksh arg1 arg2 arg3 arg4 arg5" # shift statement

 print "You specified $# arguments."
 print "The first argument is $1."

 print
 shift 1
 print "Following a shift, there are only $# arguments."
 print "The first argument is now $1."

 print
 shift 2
 print "Following a shift 2, there are only $# arguments."
 print "The first argument is now $1."
```

Executing This Script

```
$ shift_ex.ksh apricot banana carambola daikon eggplant
You specified 5 arguments.
The first argument is apricot.

Following a shift, there are only 4 arguments.
The first argument is now banana.

Following a shift 2, there are only 2 arguments.
The first argument is now daikon.
```

Table 11 illustrates what happens.

Table 11. The Influence of **shift** *on Positional Parameters*

	$1	**$2**	**$3**	**$4**	**$5**
original	apple	banana	carambola	daikon	eggplant
after first **shift**	banana	carambola	daikon	eggplant	unset
after second **shift**	daikon	eggplant	unset	unset	unset

Processing Positional Parameters with $* and $@

The KornShell expands the expressions $* or $@ to mean the value of all the positional parameters. The expressions $* and $@ are interchangeable. However, $* and "$*" have different meanings and so do $@ and "$@".

The following script averages all the integers specified on the command line.

```
USAGE="usage: average2.ksh int1 [int2 ... intN]"  # using $*

 integer running_total=0

 if (($# == 0))  # if user didn't specify any arguments, stop script
 then
   print $USAGE
   exit 1
 fi

# Each time through the loop, the KornShell will assign the value of
# the next integer on the command line to variable number.
 for number in $*
 do
   ((running_total = running_total + number))
 done

# Divide running_total by number of arguments.
 ((average = running_total / $#))
 print "The average is $average."
```

Executing This Script

```
$ average2.ksh 6 4              # average two integers
The average is 5.

$ average2.ksh 221 178 153 195 201        # average five integers
The average is 189.
```

"$*" versus "$@"

The difference between "$*" and "$@" is subtle, but a helpful difference to understand. Here's a script that explores this difference.

This script introduces the KornShell reserved variable named **IFS**. Chapter 12 details this important variable. For now though, assume that **IFS** is a string variable to which you can assign a group of characters. For example, the following statement assigns a group of five characters to **IFS**.

```
IFS='aeiou'                # set IFS to list of vowels
```

```
USAGE="usage: expand.ksh"   # demonstrates "$*" vs "$@"
# Assign apple to $1, banana bread to $2, and carambola cookies to $3.
 set apple "banana bread" "carambola cookies"
# The KornShell expands "$@" into three elements: "$1" "$2" "$3".
# Therefore, the for loop consists of three elements:
 print \"\$\@\" "expands to three elements:"
 for element in "$@"
 do
   print "\t$element"
 done

# However, the KornShell expands "$*" into one long element: "$1 $2
$3".
 print "\n"\"\$\*\" "expands to one element:"
 for element in "$*"
 do
   print "\t$element"
 done

# The first character of the IFS variable is, by default, a blank
# space; therefore, the difference between "$*" and "$@" will
# be hard to spot.
 print "\nFirst character of IFS is a blank space: "
 print "\t"\"\$\*\"": $*"
 print "\t"\"\$\@\"": $@"

# However, let's place a semicolon as the first character of IFS.
 IFS=';,.'
# Now the difference between "$*" and "$@" will become apparent because
# the KornShell will place a semicolon between each expanded element
# of "$*" and white space between each expanded element of "$@".
 print "\nFirst character of IFS is a semicolon: "
 print "\t"\"\$\*\"": $*"
 print "\t"\"\$\@\"": $@"
```

Executing This Script

```
$ expand.ksh
"$@" expands to three elements:
             apple
             banana bread
             carambola cookies

"$*" expands to one element:
             apple banana bread carambola cookies

First character of IFS is a blank space:
             "$*": apple banana bread carambola cookies
             "$@": apple banana bread carambola cookies

First character of IFS is a semicolon:
             "$*": apple;banana bread;carambola cookies
             "$@": apple banana bread carambola cookies
```

These distinctions also apply to printing arrays. For example, in the **pr_ary.ksh** example shown in Chapter 3, we used the following statement to assign four values to an array named **flowers**:

```
set -A flowers gardenia "bird of paradise" hibiscus rose
```

The following two lines are equivalent ways of printing all the elements in an array:

```
print ${flowers[*]}
print ${flowers[@]}
```

However, if we set the first character of the **IFS** variable to a semicolon and place **${...}** within a pair of double quotes, then the difference becomes more obvious. For example, the following statement:

```
print "${flowers[@]}"
```

produces the output:

```
gardenia bird of paradise hibiscus rose
```

However, substituting * for @ as follows:

```
print "${flowers[*]}"
```

generates this output:

```
gardenia;bird of paradise;hibiscus;rose
```

Processing Simple Switches with getopts

A *switch* (also called an *option*) is a command line argument that starts with a - or + and is followed by one character. One-letter switches are all the rage in the UNIX operating system. Use the **getopts** statement to analyze switches. Typically, you specify the **getopts** statement as part of a **while** loop. The body of the **while** loop usually contains a **case** statement. It is really the combination of all three KornShell statements—**getopts**, **while**, and **case**—that provides a way to analyze switches.

```
USAGE="usage: getopts1.ksh [-x] [-y]"  # a simple getopts example

# This while loop executes as long as there are switches to evaluate.
 while getopts xy arguments
 do
   case $arguments in
      x) print "You entered -x as an option.";;
      y) print "You entered -y as an option.";;
   esac
done
```

Executing This Script

The usage line in this script says that you may optionally specify **-x** or **-y** when you invoke the script. If you do specify both options, the order in which you specify them is irrelevant.

```
$ getopts1.ksh -x
You entered -x as an option.

$ getopts1.ksh -y
You entered -y as an option.

$ getopts1.ksh -x -y
You entered -x as an option.
You entered -y as an option.

$ getopts1.ksh -xy
You entered -x as an option.
You entered -y as an option.

$ getopts1.ksh -t -y          # enter an option other than -x or -y
getopts1.ksh[4]: getopts: t bad option(s)
You entered -y as an option.

$ getopts1.ksh +x             # nothing happens; user must specify -x
```

What If the User Enters an Invalid Switch?

The previous example (**getopts1.ksh**) did not handle undefined switches very gracefully. For example, when the user entered an undefined switch (such as **-t**), the script issued an error message. The following script reports undefined switches to the user, but does not end the script.

Notice the colon (:) at the beginning of **:xy**. This leading colon tells **getopts** to

- Set the value of **arguments** to **?** if the user specifies any option other than **x** or **y**.
- Set the value of a KornShell reserved variable named **OPTARG** to the name of the undefined switch.

In the **case** statement, you have to precede the **?** with the escape character \ or else the KornShell will interpret the **?** as a wildcard.

```
USAGE="usage: getopts2.ksh [-x] [-y]"  # handling undefined switches

 while getopts :xy arguments  # note the leading colon
 do
   case $arguments in
      x)  print "You entered -x as a switch.";;
      y)  print "You entered -y as a switch.";;
      \?) print "$OPTARG is not a valid switch."
          print "$USAGE";;
   esac
 done
```

Executing This Script

```
$ getopts2.ksh -k -x
k is not a valid switch.
usage: getopts2.ksh [-x] [-y]
You entered -x as a switch.

$ getopts2.ksh -x -k
You entered -x as a switch.
k is not a valid switch.
usage: getopts2.ksh [-x] [-y]
```

On and Off Switches

By convention, a minus sign (–) preceding a switch means turn something on, and a plus sign + means turn something off. For example, in the following script, a **–d** switch sets variable **compile** to "on" and a **+d** switch sets **compile** to "off."

```
USAGE="usage: getopts3.ksh [+-d] [+-q]"  # + and - switches

 while getopts :dq arguments
 do
   case $arguments in
     d)  compile=on;;  # don't precede d with a minus sign
    +d)  compile=off;;
     q)  verbose=on;;  # don't precede q with a minus sign
    +q)  verbose=off;;
    \?)  print "$OPTARG is not a valid switch"
         print "$USAGE";;
   esac
 done

 print "compile = $compile; verbose = $verbose"
```

Executing This Script

```
$ getopts3.ksh -d +q
compile = on; verbose = off

$ getopts3.ksh +d -q
compile = off; verbose = on
```

Processing Switch Arguments

The following script demonstrates how to analyze *switch arguments*. A switch argument is a word or number that follows a switch. For example, perhaps the switch **-x** requires a switch argument that specifies the number of x-coordinate pixels on the screen.

The user can enter a switch argument so that it fits snugly against the switch (for example, **-x1024**) or the user can specify any number of spaces or tabs between the switch and the argument (for example, **-x 1024**). Regardless, the **getopts** statement can still analyze the switch argument. In fact, this is one reason why **getopts** can be such a pleasure to use.

To tell **getopts** that a switch requires a switch argument, place a colon (:) after the argument name. Then, when you run the script, the KornShell will assign the switch argument to a reserved variable named **OPTARG**.

```
USAGE="usage: getopts4.ksh [-x number] [-y number]"  # switch arguments
# The colon after the x and the y tell getopts that -x and -y each
# require a switch argument.
while getopts :x:y: arguments
do
  case $arguments in
    x)  print "You entered -x as a switch."
        argument_to_x=$OPTARG # getopts sets OPTARG to switch argument
        print "You entered $argument_to_x as an argument to x.";;
    y)  print "You entered -y as a switch."
        argument_to_y=$OPTARG # getopts sets OPTARG to switch argument
        print "You entered $argument_to_y as an argument to y.";;
    \?)  print "$OPTARG is not a valid switch."
         print "$USAGE";;
  esac
done
```

Executing This Script

```
$ getopts4.ksh -x 1024 -y 800
You entered -x as a switch.
You entered 1024 as an argument to x.
You entered -y as a switch.
You entered 800 as an argument to y.

$ getopts4.ksh -x1024 -y800      # it's okay if argument is adjacent to switch
You entered -x as a switch.
You entered 1024 as an argument to x.
You entered -y as a switch.
You entered 800 as an argument to y.
```

Processing Missing Switch Arguments

There is always a chance that the user will forget to enter a required switch argument. The following script notices the mistake and gives appropriate feedback. As you've already seen, a leading colon in the list of options helps you find invalid switches. In addition, the leading colon in the following script tells **getopts** to

- Set the value of **arguments** to a colon (:) if the user forgets to specify a switch argument to **-y**.
- Set the value of **OPTARG** to the name of the switch with the missing argument.

```
USAGE="usage: getopts5.ksh [-x number] [-y number]"  # missing args

 while getopts :y: arguments
 do
   case $arguments in
     y)  height=$OPTARG;;
 # If the user forgets to specify a switch argument to x or y,
 # then the KornShell assigns a colon : to arguments.
     :)  print "You forgot to enter an argument to $OPTARG";;
    \?)  print "$OPTARG is not a valid switch."
         print "$USAGE";;
   esac
 done
```

Executing This Script

```
$ getopts5.ksh -y 800        # user remembers to enter a switch argument

$ getopts5.ksh -y            # user forgets to enter a switch argument
You forgot to enter an argument to y
```

A Command Line Containing More Than Just Switches

The following script demonstrates how to analyze a command line that contains switches, switch arguments, and arguments unassociated with switches. Consider the following command line.

```
$ getopts6.ksh -x 1024 -y 800 red green blue     # right
```

The preceding command line contains two switches (**-x** and **-y**) and two switch arguments (**1024** and **800**). The command line also contains three extra values (**red**, **green**, and **blue**) unassociated with any switches. On a mixed command line such as this, the user must specify switches and switch arguments at the beginning of the command line; that is, just after the name of the script. So, for example, **getopts** would not be able to find any switches on the following command line:

```
$ getopts6.ksh red -x 1024 -y 800 green blue     # wrong
```

The KornShell reserved variable **OPTIND** stores the OPTion INDex of the command line argument that **getopts** is currently evaluating. That is, when **getopts** is evaluating the first command line argument (assuming it's a switch), the KornShell sets the value of **OPTIND** to 1.

```
USAGE="usage: getopts6.ksh [-x width] [-y height] [color1 ... colorN]"
 while getopts :x:y: arguments
 do
    case $arguments in
      x) width=$OPTARG;;  # assign switch argument to variable width
      y) height=$OPTARG;; # assign switch argument to variable height
      \?)  print "$OPTARG is not a valid switch."
           print "$USAGE";;
     esac
 done

# OPTIND now contains a number representing the identity of the first
# nonswitch argument on the command line.  For example, if the first
# nonswitch argument on the command line is positional parameter $5,
# OPTIND holds the number 5.
 ((positions_occupied_by_switches = OPTIND - 1))
# Use a shift statement to eliminate all switches and switch arguments
# from the set of positional parameters.
 shift $positions_occupied_by_switches
# After the shift, the set of positional parameters contains all
# remaining nonswitch arguments.

 print "Screen width: $width"
 print "Screen height: $height"
 print "Screen colors: $*"
```

Executing This Script

```
$ getopts6.ksh -x 1024 -y 800 red green
Screen width: 1024
Screen height: 800
Screen colors: red green

$ getopts6.ksh -y2048 yellow cyan silver
Screen width:
Screen height: 2048
Screen colors: yellow cyan silver
```

! BEWARE: The Colon of getopts !

The colon (:) causes no end of confusion. You can place colons anywhere within the list of options. Unfortunately, the colon's purpose varies depending on where within the list you place it. A colon at the very beginning of the option list tells **getopts** how to handle undefined switches. A colon anywhere else in the option list tells **getopts** that a particular switch requires an argument.

For example, the colon in the following statement causes **getopts** to set the value of **thingy** to a question mark (?) when it encounters an undefined switch on the command line:

```
getopts :xyz thingy
```

On the other hand, the next use of the colon tells **getopts** to expect an argument right after the **-y** switch:

```
getopts xy:z thingy
```

You can specify multiple colons. For example, the following statement tells **getopts** to expect arguments with **-x** and **-z**, and to handle undefined switches by setting **thingy** to a question mark.

```
getopts :x:yz: thingy
```

There exists yet another use for the colon and this use is demonstrated in the **getopts5.ksh** example earlier in this chapter.

getopts parse command line switches.

Syntax:

getopts *possible_switches var_name* [*data1* ... *dataN*]

Where:

possible_switches	is a list of legal one-character switch names, possibly including one or more colons. (See the previous page for a lengthy discussion of the colon.)
var_name	is any variable name.
[*data1* ... *dataN*]	is one or more strings separated by white space. If you do not specify *data*, **getopts** will analyze the current set of positional parameters (usually the positional parameters passed on the command line). If you do specify *data*, **getopts** will evaluate *data* instead of the positional parameters. Generally speaking, you won't specify *data* as part of the **getopts** statement; however, specifying it this way may be helpful when debugging your script.

Quick Summary:

The primary purpose of **getopts** is to analyze command line switches and their (optional) arguments. Switches begin with a + or – and are followed by a character. A switch can optionally be followed by a switch argument.

Chapter 10
Functions

This chapter covers functions. Beginners may wish to skip over this chapter.

If You're New to Programming...

Picture yourself in Hawaii, pen in one hand, pineapple juice in the other, writing a short postcard to a jealous friend. Presumably, given the short length and inane content of the postcard, you won't need to worry much about organizing your thoughts. Now picture yourself on a January's eve in Michigan, cranking out the definitive treatise on "Our Friend the Wolverine." Since your grand project weighs in at over 600 pages, you'll find it necessary to organize your book into chapters.

In the same vein, you won't have to give a lot of thought to organizing a five-line KornShell script. However, when writing a long script, you'll probably want to organize your script into *functions.* A function is essentially a chapter of your script.

Each chapter of your wolverine book will describe a discrete aspect of wolverines; for example, "Chapter 19: Wolverine Diet." Now that the chapter has a name, you can refer to it as many times as you want from anywhere in the book. For example, in Chapter 2 you might write, "...and then the wolverine, primitive beast that he was, asked the waiter to bring a Bordeaux with the chicken. See Chapter 19 for details."

Similarly, each function will perform a discrete aspect of the script and each function will have a unique name; for example, **count_words_in_paragraph**. Now that the function has a name, you can *call* it whenever you need to count the number of words in a paragraph. You can call this function as many times as you like; perhaps you'll call it one time for every paragraph that the script analyzes.

Lest we carry the analogy too far, please note that KornShell functions can do things that chapters cannot. In particular, when you call a function, you can optionally *pass* one or more values to it. For example, suppose you define a function named **find_area_of_rectangle**. When calling this function, you pass two values to it: the length of the rectangle and the width of the rectangle. In the KornShell language, the call will look something like this:

```
find_area_of_rectangle $length $width
```

When you pass grain through a mill, the mill will produce flour. Similarly, when you pass the length and width of the rectangle through the function, the result should be the area of the rectangle. A KornShell function can optionally *return* one value to the part of the script that called it. For example, perhaps the function **find_area_of_rectangle** returns the actual area of the rectangle. In the KornShell language, the **return** statement will look something like this:

```
return $area
```

If You're an Experienced Programmer...

The KornShell, like most high-level languages, supports *functions.* (Actually, you may be more familiar with terms like procedure, subprocedure, or subprogram, instead of function.) KornShell functions provide these services to the programmer:

- KornShell functions let the programmer organize a large script into smaller, more-manageable routines.
- The code inside a KornShell function is executed only when called by some other portion of the script. However, the KornShell does check the function for syntax errors when you invoke the script, even if the function never gets called.
- KornShell functions can optionally return one or more values to the caller. In most high-level languages, the programmer must indicate whether or not the function will return a value, and if so, what data type the returned value will have. In the KornShell, there is no way to do this. If you want the function to return a value, use the **return** statement. The returned value will always be an integer.
- You can use **typeset** to declare local variables within KornShell functions.

Unlike most high-level languages, the KornShell does not provide function prototyping. That is, although you can pass values to a KornShell function, there is no way to specify the number of values or their data types.

A Disorganized Script without Functions

Here's a messy script, the kind of script you really shouldn't write. It contains a lot of redundant code.

```
USAGE="usage: funcless.ksh"  # a script that ought to have functions
 print -n "What file contains the ingredients: "
 read object
 if [[ ! -f $object ]]
 then
   print "$object is not a file."
 elif [[ ! -r $object ]]
 then
   print "You don't have permission to read $object."
 else
   print "$object contains: "
   cat $object
 fi

 print -n "\nWhat file contains the data: "
 read object
 if [[ ! -f $object ]]
 then
   print "$object is not a file."
 elif [[ ! -r $object ]]
 then
   print "You don't have permission to read $object."
 else
   print "$object contains: "
   cat $object
 fi
```

Executing This Script

```
$ funcless.ksh
What file contains the ingredients: gamma
gamma is not a file.

What file contains the data: alpha
alpha contains:
78
49
```

The Same Script Organized into Functions

Here's a better script. It's better because it's now organized into functions.

```
USAGE="usage: func1.ksh"      # a script containing a function

# This function, named examine_the_file_if_possible, won't execute
# until it is called by some other portion of the script.
function examine_the_file_if_possible
{ # The body of the function starts at the next line
   if [[ ! -f $object ]]
   then
      print "$object is not a file."
   elif [[ ! -r $object ]]
   then
      print "You don't have permission to read $object."
   else
      print "$object contains: "
      cat $object
   fi
} # The function ends here.

#######################################################################
# The script will begin execution at the next line:
 print -n "What file contains the ingredients: "
 read object
 examine_the_file_if_possible  # call the function

 print -n "\nWhat file contains the data: "
 read object
 examine_the_file_if_possible  # call the function again
```

Executing This Script

```
$ func1.ksh
What file contains the ingredients: gamma
gamma is not a file.

What file contains the data: alpha
alpha contains:
78
49
```

Simple Function with One Argument

In this script, the caller passes an integer value to a function named **sqr**. Within the confines of function **sqr**, the KornShell assigns the integer value to positional parameter **$1.** The function **sqr** takes the value (**$1**) squares it, and prints it. After the function finishes, the KornShell returns control to the statement immediately after the function call.

```
USAGE="usage: one_arg.ksh"      # passing a value to a function

########################################################################
# This is a function named sqr.  This function will be executed only
# if some other portion of the script calls it.
 function sqr
 {
# In this context, $1 is not a command line argument, but is the
# value of the argument passed by the caller.
   ((s = $1 * $1))
   print "The square of $1 is $s"
 }

########################################################################
# The shell script begins execution at the next line
 print -n "Enter an integer: "
 read an_integer

# Call function sqr and pass it the value of an_integer as an argument.
 sqr $an_integer # call function sqr and pass $an_integer to it
 print "Done."   # control returns to this line after function is done
```

Executing This Script

```
$ one_arg.ksh
Enter an integer: 6
The square of 6 is 36
Done.
```

! BEWARE: Command Line Arguments and Function Arguments !

By now, you have probably noticed that function arguments look just like command line arguments. In fact, specifying arguments on the command line or specifying arguments to a function are two different ways of setting positional parameters. However, you may mistakenly assume that a command line argument will automatically become a function argument. For example, consider the following script:

```
USAGE="usage: confused.ksh integer"  # confused function call
 function sqr  # a function to square a number
 {
   ((s = $1 * $1)) # $1 is undefined because caller didn't set it
   print $s
 }

 sqr    # call function sqr, but don't pass any arguments to it
```

Running this script produces an error message; for example:

```
$ confuse.ksh 7
sqr[2]: s =  * : syntax error
```

Although the command line argument **$1** does indeed equal 7, the function argument **$1** does not equal 7. In fact, the function argument **$1** is undefined because you did not specify any arguments to **sqr** when you called it. If you want the first command line argument to ultimately become **$1** within function **sqr**, then write the script as follows:

```
USAGE="usage: clearer.ksh integer"  # same script, done better
 function sqr  # a function to square a number
 {
   ((s = $1 * $1))
   print $s
 }

 sqr $1 # call function sqr and pass one argument to it, namely
        # the value of the first command line argument
```

And yet, command line arguments and function arguments are basically the same thing (positional parameters), just applied to different regions of the script. You might think of the part of the KornShell script that is not inside a function as being a separate function named **$0**. If you think of it that way, then the command line arguments are really just function arguments to function **$0**. If you are a C programmer, you might think of the part of the KornShell script that isn't inside a function as being analogous to the **main** function of a C program.

After the called function returns control to **$0**, the KornShell resets the positional parameters within **$0** to the value of the command line arguments.

A Function with Multiple Arguments

The following example contains a function that receives and uses multiple arguments. The arguments you pass to the function don't all have to be the same data type. In the following example, function **sqr** expects to receive two arguments. The first argument will be an integer and the second a string.

```
USAGE="usage: mul_args.ksh"  # passing multiple values to a function

########################################################################
# This is a function named "sqr".  It takes two arguments.
 function sqr
 {
   ((s = $1 * $1))
   print "$2: the square of $1 is $s"
 }

########################################################################
# The shell script begins execution at the next line.
integer an_integer
 print -n "Enter an integer: "
 read an_integer
 print -n "Enter your name: "
 read your_name

# Call function sqr and pass it the values of an_integer and your_name.
# Enclose all string arguments inside a pair of double quotes.
 sqr $an_integer "$your_name"
 print "Done."
```

Executing This Script

```
$ mul_args.ksh
Enter an integer: 20
Enter your name: Fox in Socks
Fox in Socks: the square of 20 is 400
Done.
```

A Script That Calls Another Script

One of the central dogmas of the UNIX religion is that programmers should write every program, command, or script in such a way that it can be easily called by any other program, command, or script. In the following example, the script named **call_scr** calls another script (**square.ksh**). Calling a separate script is pretty much the same thing as calling a function. However, one script cannot access a variable defined in another script.

```
USAGE="usage: call_scr.ksh"     # this script calls another script

 print -n "Enter an integer: "
 read an_integer

# Call the script named "square.ksh" and pass the value of an_integer
# as an argument to it.
 square.ksh $an_integer
```

Place this next script in a file named **square.ksh**:

```
USAGE="usage: square.ksh"    # this script is called by call_scr.ksh
# Pass one input argument to this script when you call it.

 ((s = $1 * $1))
 print "The square of $1 is $s"
```

Executing This Script

```
$ call_scr.ksh
Enter an integer: 6
The square of 6 is 36
```

Two Ways to Return Values

We've seen how the caller can send arguments to the called function or script. It is only natural to wonder how data can flow in the reverse direction, that is, from the callee back to the caller.

(Allow me a short digression. If you've programmed in high-level languages, you probably expect the callee to return values to the caller in a certain way. In fact, the KornShell's methods are rather unusual. Experienced programmers should momentarily suspend their experience and keep an open mind while reading this passage. Let's return to the discussion, already in progress.)

The KornShell provides two independent ways for the called function or script to send information back to the callee:

- The callee can send one integer value back to the caller by using the **return** statement. The **return** statement assigns an integer value to the predefined variable **$?**. The caller can then use or ignore the value of **$?**. On many operating systems, the integer returned by **$?** must be in the range 0 to 255. As such, it is useful for returning error codes and other small numbers, but little more than that.

- The callee can send any quantity or type of data back to the caller, if the caller uses the command output return parameter **$(...)**. This parameter tells the callee to pipe all function or script output into a variable selected by the caller.

These two methods are independent of each other. For example, the callee can return an integer value with **return** and return string data back to the caller if the caller uses **$(...)**. We explore both methods in the next few scripts.

Actually, there are two other ways for a function to communicate with its caller:

- The function could write information into a global variable and the caller could read that value. However, a lot of programming purists frown on this method.

- The function could write information into a file and the caller read data out of the file. Chapter 12 details file input and output.

Returning a Value from a Function with return

In the following script, the callee uses **return** to send one integer value back to the caller. The KornShell stores the returned integer value in variable **$?**. The caller assigns **$?** to a variable named **returned_value**.

```
USAGE="usage: return1.ksh"    # demonstrates the return statement
function sqr        # square the input argument and return the result
{
  ((s = $1 * $1))
  return $s         # return the value of s to the caller
}
#######################################################################
# The shell script begins execution at the next line:
 print -n "Enter an integer: "
 read an_integer
# Call function "sqr" and pass the value of an_integer as
# an argument to the function.
 sqr $an_integer

# The value returned by function sqr is stored in variable $?.
 returned_value=$?
 print "The square of $an_integer is $returned_value"
```

Executing This Script

```
$ return1.ksh
Enter an integer: 6
The square of 6 is 36
```

! BEWARE: $? Doesn't Stick Around Long !

If you intend to use the value of **$?** returned by the **return** statement, you had better use it right away because it won't last past the next command. In fact, every KornShell statement, KornShell script, operating system command, and user program modifies the value of **$?**. So, for example, if you mistakenly add a **print** statement after the function call, the exit status of the **print** statement will overwrite the value returned by function **sqr**:

```
sqr $an_integer # call function
print "Back"    # this statement overwrites the value of $?
returned_value=$? # assign exit status of print to returned_value
```

Using $(...) to Return Values from a Function

In the preceding script, the function **sqr** needed to return only an integer value back to the caller. In this next script, the function **sqr** will return a string. Since we cannot use **return** to return a string, the caller will have to call the function with the command output return parameter $(...).

```
USAGE="usage: retprmtr.ksh"     # returning values from functions

function sqr  # square the input argument
{
  ((s = $1 * $1))
  print "Input -> $1; Output -> $s"
}

################################################################
# The shell script begins execution at the next line.
 print -n "Enter an integer: "
 read an_integer

# Call function "sqr" and pass the value of an_integer as an
# argument to the function.  Assign all the output of function
# sqr to the returned_value variable.
 returned_value=$(sqr $an_integer)
# By surrounding the function call in a pair of parentheses, we've
# effectively "bottled" all the output from function sqr and stored
# it in the variable "returned_value".

 print "Function sqr returned this value: $returned_value"
```

Executing This Script

```
$ retprmtr.ksh
Enter an integer: 6
Function sqr returned this value: Input -> 6; Output -> 36
```

Local Variables versus Global Variables

By default, all KornShell variables are *global*. You can use a global variable anywhere within the script. However, if you use **typeset** (or **integer** or **readonly**) within a function, the newly declared variable will be a *local* variable. That is, you will be able to use that variable only within the function in which it is defined. If you do not explicitly declare a variable before using it, then the variable is automatically global.

In the following script, variables **ocean**, **sky**, and **earth** are global. Variable **ocean** is global because it is explicitly declared in a region of the script that is not within a function. Variables **sky** and **earth** are global because they are implicitly declared; that is, they are not created with **typeset**.

Variable **rain** is local to function **think** and variable **cloud** is local to function **act**. These two variables are local because they are explicitly declared within functions.

```
USAGE="usage: lcl_glbl.ksh"      # comparing local and global variables

integer ocean=10  # ocean is global
######################################################################
function think
{
 integer rain=5  # rain is local to function think

 ((rain = rain * 10))     # okay to modify rain within think
 print "rain = $rain"
 ((ocean = ocean * 100)) # okay to modify ocean within think
 print "ocean = $ocean"
}
######################################################################
function act
{
 typeset cloud  # cloud is a string variable local to function act

 cloud="cirrus"          # okay to modify cloud
 print "cloud = $cloud"
 sky="blue"              # sky is global because it isn't declared
                         # with typeset
}
######################################################################
# The script begins execution at the next line:
 think                   # call function think
 act                     # call function act
 print "sky = $sky"      # access global variable sky
 print "ocean = $ocean"  # access global variable ocean
 earth="mother"          # create a global variable named "earth"
```

Executing This Script

```
$ lcl_glbl.ksh
rain = 50
ocean = 1000
cloud = cirrus
sky = blue
ocean = 1000
```

! BEWARE: Global and Local Variables with the Same Name !

It is perfectly legal, though not advisable, to declare a local variable and a global variable with the same name. For example, the following script contains two variables named **x**, one of them global and the other local to function **foo**. Note that these are two distinct variables, each having a distinct value. Assigning a new value to one of the variables has no effect on the value of the other variable.

```
USAGE="usage: samename.ksh"  # confusing local and global variables
 integer x    # this is global variable x

function foo
{
  integer x   # this is local variable x

  x=3  # this statement doesn't change value of global variable x
  print "Within foo, the value of local x is $x"
}

#################################################################
# Script starts execution at next line.
 x=10
 print "The current value of global x is $x"
 foo
 print "The current value of global x remains $x"
```

Executing this script produces the following output:

```
$ samename.ksh
The current value of global x is 10
Within foo, the value of local x is 3
The current value of global x remains 10
```

The moral is that you should take care not to confuse global and local variables having the same name.

By the way, you can declare two local variables in two separate functions, each having the same name. For example, function **A** might contain a local variable named **counter** and function **B** might also contain a local variable named **counter.** Although these two variables share the same name, they are distinct variables because they are local to two different functions. Changing the value of one variable has no effect on the value of the other variable.

Passing Arrays as Arguments to Functions

You can pass an array as an argument to a function; however, the method you use is rather different from most high-level languages (like C). In most high-level languages, you pass a pointer to the starting element of the array. In the KornShell, there is no way to do this, so you must pass the entire array. For example, the following statement calls a function and passes every element of **array** to that function:

```
function_call ${array[*]}
```

The called function (for example, **find_minimum** in the following script) converts all the array elements into positional parameters.

```
USAGE="usage: pasarray.ksh"         # passing an array to a function
######################################################################
# This function finds the lowest number in the array.
function find_minimum
{
   set -s  # sort all positional parameters in lexical order,
           # from lowest to highest
# Since the positional parameters are now sorted, the first one ($1)
# must contain the lowest value.
   print "The minimum is $1"
}
######################################################################
# Read input and assign it to an array.
function gather_input
{
 integer counter=0
# Store values in array as three-digit numbers. If an input value takes
# up less than three digits, pad with leading zeros.
 typeset -Z3 array
 while read value  # read numbers out of $datafile and assign to array
 do
   array[$counter]=$value
   ((counter = counter + 1))
 done < $1        # (See Chapter 12 for information about this line.)
 find_minimum ${array[*]}     # call function; pass it all the elements
                              # of the array
}
######################################################################
# The script begins execution at the next line.
 print -n "Enter the pathname of the data file: "
 read datafile
 gather_input $datafile
```

Executing This Script

Before running the script, you need to place some numbers into a file. The numbers you specify must be between 0 and 999. Here's what I used.

```
$ cat data       # cat is the UNIX command to display the contents of a file
97
3
920
517
19
265
```

Now you can run the script as follows:

```
$ pasarray.ksh
Enter the pathname of the data file: data
The minimum is 003
```

Why was it necessary to declare **array** as follows?

```
typeset -Z3 array
```

The answer is quite complicated. Before I get into the whys and wherefores, I'd like you to try a little experiment. Delete **typeset –Z3 array** from the script and then re–execute the script; for example:

```
$ pasarray.ksh
Enter the pathname of the data file: data
The minimum is 19
```

Aha, the wrong answer, but why? The reason is that **set –s** sorts positional parameters in lexical order rather than numerical order. Since 19 has a lower lexical value than 3 (1 precedes 3 in the ASCII table), **set –s** sorts 19 before 3. However, specifying **typeset –Z3 array** causes the KornShell to store the array values like this:

```
097    003    920    517    019    265
```

In a sense, **typeset –Z3 array** levels the playing field. That is, now a lexical sort will correspond to a numerical sort.

Autoloading Functions

(Inexperienced programmers should probably skip over this section; it's hard.)

To explain autoloading, let me draw an analogy to programming in a compiled language. Suppose you write a large C program containing many functions. The C compiler has to compile every function in that program whether it ends up being called or not. Consequently, you end up with a program that is larger and slower than it theoretically has to be.

One solution, available on certain operating systems, is dynamic (run time) linking. In this solution, the programmer extracts certain functions from the program and places them into one or more function libraries. When the program makes a call to a function not inside the program, the operating system loader utility searches for the desired function inside the function libraries.

Autoloading in the KornShell is a lot like dynamic linking. With KornShell autoloading, you create one or more directories containing files of functions. Then, you can write KornShell scripts that call any of these functions, even though the code for these functions isn't actually inside your KornShell scripts. There are two important benefits:

- Your KornShell scripts will run faster because the KornShell won't have to interpret uncalled functions. That is, the KornShell ignores autoload functions unless the calling script specifically invokes them.

- You won't have to "reinvent the wheel." That is, every time you create a new function, you can place it inside one of the autoloading directories.

Now let's turn our attention to a working example. First, create a new directory to hold autoloaded functions. If you are on the UNIX operating system, you can use the **mkdir** command to create a directory, as follows:

```
$ mkdir $HOME/my_funcs
```

Next, using a text editor, type the following autoload function into a file. You must name the file **$HOME/my_funcs/sqr**. If you give it some other name, then this demonstration won't work.

```
# This is a function named sqr.  This function will be executed only if
# some other script calls it.
 function sqr
 {
   ((s = $1 * $1))
   print "The square of $1 is $s"
 }
```

Next, type the following script into a file named **callauto.ksh**. The directory in which you place **callauto.ksh** is irrelevant.

```
USAGE="usage: callauto.ksh"  # calling an autoloaded function

# Tell the KornShell that sqr is defined outside this file:
 autoload sqr

# Assign two directories to FPATH:
 FPATH=$HOME/my_funcs:/usr/groupfun

 print -n "Enter an integer: "
 read an_integer

# Call function sqr and pass it the value of an_integer.
 answer=$(sqr $an_integer)      # call the function
 print "$answer"
```

A few extra words of explanation are in order. The following statement:

```
autoload sqr
```

tells the KornShell that function **sqr** is to be autoloaded. (C language programmers may recognize that **autoload** is vaguely analogous to **extern** in C.)

FPATH is a KornShell reserved variable. This variable holds the names (separated by colons) of all the directories containing autoload functions. There is no default value for **FPATH**. The following statement assigns two directories to **FPATH**:

```
FPATH=$HOME/my_funcs:/usr/groupfun
```

Therefore, when **callauto.ksh** calls **sqr**, the KornShell will look for **sqr** inside directory **$HOME/my_funcs**. If **sqr** isn't there, the KornShell will search for it inside directory **/usr/groupfun**. If **sqr** isn't there either, the KornShell will issue the error message:

```
sqr: not found
```

Executing This Script

```
$ callauto.ksh
Enter an integer: 7
The square of 7 is 49
```

---

function a section of a script that can be called from any other section of a script.

Syntax:

function *name*
{
variable_decl

code
}

Where:

name is the name of the function. Function names follow the same rules as variable names. See Chapter 2 for details on variable names.

variable_decl is zero or more variable declarations (see Chapter 3). Any explicitly declared variables will have a value and scope local to the function in which they are defined. In other words, if you explicitly declare a variable (with **typeset** or one of its aliases), then that variable only has meaning within the function. If you implicitly declare a variable (by using it within a KornShell statement), then that variable has global scope. By the way, you can explicitly declare a local string variable with the syntax **typeset** *variable_name*.

code is any command or group of commands that could appear outside a function. For example, *code* could be a KornShell statement, an operating system command, or a call to another function or script. In fact, *code* could be anything except another **function** statement. (In other words, you can't nest a function inside another function.)

Quick Summary:

A function is a named section of your script. To invoke a function, the caller must specify the function's name optionally followed by one or more arguments. The optional arguments become positional parameters within the called function.

You cannot call a function unless it appears earlier in the script. In other words, you cannot make a "forward reference" to a function.

---

exit unconditionally halt execution of the current script and return to the caller.

return unconditionally halt execution of the current function and return to the caller.

Syntax:

exit *number* **return** *number*

Where:

number (optional) is any integer value representing the error status of the script (**exit**) or the function (**return**). The KornShell stores this value inside the **$?** variable. If you don't specify *number*, the KornShell sets *number* to 0.

Quick Summary:

A KornShell script stops running when one of the following happens:

- The KornShell executes the last line of the script.
- Your script receives an outside signal (like <CONTROL>c) telling it to stop running.
- Your script issues an **exit** statement.

A KornShell function stops running and returns to the caller when one of the following happens:

- The KornShell executes the last line of the function.
- Your script issues a **return** statement.

Chapter 11
Start–Up Scripts and Environments

This chapter explains start–up scripts, environment inheritance, dot scripts, and aliases. The information in this chapter is particularly relevant to system administrators. If you are a newcomer to the KornShell, you may want to hold off reading this chapter until you gain a little more experience.

Start–Up Scripts

Many programs run *start–up scripts* when you invoke them. Generally speaking, the purpose of a start–up script is to ensure that certain things happen to a program whenever it is invoked (that is, whenever it starts up). For example, the start–up script for a certain graphics program may tell the program what kind of terminal it is running on.

An operating system is itself a program. Typically, an operating system reads and executes one or more start–up scripts when you boot (start) it. For instance, the UNIX operating system usually reads and executes the start–up script located at pathname **/etc/rc**. This start–up script may, in turn, call other start–up scripts.

(At this point, let me pause to warn you that the following discussion is meaningful only if you're running the KornShell on a generic UNIX system. In other words, if you're running the KornShell on something other than a generic UNIX system, then start–up scripts probably do not work in the way that I'm about to describe. Also, I'd like to point out that there's currently no such thing as a generic UNIX system. Therefore, the following discussion is an approximation. I'd encourage you to read the documentation that describes login for your system.)

The KornShell supports three start–up scripts. The first two are *login scripts;* they are executed when you log in. A third start–up script runs whenever you create a KornShell or run a KornShell script.

When you log in, the system has to know which kind of shell to log you into. (After all, most UNIX systems support several different kinds of shells.) Typically, the system administrator at a UNIX site stores the identity of your login shell inside the **/etc/passwd** file. If your login shell is a KornShell, then the system automatically executes the following two login scripts immediately after starting the KornShell:

- **/etc/profile**
- **$HOME/.profile**

The **/etc/profile** script runs first. Every KornShell user on the system will share this script; therefore, it is a good place for the system administrator to store information that every user should have. The **$HOME/.profile** script runs second. Because this script is inside each user's **$HOME** directory, each user can customize the script to his or her needs. Figure 2 summarizes KornShell start–up scripts.

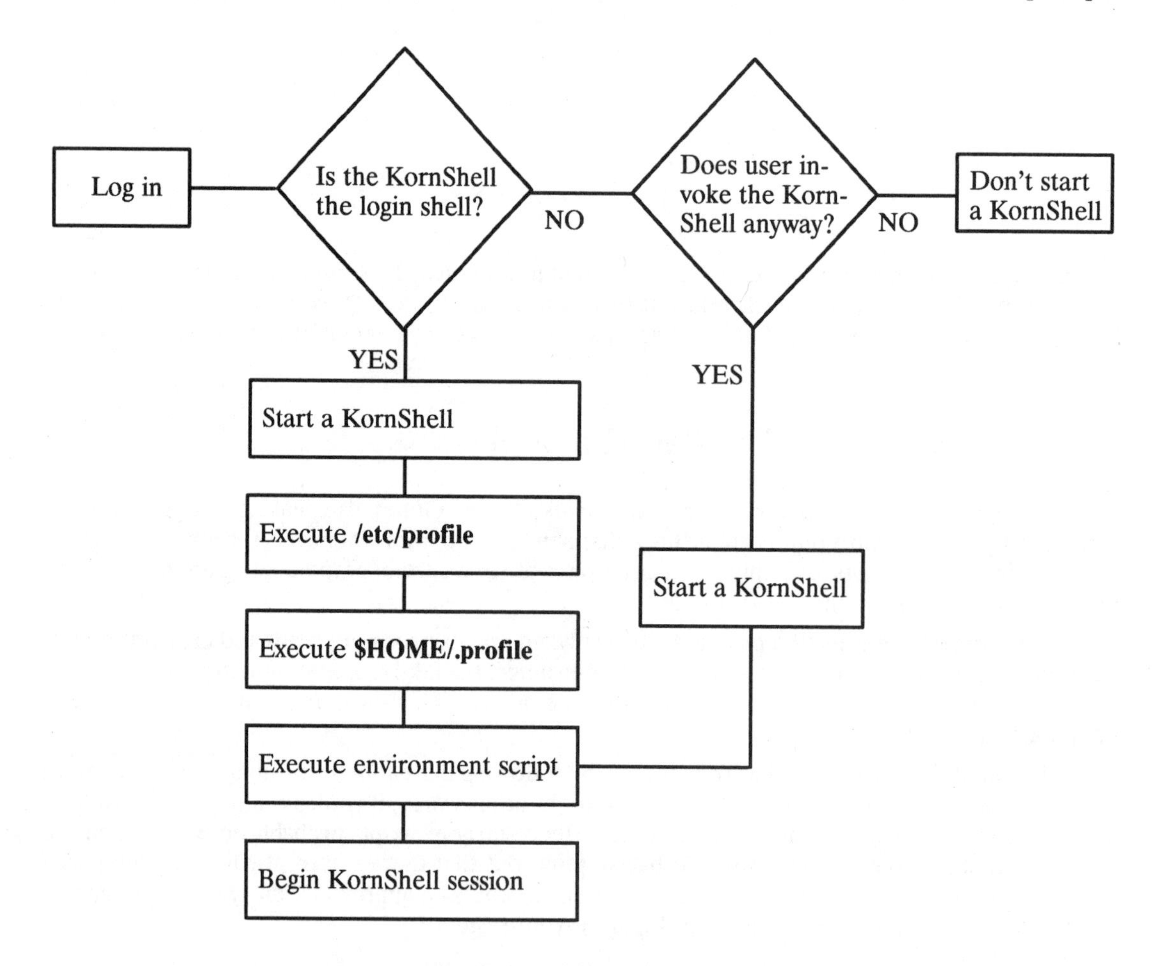

Figure 2. Sequence of KornShell start–up scripts

Whenever you start up a new KornShell or run a KornShell script, the system automatically invokes the *environment script*. The KornShell variable **ENV** holds the pathname of the environment script. For example, if the value of **ENV** is **$HOME/.kshrc**, the system will automatically invoke the script located at **$HOME/.kshrc** whenever you start up a KornShell or run a KornShell script.

The end of this chapter contains a sample **$HOME/.profile** script and a sample environment script.

Environments

A boy was arrested and dragged before the town judge. Before passing sentence, the judge asked the boy if he had anything to say. "Please have mercy, Your Honor," the child begs. "I'm the product of a bad environment."

The preceding bit of melodrama has a certain relevance to KornShell users. In fact, when bad things happen to good shell scripts, the environment may be to blame. Sometimes even a well–meaning parent will fail to give the proper environment to a child. But I'm getting ahead of myself. What's an environment? What's a parent? What's a child?

Suppose you are in the KornShell and you invoke a script by typing its pathname, for example:

```
$ myscript.ksh
```

The running script, **myscript.ksh**, is the *child* of the KornShell. The KornShell is the *parent* of the script. Other parent–child relationships exist on the system, but for the following discussion assume that the parent is the KornShell itself and the child is a KornShell script.

Every parent or child has an *environment*. This environment is really a collection of traits, privileges, and resources. (For a complete list, see the lefthand column of Table 12.)

A parent cannot inherit environmental traits from its child. For example, the KornShell variable **PWD**, which holds the current directory, is part of an environment. Changing the value of **PWD** within a script (the child) does not change the value of **PWD** within the parent. Consider the following script:

```
USAGE="usage: talky_cd.ksh"  # child can't change parent

 cd $1       # change current directory (which also changes PWD)
 print $PWD
```

Now we'll experiment:

```
$ print $PWD                   # what is current directory before running the script?
/usr/kalonymus

$ talky_cd.ksh /usr/jessica    # run the script
/usr/jessica

$ print $PWD                   # but the script didn't change the KornShell environment
/usr/kalonymus
```

The plus side to this behavior is that a child can't damage the environment of its parent.

Table 12. What a Child Inherits from Its Parent

Environmental characteristic	**Does child inherit this from parent?**
The parent's ability to read, write, or execute objects; that is, the parent's access rights to files, directories, etc.	yes
The files that the parent has opened.	yes
The parent's resource limits; you can use the **ulimit** statement to set or display these limits (see Appendix). An example of a resource limit is the amount of main memory that a process is allowed to use.	yes
The parent's response to signals (see Chapter 15).	yes
Aliases defined by the parent.	no
Functions defined by the parent.	yes, if function is exported; otherwise, no
Variables defined by the parent.	yes, if variable is exported; otherwise, no
The values of the parent's KornShell reserved variables (like **PWD**, **EDITOR**, **PATH**, etc.), except for **IFS** (see Chapter 14).	yes, if variable is exported; otherwise, no
The value of the **IFS** variable in the parent (see Chapter 14).	yes, even if not exported
The parent's option settings; typing **set –o** will give you a list of the parent's option settings.	no

Now let's look at the flip side of the parent–child relationship. In other words, what does a parent pass to its child?

By default, a parent passes its rights and privileges to its children. For example, if the parent has permission to read a particular file, then so do its children. However, by default, the parent does not pass variables, aliases, or functions to the child. For example, suppose you declare a variable named **st** on the KornShell command line as follows:

```
$ st="world enough and time"
```

If you try to access **st** inside a KornShell script, then the script won't have any idea what **st**'s value is. In other words, the KornShell script can't "see" **st**. For a child to "see" a variable or function of the parent, the parent must **export** it (as illustrated in Figure 3) to the child.

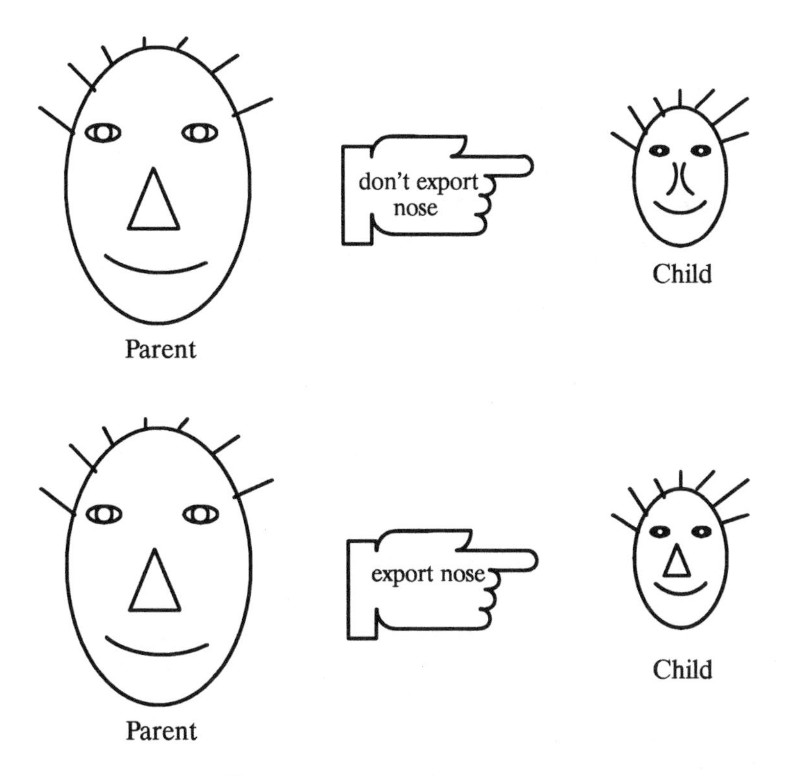

Figure 3. Children inherit all variables explicitly exported by their parents

For example, suppose you issue the following statements in the KornShell itself:

```
$ st="world enough and time"          # declare variable st

$ export st                           # export st
```

Here's a script that accesses **st**:

```
USAGE="usage: marvel.ksh"             # experiment with export

 print "st = $st"         # access the exported variable named st
 st="would be no crime." # change its value within the script
 print "st = $st"         # print its new value
```

Remembering that the KornShell is the parent and the script is the child, here's what happens when we run the script:

```
$ marvel.ksh
st = world enough and time
st = would be no crime
```

However, after running **marvel.ksh** and returning to the KornShell, **st** returns to its original value

```
$ print $st                    # what's in st now?
world enough and time
```

That's because a parent cannot inherit from its child.

By the way, you can use the following statements to get a list of exported objects available to the current environment:

```
$ typeset -x                   # list exported variables
$ typeset -fx                  # list exported functions
```

Aliases, which we'll explain shortly, cannot truly be exported.

Dot Scripts

It is pretty easy to get frustrated by the parent–child rules. For example, the rule about a child not being able to change its parent can be a nuisance in programming. Fortunately, the KornShell provides an interesting workaround to this problem called the *dot script*.

A dot script is a script that runs in the parent's environment. In other words, unlike a regular script, a dot script is *not* a child of the caller. The dot script inherits all of the caller's environment, including variables that haven't been exported.

A dot script can contain any code that a regular script can. In fact, the only difference between a regular script and a dot script is how you invoke them. To invoke a regular script, you usually type its name; for example:

```
$ ficus.ksh
```

To invoke a dot script, you preface the name of the script with a dot and then a space; for example:

```
$ . ficus.ksh
```

In other words, a regular script becomes a dot script when you invoke it as above.

Let's go back to the **talky_cd.ksh** script introduced earlier in this chapter. Here it is again:

```
USAGE="usage: talky_cd.ksh"  # an earlier example revisited

 cd $1       # change the working directory (which changes PWD)
 print $PWD
```

Running **talky_cd.ksh** as a regular script cannot actually change the working directory of the KornShell. However, running **talky_cd.ksh** as a dot script can; for example:

```
$ print $PWD                   # where are we now?
/usr/kalonymus

$ . talky_cd.ksh /usr/jessica  # run talky_cd.ksh as a dot script...
/usr/jessica

$ print $PWD                   # which changes the current directory of the KornShell
/usr/jessica
```

You might be surprised to find that the environment script (**ENV**) is itself a dot script. That is, whenever you create a KornShell or run a KornShell script, the system automatically runs the environment script as a dot script. By the way, if you make any changes to the **ENV** file, you can test these changes by explicitly running the environment script as a dot script; for example:

```
$ . $ENV
```

Aliases

An alias is a nickname for a KornShell statement, KornShell script, user program, or operating system command. KornShell users sometimes create aliases to reduce typing. For example, I used to type the UNIX command **ls –l** all the time. Since I was forever typing **ls –l**, I decided to create an alias named **g** as a nickname for **ls –l**. I created this alias by placing the following command in my environment file:

```
alias g='ls -l'
```

With this alias in place, I can now issue the simple command

```
$ g
```

instead of the longer **ls –l**. Since the KornShell expands **g** to **ls –l**, the following commands are synonymous:

```
$ g $HOME
$ ls -l $HOME
```

Another good reason to create aliases is to change the name of a poorly named command. For example, perhaps you're one of the multitudes of newcomers to the UNIX operating system who have trouble remembering the name of the pattern matching utility, **grep**. For this reason, you might place the following alias definition in your environment file:

```
alias pattern='grep'
```

Now that **pattern** and **grep** are equivalent, a user can use either to search for a pattern; for example, the following two commands are equivalent:

```
$ grep 'poodle' canines
$ pattern 'poodle' canines
```

Aliases can also keep you out of harm's way. For example, consider the UNIX command **rm**, which deletes objects off the disk. By default, the **rm** command does not ask users for confirmation ("Do you really want to delete this file?") before blasting it to bits. To get a confirmation prompt, you have to use **rm –i** instead of **rm**. If you're a paranoid user who always wants to get confirmation, you might consider setting up the following alias in an environment script:

```
alias rm='rm -i'              # whenever you specify rm, KornShell substitutes rm -i
```

The KornShell comes with a few predefined aliases of its own. For example, the KornShell predefines **history** as an alias for **fc –l** because the word **history** is easier to remember than **fc –l**. If you want to see a list of all aliases, including those defined by the KornShell itself, just type:

```
$ alias
```

If an alias should become tiresome, you can use the **unalias** statement to remove it. For example, here's how to delete the alias **g**:

```
$ unalias g
```

An alias definition can include the value of a variable; for example, if you wanted a little shortcut for printing the current values of the positional parameters, you might put the following alias definition in your environment script:

```
alias pp='print $*'        # whenever you specify pp, KornShell substitutes print $*
```

Before you start going wild with alias definitions, I'd better warn you that aliases are not as powerful as functions or scripts. For example, you can pass arguments to scripts or functions when you call them; the KornShell will convert the arguments into positional parameters. By contrast, if you try to pass arguments to an alias, the KornShell won't convert them into positional parameters. Instead, the KornShell will simply append the arguments to the end of whatever the alias expands into. For example, consider the following alias declaration:

```
alias pm='print "Try to pass $1 as an argument to this alias."'
```

The KornShell will expand the **$1** in the alias definition into the value of the first positional parameter, not the first argument to the alias. Let's experiment:

```
$ set apple banana            # assign "apple" to $1 and "banana" to $2

$ pm                          # call pm without any arguments
Try to pass apple as an argument to this alias.

$ pm MYARG                    # append MYARG to the end of the expanded alias
Try to pass apple as an argument to this alias. MYARG
```

Example of a $HOME/.profile Start-Up Script

The **$HOME/.profile** script is a very good place to specify the values of KornShell reserved variables. (See Chapter 14 for details on KornShell reserved variables.) Although you can put function definitions inside this script, it would be better to put them into one of your **FPATH** directories. (See Chapter 10 for details on **FPATH**.)

```
# The set -o allexport statement tells the KornShell to export all
# subsequently declared variables.
 set -o allexport

  PATH=.:/bin:/usr/bin:$HOME/bin:/usr/ucb  # define command search path
  CDPATH=.:$HOME:$HOME/games    # define search path for cd
  FPATH=$HOME/mathlib:/usr/common/funcs    # define path for autoload
  PS1='! $PWD> '                # define primary prompt
  PS2='Line continues here> '   # define secondary prompt
  HISTSIZE=25                   # define "size" of history file
  FCEDIT=/usr/ucb/vi            # use vi when editing fc commands
  ENV=$HOME/.kshrc              # pathname of environment script
  TMOUT=0                       # KornShell won't be timed out
  VISUAL=vi                     # make vi the command line editor

 set +o allexport         # turn off allexport feature
```

Example of an Environment (ENV) Script

You should divide your environment script into two regions:

- Start-up information appropriate for the KornShell command line only
- Start-up information appropriate for both the KornShell command line and KornShell scripts.

The sample environment script shows you how to create these two regions.

In general, you should try to keep as short as possible the region that KornShell scripts will use. That's because the KornShell has to execute all the commands in the region before it executes the commands in the script itself. So, in a sense, the environment script is extra baggage that every script has to carry around with it. Pack wisely.

The environment script is a very good place to put aliases. You can also put function definitions inside the environment script, but putting them inside of an autoload function directory (see Chapter 10) is more efficient.

```
# Example environment script.  Store this file at the pathname
# assigned to the ENV variable.

# The information in this region will be accessible to the KornShell
# command line itself and to KornShell scripts.  If you want an
# alias to be accessible to a KornShell script, you must specify
# alias -x.  The -x option does not truly export the alias definition
# to children, but does make it accessible to KornShell scripts.
 alias -x pattern='grep'
 alias -x disk='du'

# Now we'll use a peculiar looking case statement to create another
# region.  The information in this region will be accessible to the
# KornShell itself, but not to KornShell scripts.  If you want to
# create a function that is accessible to the KornShell itself but not
# to scripts, then place the function definition within this region.
 case $- in
   *i*)      # if $- matches *i*, then it means that the KornShell is
             # running interactively.  That is, you are in a KornShell,
             # not a KornShell script.
       alias copy='cp'
       alias rm='rm -i'
       alias g='ls -l';;
 esac
```

Chapter 12
Input and Output

This chapter details input and output in the KornShell.

If You're New to Programming...

Even people whose experience with computers is limited to reading science fiction novels seem to have a pretty good idea what input and output mean. The term *input* refers to information that the computer gathers from the outside world. The term *output* refers to data that the computer presents to the outside world. Collectively, they are known as I/O.

Your body acquires all sorts of sensory input (for example, the things that you hear), processes it, and presents output (for example, the things you say) to the outside world. Similarly, KornShell scripts can acquire input, process it, and present output. For example, a KornShell script can gather 500 numbers (acquire input), find their average (process it), and write the average to a computer monitor (present output).

A wide variety of devices (for example, a mouse, a trackball, a light pen) can gather input for modern computers, but the KornShell is only interested in input from two sources:

- Input typed on a keyboard
- Input read from a file

You use the **read** statement to gather both kinds of input. Similarly, you can use the **print** statement to generate two kinds of output:

- Output written to the screen (that is, the monitor or the CRT)
- Output written to a file

(By the way, to a UNIX guru, keyboards and monitors *are* files.)

A third I/O statement, **exec**, allows KornShell programmers to explicitly open files before reading from or writing to them. Some beginners may find the **exec** statement rather complicated, and may wish to skip over it.

Finally, you should understand what standard input, standard output, and standard error mean.

Standard input refers to the default source of input data. By default, the standard input source is the keyboard. Therefore, the **read** statement will, by default, gather data typed on the keyboard. You may redirect standard input by specifying the **<** operator. In other words, if you specify an alternate source of standard input (with **<**), then the **read** statement will gather data from the alternate source instead of the keyboard.

Standard output refers to the default destination of output data. By default, the standard output destination is the monitor. Therefore, by default, the **print** statement sends output to the computer monitor. However, you can use the **>** operator to redirect standard output to a disk file.

Standard error refers to the default destination of error messages. By default, the standard error destination is the monitor, meaning that error messages are written to the monitor. You may redirect standard error to a disk file by specifying **2>**.

If You're an Experienced Programmer...

I/O in the KornShell looks deceptively simple-minded. After all, the total KornShell I/O arsenal consists of the following:

- A **read** statement for doing input
- A **print** statement for doing output
- An **exec** statement for opening and closing streams
- Several operators (for example, **|**, **<**, and **>**) for redirecting input and output

However, after a little experimentation, you will discover the true power of these simple statements, particularly **read**.

The **read** statement gathers a line of input and then parses the line into tokens. This statement should remind C programmers of the **scanf** function. The KornShell **read** statement is more versatile, however, because it permits you to define token delimiters. For example, you might specify that commas and periods are token delimiters, but white space is not. To define a token, assign a set of token delimiters to the **IFS** variable.

Use the **print** statement to output anything. An old artifact of the Bourne shell named **echo** is also available for your outputting pleasure, but **print** works better. Compared to most high-level languages, there's nothing very fancy about **print**. You don't have to worry about conversion specifiers (like **%d** in the C language), because there aren't any. In other words, you can output the value of an integer the same way you'd output the value of a string. In fact, there's just one slightly odd thing about outputting in the KornShell. As in many high-level languages, the KornShell does permit you to control leading and trailing blanks and zeros in output values. That's not so odd. What is odd is that you specify these things when you *declare* the variable, not when you write its value. In other words, leading and trailing blanks are attributes of the variable itself rather than something specified in a **print** statement.

The KornShell provides three default streams: standard input, standard output, and standard error. You can get plenty of work done with these three streams. However, the KornShell also provides the **exec** statement so that you can create and manipulate additional streams. The **exec** statement is like the **OPEN** procedure of many Pascal implementations or the **fopen** function of the C library. However, you don't have to open a file with **exec** before reading from or writing to it. Most of the time, you can use the input and output redirection operators instead of **exec**.

read, REPLY, and Prompts

The following script demonstrates the humble **read** statement. Since the book already contains lots of other **read** statements, the following script shows off a few new twists. In particular, this script shows how to combine a prompt and **read** into one statement. It also demonstrates one use of the KornShell reserved variable called **REPLY**.

```
USAGE="usage: read1.ksh"  # fancy footwork with simple read statements

# You can prompt with a print statement then gather input with a read
# statement:
 print -n "Enter any string: "
 read st     # variable st is a string
 print "st = $st"

# Or, you can prompt and gather input in the same statement:
 read name?"Enter a name: "
 print "$name"

# If you specify read and don't specify a variable with it, then
# KornShell assigns the input to a special KornShell variable
# named REPLY.
 print -n "Enter a country: "
 read
 print "The value of variable REPLY is $REPLY"
 place=$REPLY
 print "The value of place is $place"
```

Executing This Script

```
$ read1.ksh
Enter any string: The Rain in Spain
st = The Rain in Spain
Enter a name: Don Quixote
Don Quixote
Enter a country: Denmark
The value of variable REPLY is Denmark
The value of place is Denmark
```

Reading Three Values

The following script illustrates a **read** statement that assigns values to three variables. The **read** statement divides up user input into tokens. In the following script, a token is any consecutive group of characters (letters, numbers, or punctuation marks). The first character in the group marks the start of the token and any white space character marks the end of the token. The KornShell assigns the first input token to variable **first**, the second input token to variable **second**, and all remaining input to variable **last**.

```
USAGE="usage: read_tok.ksh"  # read three tokens

 print -n "Enter your full name (first middle last): "
 read first middle last
 print "First Name: $first"
 print "Middle Name: $middle"
 print "Last Name: $last"
```

Executing This Script

If the user enters only two words, the KornShell assigns the null value to variable **last**:

```
$ read_tok.ksh    # user enters only two words
Enter your full name (first middle last): Rachel Rosenberg
First Name: Rachel
Middle Name: Rosenberg
Last Name:

$ read_tok.ksh    # this works well because user enters exactly three words
Enter your full name (first middle last): Rachel Elisa Rosenberg
First Name: Rachel
Middle Name: Elisa
Last Name: Rosenberg

$ read_tok.ksh    # what happens if user enters four words?
Enter your full name (first middle last): Mar Joyce Tucker Rosenberg
First Name: Mar
Middle Name: Joyce
Last Name: Tucker Rosenberg
```

Ignoring Extraneous Input

The following script shows how to ignore extraneous input. For example, in the following script, the **read** statement expects to receive exactly three input tokens. If the user enters more than three tokens, then all input after the third token will be assigned to a variable called **ignore_others**.

```
USAGE="usage: read3.ksh"  # ignoring extra input

 print -n "Enter the three top finishers in the race: "
 read win place show ignore_others

 print "Winner: $win"
 print "Second Place: $place"
 print "Third Place: $show"
```

Executing This Script

```
$ read3.ksh                    # user enters exactly three tokens
Enter the three top finishers in the race: Carl Ben Jessie
Winner: Carl
Second Place: Ben
Third Place: Jessie

$ read3.ksh                    # user enters more than three tokens
Enter the three top finishers in the race: Carl Ben Jessie Bob Houston
Winner: Carl
Second Place: Ben
Third Place: Jessie
```

Reading Values Having Different Data Types

The variable arguments of a **read** statement don't all have to be of the same data type. For example, in the following script, variables **month**, **day**, and **year** are all arguments to the same **read** statement even though **month** is a string and **day** and **year** are integers.

```
USAGE="usage: read4.ksh"      # input of various data types

 integer day
 integer year
# Read in one line containing three tokens.  The first token is a
# string, but the last two are integers.
 print -n "Enter today's date as Month Day Year: "
 read month day year   # month is a string; day and year are integers
 print "The current year is $year."
```

Executing This Script

```
$ read4.ksh       # user enters exactly three words
Enter today's date as Month Day Year: February 20 1991
The current year is 1991.
```

The IFS Variable

By default, the **IFS** variable equals *white space.* In other words, white space marks the end of one token, and any non-white-space character marks the beginning of the next token. The KornShell defines *white space* as the following three characters: space, tab, and newline in that order. (You usually generate a newline character when you press the <RETURN> key on your keyboard, and you generate a space character when you press the long space bar at the bottom of your keyboard.)

The KornShell allows you to specify a new value of **IFS**. For example, the following script parses input into sentences by specifying a value of **IFS** equal to any character that ends a sentence (.!?).

```
USAGE="usage: read_IFS.ksh"  # the IFS variable

# We haven't redefined IFS, so IFS is white space.
 print -n "Enter three words: "
 read word1 word2 word3
 print "First word: $word1"
 print "Second word: $word2"
 print "Third word: $word3"

 IFS=".!?"  # redefine IFS; IFS is now the three characters: . ! ?
# (The newline still marks the end of input.)
 print -n "\nEnter three sentences: "
 read sent1 sent2 sent3 junk
 print "First sentence: $sent1"
 print "Second sentence: $sent2"
 print "Third sentence: $sent3"
```

Executing This Script

```
$ read_IFS.ksh
Enter three words: red green blue
First word: red
Second word: green
Third word: blue

Enter three sentences: The cat.  A fog?  Silent shores of sand!
First sentence: The cat
Second sentence:   A fog
Third sentence:   Silent shores of sand
```

Notice that **sent1**, **sent2**, and **sent3** do not contain any periods, question marks, or exclamation points. Also, notice that the KornShell does not strip white space. Both of these effects are due to the redefinition of **IFS**.

Input Longer Than One Line

You may sometimes want a single **read** statement to gather more than one line. If the last character in an input line is a backslash (\), **read** assumes that the input continues on the next line. If this next line ends in a backslash, **read** assumes that the input line continues on the third line, and so on.

Nothing, not even white space, can follow the backslash. If it does, then the backslash won't mean line continuation.

In some cases, you don't want the terminating \ to mean line continuation. That is, you might want to read in only one line at a time but the input line might just end on a \. For that reason, the KornShell provides **read -r**. The **-r** tells the KornShell to treat a terminating \ as just another character of input.

```
USAGE="usage: read_r.ksh"  # reading input longer than one line

 print "Enter a paragraph.  End each line (except the final) "
 print "with a backslash:"
 read paragraph
 print "$paragraph"

# Try it again; this time with read -r:
 print "Enter another paragraph.  End each line (except the final) "
 print "with a backslash:"
 read -r paragraph  # ignore special meaning of closing backslash
 print "$paragraph"
```

Executing This Script

```
$ read_r.ksh
Enter a paragraph.  End each line (except the final)
with a backslash:
The cat. \
A fog? \
Silent shores of sand!
The cat. A fog? Silent shores of sand!

Enter another paragraph.  End each line (except the final)
with a backslash:
The cat. \
The cat. \
```

Using a Loop to Process Input

As noted back in Chapter 7, a **while** loop runs as long as its condition is true, but what is truth?

All UNIX commands and all KornShell statements return an error status (or exit status) upon completion. This error status is 0 if the command ran successfully, and some integer other than 0 (usually 1 or 2) if it did not. The value 0 corresponds to a true condition, and any value other than 0 corresponds to a false condition.

In the following loop, the **read** statement returns the error status 0 when it can successfully gather input. Since the value 0 corresponds to a true condition, the **while** loop will continue running. When the **read** statement sees an end-of-file mark, the **read** statement returns 1 as an error status. Since the value 1 corresponds to a false condition, the **while** loop stops running.

```
USAGE="usage: readloop.ksh"     # reading data until end of input

 integer running_total=0
 integer a_number

 print "Enter integer values, one per line.  When you are finished,"
 print "enter an end-of-file mark (usually <CONTROL>d or <CONTROL>z)"

# This loop will execute until the read statement reaches an
# end-of_file mark.
 while read a_number  # read until end of input
 do
   ((running_total = running_total + a_number)) # sum input integers
 done
 print "\nTotal = $running_total"
```

Executing This Script

```
$ readloop.ksh
Enter integer values, one per line.  When you are finished,
enter an end-of-file mark (usually <CONTROL>d or <CONTROL>z)
10
15
11
<CONTROL>d*** EOF ***

Total = 36
```

Reading Text out of a File with <

This script is almost identical to the previous script. However, in the previous script, you provided input by typing data on the keyboard. By contrast, the following script takes input data from a file. The difference in the two scripts is the way you invoke them.

Before running this script, create a separate file named **scores** containing only integers (one per line). You can create this separate file with a text editor. The text editor automatically writes an end-of-file marker at the end of your file.

Use the < symbol to redirect standard input. If you don't specify the < symbol, the **read** statement will take its input from the keyboard. The < symbol tells the **read** statement to take its input from the specified file.

```
USAGE="usage: rdrctin1.ksh < datafile"     # redirecting standard input

  integer a_number
  integer running_total=0

# This loop sums all the integers in a given file.
 while read a_number  # read until end-of-file
 do
   ((running_total = running_total + a_number))
 done

 print "Total = $running_total"
```

Executing This Script

Before running this script, use a text editor (like **vi**) to place some numbers into a file named **scores**.

```
$ cat scores              # this UNIX command displays the contents of file scores
10
15
11

$ rdrctin1.ksh < scores  # read data from file scores
Total = 36
```

With only 3 input integers, the advantages of input redirection might not be very obvious. However, with 300 input integers the advantages become clearer. Typing those 300 integers every time you ran the script would be an awful job. Putting them into a file like **scores** once and then having your script read from **scores** would be a far simpler solution.

Putting < within a Statement

This script is similar to the previous script. However, unlike the previous script (in which we redirected standard input for the entire script), the following script redirects input within one loop only. So, within the loop the script reads from a file named **scores,** and outside the loop the script reads from standard input, which is probably the keyboard. Therefore, this script has two different sources of input.

The script will read from file **scores** even if the user redirects standard input on the command line.

```
USAGE="usage: rdrctin2.ksh"          # input redirection within a loop
 integer a_number
 integer running_total=0

# This loop sums all the integers in file scores.
 while read a_number
 do
   ((running_total = running_total + a_number))
 done < scores    # redirect input within this while loop

# Since the while loop has finished, we can now get input
# from the keyboard.
 print -n "Enter one more integer: "
 read a_number
 print "Total = $((running_total + a_number))"
```

Executing This Script

Before running this script, use a text editor (like **vi**) to place some numbers into a file named **scores**.

```
$ cat scores          # this UNIX command displays the contents of file scores
10
15
11
```

Now run the script.

```
$ rdrctin2.ksh
Enter one more integer: 20
Total = 56
```

! BEWARE: Common Input Mistakes !

The **read** statement is a feast to the trained KornShell script writer, but beginners should be wary of the following sources of indigestion:

- If you want to redirect input within a loop, remember to place the < operator right after the keyword **done**. Do not put the < operator on the line that contains the **read** statement. Doing so will probably create an infinite loop. For example, the following statement causes the **read** statement to gather input from the same line (the first line of **file**) on each iteration of the loop:

```
while read < file # this will create an infinite loop
```

- Make sure that the file you are trying to read from exists and is readable. To do so, use the object tests **-f** and **-r** before reading from the file.
- Most experienced KornShell script writers are in the habit of using **read -r** instead of **read**. The **read -r** tends to keep you out of trouble more often than **read**.
- Extraneous input information can ruin your script unless you remember to supply an additional variable argument to every **read** statement (as in the **read3.ksh** example).

The print Statement

You've already seen **print** at least a zillion times in this book. Here though, we focus on some of the lesser-known options and escape sequences that you can specify within a **print** statement.

```
USAGE="usage: print1.ksh"                    # escape sequences
 print "Ring a bell: \a"
# Notice how the b causes print to overwrite the 'k'.
 print "Overwrite the k: Back\bspace"
# Use the -r option to turn off the special significance of the
# backslash.
 print -r "Interpret \b literally: Back\bspace"

# Use the -- option to turn off the special significance of minus signs
# embedded in text.
 print -- "-5 + 7 is +2"  # need the -- option to print this correctly

# Backslashes are a pain to output because they have special
# significance to the KornShell.  To avoid trouble, place the text
# inside a pair of single quotes and specify the -r (or -R) option:
 print -r 'The \ is difficult to output.'
# or place the text inside a pair of double quotes and specify \\:
 print "The \\ is difficult to output."
```

Executing This Script

```
$ print1.ksh        # you'll hear a bell ring when you run this script
Ring a bell:
Overwrite the k: Bacspace
Interpret \b literally: Back\bspace
-5 + 7 is +2
The \ is difficult to output.
The \ is difficult to output.
```

! BEWARE: Bad Options !

At some point or another, you're bound to encounter this cryptic error message:

```
print: bad option(s)
```

Let me guess: you were trying to print some text that started with a minus sign (-), weren't you? The solution is to use the double minus sign option (—) of **print**.

! BEWARE: Wildcards within Strings !

Suppose that you assign input to a variable and then try to print the variable, but instead of getting the expected output, the **print** statement starts printing all sorts of gibberish that looks like filenames or directory names. The culprit could be wildcards inside the input string. For example, consider the following innocent-looking code:

```
USAGE="usage: wildstr.ksh"      # wildcards in input
 print "Enter a line: "
 read line
 print $line
```

Let's run it and feed it an input string containing wildcards; for example:

```
$ wildstr.ksh
Enter a line: The *s shine bright.
The my_mistakes numbers scores words shine bright
```

Uh oh, the **print** statement expanded ***s** into the list of all objects in the current directory that end with the letter s. If that's a problem, you can tell the KornShell not to *glob* the input. If you're not familiar with the term, globbing is a verb (I glob, you glob, the script globs) that means "try to expand that pattern into a pathname." We've seen several instances (particularly within **for** loops) where glob is a many-splendored thing; however, in some instances (for example, in script **wildstr.ksh**) globbing is a nuisance. To turn off globbing, put this statement somewhere before the **print** statement:

```
set -o noglob
```

Use this statement to turn globbing back on:

```
set +o noglob
```

Output Redirection with >

This script demonstrates one way of sending output to a file.

By default, the KornShell sends output to standard output, which is usually the monitor. You can redirect standard output by specifying the > symbol followed by a filename. If you do specify the > symbol when you invoke the script, then all commands that produce output will write the output to the specified file.

```
USAGE="usage: rdrctout.ksh > any_filename"       # redirecting output

 read a_string            # gather input from standard input
 print "$a_string"        # write to standard output

 read a_number            # gather input from standard input
 print "$a_number"        # write to standard output
```

Executing This Script

There are no prompts in this script. After typing the name of the script, you must enter a string and then an integer. If there were prompts in the script, the KornShell would write them to the specified file rather than to the monitor.

```
$ rdrctout.ksh                # no output redirection
Silent sand.
Silent sand.
175
175

$ rdrctout.ksh > stuff        # redirect output to file stuff
Silent sand.
175
```

Let's check file **stuff** just to make sure that the data really did end up there:

```
$ cat stuff                   # cat is the UNIX command that displays a file
Silent sand.
175
```

! BEWARE: "But it was right there a second ago!" !

You can wipe out a file in the wink of an eye with output redirection. Watch this:

```
$ rdrctout.ksh > file_that_took_days_to_create
Silent sand.
175
```

It is my unfortunate duty to inform you that the former contents of **file_that_took_days_to_create** have been replaced by "Silent Sand. 175." You had a backup version, didn't you? You, er, didn't?

Let's replay this unfortunate incident, shall we? This time we'll do it the play–safe way.

```
$ set -o noclobber  # turn on the noclobber option

$ rdrctout.ksh > file_that_took_days_to_create
ksh: file_that_took_days_to_create : file already exists
```

By turning on the **noclobber** option, we're telling the KornShell not to overwrite any existing files when we redirect output with >. Therefore, when we tried to write to **file_that_took_days_to_create**, the KornShell wouldn't allow it.

If you really do want to overwrite the file anyway, use **>|** in place of **>**; for example:

```
$ rdrctout.ksh >| file_that_took_days_to_create  # but who cares
Silent sand.
175
```

If you're the squeamish type, you should probably put the **set –o noclobber** statement inside your KornShell start–up script. Otherwise, you might not remember until it's too late.

Another way to protect a file is to deny write permission to anyone (including yourself). For example, if you're working in the UNIX operating system, you could issue this command:

```
$ chmod -w file_that_took_days_to_create
```

Unfortunately, most people find it hard to remember to change the write permission after every single time they change a file.

Appending with > >

The following script demonstrates how to append data to the end of a file with the >> operator. Specifically, the script adds all the integers stored in a file named **values** and then writes their sum at the end of the file.

If you specify >> *file* and *file* doesn't exist, the KornShell will create it. In a sense, the paranoid KornShell user may wish to use >> in place of > because >> never overwrites anything.

```
USAGE="usage: append.ksh filename"  # using >> to append

 integer running_total=0
 integer number

# Read data as long as there is data.
 while read number
 do
   ((running_total = running_total + number))  # add numbers
 done < $1

# Append the total to the end of the file that is symbolized by $1
 print "TOTAL: $running_total" >> $1
```

Executing This Script

Use a text editor (like **vi**) to store some integers into a file named **numbers**.

```
$ cat numbers                  # cat is the UNIX command that displays a file
3
7
6
```

Now run the script:

```
$ append.ksh numbers           # run the script


$ cat numbers                  # what's in file numbers now?
3
7
6
TOTAL: 16
```

Mixing < and >

The following script shows how one loop can read from one file and write to another.

```
USAGE="usage: rdrct_io.ksh"   # using both < and > in a loop

 print -n "Pathname of input file: "
 read input_file
 print -n "Pathname of output file: "
 read output_file

# Read each line of the input file and write the first word of each
# input line to the output file.
 while read first_token rest_of_line
 do
   print "$first_token"
 done < $input_file > $output_file       # redirect input and output
 print "Done!"
```

Executing This Script

Use a text editor (like **vi**) to put some text into a file named **poetry**. Here's what I put into **poetry**:

```
$ cat poetry
Now you see a trick that I've never seen,
but wait!  Am I lying?  Is this part of some scheme?
For how can I who rely on matching hand to eye
still use my hands when my eyes are denied?
```

Now run the script as follows:

```
$ rdrct_io.ksh
Pathname of input file: poetry
Pathname of output file: words
Done!
```

The preceding script created a file named **words** which should contain the first word of every line; let's verify:

```
$ cat words    # cat is the UNIX command that displays a file
Now
but
For
still
```

Pipes

The pipe operator (|) tells the KornShell to take the output from one command and use it as the input to another command. For example, the following three command lines:

```
$ command1 > /tmp/file     # redirect command1's output to a file named /tmp/file
$ command2 < /tmp/file     # tell command2 to get its input from /tmp/file
$ rm /tmp/file             # delete /tmp/file
```

are equivalent to the following single pipe command line:

```
$ command1 | command2    # make command1's output into command2's input
```

Some beginners find the concept of pipes a little daunting, perhaps because experts tend to use them with wild abandon. Try to imagine a metallic tube (a pipe) connecting two commands. Imagine that data flows out of the command on the left and into the command on the right.

Let's consider an example that uses actual UNIX commands. These two command lines:

```
$ ls -l > mydir              # write output of ls -l to file mydir
$ grep 'Nov 14' < mydir      # read
```

are equivalent to this command line:

```
$ ls -l | grep 'Nov 14'      # don't have to create mydir and then delete it
```

The following command line uses three pipes to connect four UNIX commands. The purpose of the command line is to count the number of unique lines in file **canine_journal** that start with the word **dog**:

```
$ grep '^dog ' canine_journal | sort | uniq | wc -l    # multiple pipes
17
```

Table 13 details how this lengthy command line works.

Table 13. What Did Each Pipe Do?

Step	Input to command	Command	Output of command
1	contents of **canine_journal**	**grep '^dog ' canine_journal**	all lines in file **canine_journal that** start with the word **dog.**
2	all lines starting with **dog**	**sort**	same as input, but sorted
3	sorted lines	**uniq**	same as input, except all redundant lines have been removed
4	unique lines starting with **dog**	**wc -l**	an integer representing the number of unique lines starting with **dog**

Streams

Imagine yourself at a picnic on a gentle summer day. It's a hot day so you dip your toes in a nearby stream. The water from the stream flows past your feet, carrying cold water from a mountain lake past your toes and out towards the sea. The water in the stream flows in one direction.

Now picture yourself running a KornShell script on a dark, depressing winter's night. The KornShell script generates output. It is almost as if that output flows from the script to your monitor. In fact, you might say that this flow is a kind of output data *stream.* Furthermore, an input data stream seems to carry data from the keyboard into your script.

Each KornShell script provides the following three default streams (which can all be redirected):

- An input stream named *standard input* and numbered 0. By default, the standard input stream flows from the keyboard to your script.
- An output stream named *standard output* and numbered 1. By default, the standard output stream flows from your script to the monitor.
- An output stream named *standard error* and numbered 2. By default, the standard error stream flows from your script to the monitor.

By default, the **print** statement sends data on stream number 1 and the **read** statement gathers data from stream number 0. However, both **print** and **read** take an optional argument named **–u** that allows you to specify the stream number that you are writing to or reading from. For example, to send data out on the standard error stream (number 2), you specify **print –u2**.

In addition to these three default streams, you can use the **exec** statement to create other input and output streams. Figure 4 shows a script with five streams: three output and two input. In addition to streams 0, 1, and 2, the script supports an output stream (number 3) that carries data from the script to **fileB** and an input stream (number 4) that carries data from **fileA** to the script.

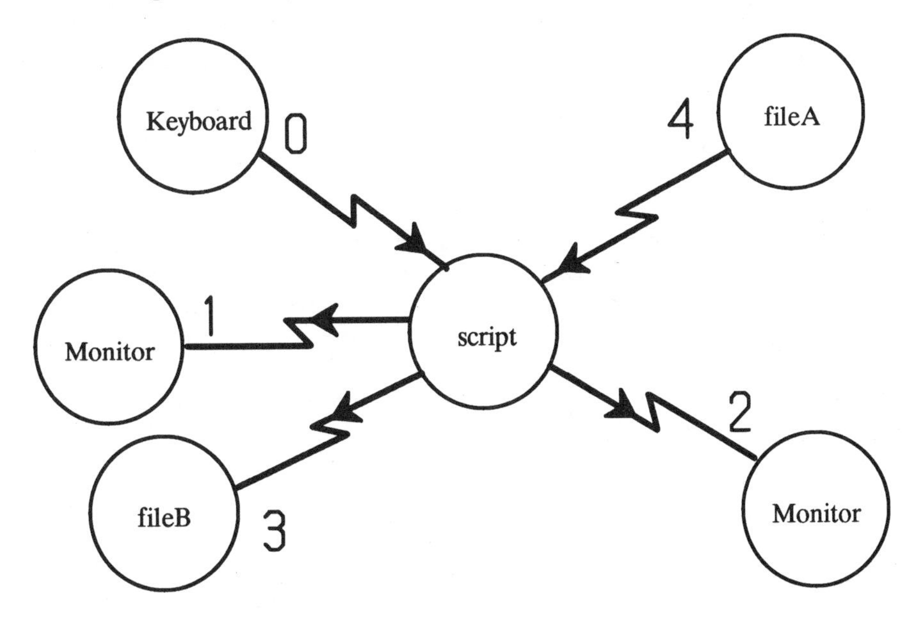

Figure 4. Input and output streams of a typical script

Redirecting Standard Error

By convention, all user programs, operating system commands, KornShell statements, and KornShell scripts are supposed to send error messages to the standard error stream. By default, the standard error stream flows to the monitor. However, the standard output stream also flows to the monitor. Therefore, by default, error messages and regular output are interspersed. When writing an interactive script, it's usually helpful to have error messages go to the monitor. However, there will be times when it would be better to send the error messages and regular output to different destinations.

To redirect the standard output stream, you use the operator >. To redirect the standard error stream, use the same > operator, but precede it with the stream number, which is 2.

Here's a script for C programmers. It compiles C source code and produces two compilation reports: a brief report written to standard output and a detailed report (complete with error messages) written to standard error.

```
USAGE="usage: std_err.ksh C_file1 ... [C_fileN]  2> error_file"
# demonstrates standard error stream

 for file in $*    # compile the files specified on the command line
 do
  print -n     "$file: "  # write name of file to standard output
  print -n -u2 "$file: "  # write name of file to standard error

# Compile the source code.  The cc command automatically sends its
# error messages to standard error.
   cc -c $file

# The cc command also returns an error status (not to be confused with
# an error message) that symbolizes the success or failure of the
# compilation.  An error status of 0 means that there were no compiler
# errors; a nonzero error status means that there were compiler errors.
   if (($? == 0))
   then   # write text to standard output and standard error
     print      "no errors."
     print -u2  "no errors."
   else   # write text to standard output only
     print      "errors, see error message file."
   fi
 done
```

This script won't work unless you can feed it some files of C source code as input. By convention, compilable C source code filenames end with the **.c** suffix. So, the pattern ***.c** should match all C source code files in the current directory.

For best results, you should redirect the standard error stream when you invoke the script. The phrase **2> mistakes** redirects the standard error stream to a file named **mistakes**.

Executing This Script

```
$ std_err.ksh *.c 2> mistakes  # redirect standard error stream
events.c:  no errors.
boffo.c:  errors, see error message file.
start.c:  no errors.
```

Now let's read the "detailed report" stored in file **mistakes**:

```
$ cat mistakes
events.c: no errors.
boffo.c:
 (0143)     ab7="arf"
******** Line 143 of "mistake.c": "ab7" has not been declared.
start.c: no errors
```

Opening Files with exec

The following script explicitly uses the **exec** statement to open an input stream from file **poem** to the script. The stream number is 8. If you're used to programming in the C language, then you might find the **exec** statement analogous to the **fopen** function of the C library. (If you haven't programmed too much, you might find the next few examples rather difficult.)

```
USAGE="usage: openfile.ksh"  # opening a file with exec

# Use exec to open a file for reading.
 exec 8< poem         # make file descriptor 8 a synonym for file "poem"
# We have now opened a named input stream from the file "poem"
# to our KornShell script.

# Read the first three lines of this file.
 read -u8 first_line  # read the first line of file descriptor 8
 read -u8 second_line
 read -u8 third_line
 print "$first_line $second_line $third_line"

# Using read without -u8 won't work quite as well.
 read first_line < poem  # this reads the first line
 read second_line < poem # this also reads the first line
 read third_line < poem  # this also reads the first line
 print "$first_line $second_line $third_line"
```

Executing This Script

Use a text editor (like **vi**) to place the following sophomoric lines inside file **poem**:

```
$ cat poem
A blue wave thunders.
Sand swirls in a summer storm.
Now all is quiet.
```

Now run the shell script:

```
$ openfile.ksh
A blue wave thunders. Sand swirls in a summer storm. Now all is quiet.
A blue wave thunders. A blue wave thunders. A blue wave thunders.
```

Closing Files

If you don't explicitly close a stream, the KornShell will close it for you when the script ends. However, it is usually best to keep streams open for only a short time. Your operating system probably imposes a limit on the number of streams that a process can open. As you bump up against that limit, you will have to close some streams.

The following script opens a stream, prints the file's second line to standard output, then closes the file. The script repeats this procedure for every regular file in the current directory.

```
USAGE="usage: closfile.ksh"       # opening and closing streams

 for object in *                  # list of objects in current directory
 do
   if [[ -f $object ]]            # act on regular files only
   then
     print -n "$object: "
     exec 3< $object              # open file $object for reading
     read -u3 first_line          # read the first line of this file
     read -u3 second_line         # read the second line of this file
     print "$second_line"         # print second line to standard output
     exec 3<&-                    # close file symbolized by 3
   fi
 done
```

Executing This Script

```
$ closfile.ksh    # print second line of each object in current directory
apple: granny smith's closed higher today.
matching: and a tiny tot's shoe
poetry: A mourner cried.
sky:                                   # second line of this file is blank
why1: print "q"
```

Using exec to Do I/O on Multiple Files

The following script demonstrates a fairly sophisticated use of **exec**. This script does a line-by-line comparison of two files (rather like the UNIX **diff** command). If line *N* in the first file matches line *N* in the second file, then the script writes line *N* to a file named **match**. However, if line *N* in the first file does not match line *N* in the second, the script writes both nonmatching lines to a file named **nomatch**.

All together, the script uses **exec** to open four different streams (the two input files, file **match**, and file **nomatch**).

```
USAGE="usage: exec_ex.ksh file1 file2"  # complex exec
 if (($# != 2))   # if user forgets command line arguments, stop script
   then
     print "$USAGE"
     exit 1
   elif [[ (-f $1) && (-f $2) && (-r $1) && (-r $2) ]]
# Both objects must be readable regular files.
   then    # use exec to open four files
     exec 3< $1           # open $1 for input
     exec 4< $2           # open $2 for input
     exec 5> match        # open file "match" for output
     exec 6> nomatch      # open file "nomatch" for output
   else    # if user enters bad arguments, stop script
     print "$USAGE"
     exit 1
 fi

 while read -u3 lineA  # read a line out of $1
 do
   read -u4 lineB   # read a line out of $2
   if [ "$lineA" = "$lineB" ]  # compare the two input lines
   then   # send matching lines to one file.
     print -u5 "$lineA"
   else   # send nonmatching lines to another file
     print -u6 "$lineA; $lineB"
   fi
 done

 print "Done!"
```

Executing This Script

Before running the script, use a text editor to create two different files. Ideally, the two files should be similar, though not identical. I created these two files:

```
$ cat poemA                      # cat is the UNIX command to display a file
I can juggle my hat
and this marble so round
and a tiny tot's shoe
that I saw on the ground.

$ cat poemB
I can juggle my hat
and this marble I found
and a tiny tot's shoe
that I saw on the ground.
```

Now let's run the script:

```
$ exec_ex.ksh poemA poemB   # compare poemA to poemB
Done!
```

Running the script produced two files: **match** and **nomatch**. Here are their contents:

```
$ cat match                      # these lines match
I can juggle my hat
and a tiny tot's shoe
that I saw on the ground.

$ cat nomatch                    # these lines don't match
and this marble so round; and this marble I found
```

Using $(...) to Assign the Output of a Command to a Variable

By default, the KornShell writes the output of every script, user program, or operating system command to standard output. As shown earlier in this chapter, you can redirect standard output to a new file. Another place to redirect output is into a variable. In other words, you can tell the KornShell to suppress writing output to a file or the monitor and write it into a variable instead. To accomplish this feat, use this syntax:

variable = $(*command*)

The following script explores some of the things that you can do with this syntax.

```
USAGE="usage: cmd_out.ksh file word1 word2" # capturing command output

# Specifying $(date) tells the KornShell to run the date command
# and insert the output of the date command in the text.
 print "Today's date is $(date)"  # call date command
# You can also assign the output of the date command to a variable.
 date_variable=$(date)    # call date command again
 print "Today's date is $date_variable"

# The grep command returns the lines of a file that contain a
# certain word.  We can assign all these lines to a variable.
 lines_containing_pattern=$(grep "$2" $1)
 print "\nAs of $date_variable, the word $2 appears in"
 print "file $1 within these lines:"
 print "$lines_containing_pattern"

# The grep -c command returns a count of the number of lines
# containing a certain word.
 if (( $(grep -c "$2" $1) > $(grep -c "$3" $1) ))
 then
    print "\n$2 appears in more lines of file $1 than $3."
 elif (( $(grep -c "$2" $1) < $(grep -c "$3" $1) ))
 then
    print "\n$3 appears in more lines of file $1 than $2."
 else
    print "\n$3 and $2 appear in the same number of lines."
 fi
```

Executing This Script

Using a text editor, put some text into a file. Here's the text that I used:

```
$ cat my_text                    # cat is the UNIX command to display a file
sunflower sam
ate peanuts and jam
while sunflower sue
had nothing to do.
```

Now, we'll run the script, specifying the name of the file **my_text** as the first argument, and two words from the file, **sunflower** and **peanut**, as the second and third arguments, respectively.

```
$ cmd_out.ksh my_text sunflower peanut
Today's date is Fri Feb 22 10:55:26 EST 1991
Today's date is Fri Feb 22 10:55:27 EST 1991

As of Fri Feb 22 10:55:27 EST 1991, the word sunflower appears in
file my_text within these lines:
sunflower sam
while sunflower sue

sunflower appears in more lines of file my_text than peanut.
```

Here Documents

Pretend for a moment that you are so spiritually bankrupt that you are willing to meditate Zen–like on the nature of command lines. As you sit cross–legged on a tatami mat focusing on your breathing, the *truth* about command lines will float to you. You will understand in a very deep sense that a command line contains all the information that the command needs to start up. Do you see that? Good. Keep breathing. Now try to imagine a lengthy command line that has all the information necessary to start up a command, but also contains instructions to the command once it has been started. Do you see that? Good. You'll need to invoke such a command as a *here document.* Leave the trance slowly.

The syntax of a here document is as follows:

```
command invocation_arguments <<word
                  instruction1_to_command
                  .
                  .
                  .
                  instructionN_to_command
word
```

In other words, the here document starts with a normal command invocation but at the end of the first line, you specify <<*word.* This ending tells the KornShell that a here document follows. The here document can contain as many lines as you want. You end the here document by specifying the same word that you started it with. Make sure that *word* is flush left; that is, don't allow any white space to the left of *word.* Don't put anything after *word.*

```
USAGE="usage: here_doc.ksh file replace_this with_this"

# The following command invokes ex, a UNIX text editor, as a here
# document.  This command starts ex and tells it that $1 will
# be the file to process.  After startup, ex will begin executing the
# two instructions stored in the here document.  The first instruction
# tells ex to substitute all occurrences of $2 with $3, and the second
# instruction, wq, tells the KornShell to save the substitutions.
ex - $1 <<EOD
%s/$2/$3/g
wq
EOD
# Notice that EOD is flush left.
```

Executing This Script

Using a text editor, put some text into a file. Here's the text that I used:

```
$ cat my_text                    # cat is the UNIX command to display a file
sunflower sam
ate peanuts and jam
while sunflower sue
had nothing to do.
```

Now, we'll run the script, specifying the name of the file **my_text** as the first argument, and two words, **sunflower** and **cornflower**, as the second and third arguments, respectively. The script should replace all occurrences of **sunflower** with **cornflower**.

```
$ here_doc.ksh my_text sunflower cornflower    # run the script
```

We'll find out what's inside of **my_text** just to be sure:

```
$ cat my_text
cornflower sam
ate peanuts and jam
while cornflower sue
had nothing to do.
```

If you run this script and the KornShell reports this:

```
ex not found
```

then you'll have to specify the full pathname of the **ex** utility. On some UNIX systems, the **ex** utility is stored in pathname **/usr/ucb/ex**, so try changing this line:

```
ex - $1 <<EOD
```

to this:

```
/usr/ucb/ex - $1 <<EOD
```

read gather input from the keyboard or from a file.

Syntax:

read *options variable1* [... *variableN*]

read *options variable?prompt*

Where:

options are zero, one, or more of the following:

-p reads input from the co-process.

-r by default (if you don't specify **-r**), the **read** statement interprets the backslash character (\) at the end of a line to indicate that the line logically continues on the next physical line. That is, the \ means that the text was too big to fit on one physical line, so it was continued on the next. If you do specify -r, then each input line is exactly one physical line long, even if it ends with a backslash.

-s places the input from this **read** statement into your history file. (See Chapter 17 for information on the history file.) By default (if you don't specify **-s**), the KornShell does not write input into the history file.

-u if you don't specify **-u**, the KornShell reads from standard input. If you do specify **-u**, but don't specify a number *n* after it, then the KornShell also reads from standard input. If you specify **-u** followed by a number *n* other than 0 or 2, then the KornShell reads from the file symbolized by *n*. (You use the **exec** statement to associate *n* with a file.) By the way, a value of 0 for *n* refers to the standard input stream (stuff from the keyboard) and a value of 2 refers to the standard error.

variable1 ... variableN
is one or more variables separated by white space. (Do not put commas between the variables.)

variable?prompt
is the name of one (and only one) variable, followed by a question mark (?), followed by a prompt. If the prompt contains more than one word, you must enclose it in a pair of single or double quotes. If you specify a prompt, the KornShell will write the prompt to standard output, and then perform the input. Don't put any white space between *variable* and ? or between ? and *prompt*.

Quick Summary:

Use the **read** statement to gather input and assign the input to one or more variables.

When you issue a **read** statement, the KornShell performs the following actions:

- First, the KornShell identifies the source of input. The source will be standard input (the default), an alternate file (specified by **-u**), or the co-process (specified by **-p**).
- Second, the KornShell reads in one line of input from the source. (See **-r**.)
- Finally, the KornShell divides up the line into tokens and assigns the first token to *variable1*, the second token to *variable2*, and so on. If the number of tokens in the input line exceeds the number of variables, then the KornShell assigns all remaining tokens to *variableN*. If you have not specified any *variables* as arguments to **read**, then the KornShell assigns input to the reserved variable named **REPLY**.

---

print write output to the screen or to a file.

Syntax:

print *options text*

Where:

options are zero, one, or more of the following:

-n by default, **print** writes a newline at the end of *text*. However, if you specify **-n**, then **print** won't write a newline at the end of *text*.

-p writes *text* to a co-process.

-r the backslash (\) is the *escape character* of the KornShell. If a backslash is followed by a particular character, the pair of characters is called an *escape sequence*. (See the list of escape sequences in Table 14.) For example, if you specify the escape sequence **\t** as part of *text*, then the KornShell doesn't print the two characters \ and **t**, but prints a tab character instead. In most cases, these escape sequences are very useful for creating tabs, backspaces, newlines, and the like, but, occasionally, you'd like **\t** to be printed as the two characters **\t** instead of as a tab. For those instances, use **-r**. This option turns off the special meaning of the backslash.

-- (two minus signs in a row) Ordinarily, you will want **print** to interpret anything beginning with a minus sign (-) as an option. For example, you usually want **print** to interpret **-n** as an option. If, however, you actually want **print** to output the two characters - and **n**, then use the -- (two minus signs) option to turn off the special significance of the **-n** option. Therefore, the entire statement would look like this: `print -- -n`

-R this option is something like a combination of the **-r** option and the -- option. Like the **-r** option, **-R** turns off the special meaning of the backslash. Like the -- option, **-R** turns off the significance of the minus sign. However, unlike the -- option, **-R** still honors the significance of the **-n** option. That is, if **-n** appears after **-R** on the command line, then the **print** statement will suppress the trailing newline at the end of *text*.

-s this option writes a copy of *text* into your history file. See Chapter 17 for a brief description of the history file.

-u *n* if you do not specify **-u**, the KornShell writes *text* to standard output. If you specify **-u** without a number *n*, then the KornShell also writes *text* to standard output. In addition, if you specify **-u** followed by the number 1, the KornShell also writes to standard output. If you specify **-u** followed by the number 2, the KornShell writes *text* to standard error. If you specify **-u** followed by a number *n* other than 1 or 2, then the KornShell writes *text* to the file symbolized by *n*. However, you can only specify a value of *n* other than 1 or 2 if you have previously defined *n* in an **exec** statement.

text This is the information that you want to output. You can optionally enclose *text* in a pair of single or double quotes. See the end of Chapter 2 for complete details. By the way, *text* is optional; if you don't specify any *text*, **print** writes a blank line. The *text* can include zero, one, or many of the escape sequences shown in Table 14.

Table 14. Escape Sequences

Escape sequence	**ASCII value in octal**	**Does this...**
\a	007	rings the bell on your terminal
\b	010	prints the backspace character; the character that follows **\b** will overwrite the character that precedes **\b**
\c	none	prints everything preceding it and suppresses printing of everything that follows it; suppresses concluding newline
\f	014	prints a formfeed character; if the output is sent to a printer, the formfeed character tells the printer to start printing on a new page
\n	012	prints a newline character (also known as a linefeed character)
\r	015	prints a carriage return character
\t	011	prints a horizontal tab
\v	013	prints a vertical tab
****	134	prints a backslash; in other words, you have to specify two backslashes in order to get one printed
\0*number*	*number*	prints the character whose octal ASCII value is *number;* for example, **print \0124** will output **T** because octal ASCII value 124 corresponds to **T**

Quick Summary:

Use the **print** statement to write output to the terminal or to a file. When you issue a **print** statement, the KornShell performs the following actions:

- First, the KornShell identifies the output destination. In other words, the KornShell figures out where it's supposed to write the output. The destination will be standard output (the default), an alternate file (specified by **–u**), or the co-process (specified by **–p**).
- Second, the KornShell writes *text* to the output destination.

exec — open or close a stream. (For advanced users only.)

Syntax:

exec *numberaction target*
exec *program*

Where:

number — is an integer. Numbers greater than 9 must be enclosed within braces; for example, {12}. The number 0 corresponds to standard input, the number 1 corresponds to standard output, and the number 2 corresponds to standard error.

action — is one of the I/O redirection operators shown in Table 15. Do not put any white space between *number* and *action.*

target — is the pathname of a file, the *number* of another stream, or a minus sign (–). A minus sign signifies that you are closing a stream. If *action* is **<&** or **>&**, then *target* cannot be a pathname.

program — the pathname of a program that will replace the KornShell program.

Quick Summary:

Use the **exec** statement to do the following:

- Open or close a stream.
- Duplicate input or output streams.
- Replace the current KornShell with *program* so that *program* occupies the same process space now occupied by the KornShell.

Table 15. I/O Actions

Action	Does this...
<	redirects standard input to *target*
<&	duplicates input stream
> or >|	redirects standard output to *target*
>&	duplicates output stream
>>	appends output
<>	opens stream for both input and output; (has limited use in scripts and should be avoided)

Chapter 13

Manipulating Strings

This chapter illustrates string manipulation. The string is the primary data type of the KornShell. Just about everything is a string, including letters, phrases, sentences, pathnames, and numbers (as long as the numbers haven't been explicitly declared as integers).

Using KornShell, you can do the following:

- Compare one string to another string. We did that in Chapter 6.
- Compare one string to a pattern. We did that in Chapter 6, also.
- Assign a new value to a string variable. We did that in Chapter 2.
- Convert a string to uppercase or lowercase.
- Specify leading or trailing blanks for string values.
- Concatenate one string to another string.
- Remove a portion (that is, a substring) of a string.
- Parse a string according to specified rules; for example, parse a string into words or sentences.
- Determine whether or not a string variable has been given a value, and take an action depending on the outcome.

Some users think of the KornShell as a string manipulation language first and a command processor second. In fact, gaining experience with the string manipulation features will allow you to write powerful text processing scripts in the KornShell far quicker than you could write them with C or FORTRAN.

Uppercase and Lowercase

The following script demonstrates how to convert strings to uppercase or lowercase. Use the **typeset -u** attribute to convert a string to all uppercase. Use the **typeset -l** attribute to convert a string to all lowercase. Use **typeset +u** or **typeset +l** to revert to the case sensitivity of the original string.

```
USAGE="usage: U_and_lc.ksh"  # upper and lowercase strings

# Ordinary string input.
 print -n "Enter a string: "
 read a_string
 backup_string=$a_string
 print "\nCase sensitive: $a_string"

# Convert a_string to uppercase.
 typeset -u a_string
 print "UPPERCASE: $a_string"

# Convert a_string to lowercase.
 typeset -l a_string     # turn on lowercase attribute; turn off
                         # uppercase attribute
 print "lowercase: $a_string"

# Revert to case sensitivity.
 typeset +l a_string    # turn off lowercase attribute
 print "Still in lowercase: $a_string"
 a_string=$backup_string
 print "Case sensitive: $a_string"
```

Executing This Script

```
$ U_and_lc.ksh
Enter a string: The Rain in Spain.

Case sensitive: The Rain in Spain.
UPPERCASE: THE RAIN IN SPAIN.
lowercase: the rain in spain.
Still in lowercase: the rain in spain.
Case sensitive: The Rain in Spain.
```

Left Justification

This shell script demonstrates various uses of the **typeset -L*n*** and **typeset -LZ** attributes. You can use these attributes to do the following:

- Make nice, neat output columns (with **-L*n***) when you're writing a report.
- Copy the first *n* characters of a string to another string. This can be useful if you're only interested in the first *n* characters and want to ignore the rest of the string.
- Strip leading zeros (**-LZ**) from strings.

The KornShell also supports string attributes **typeset -R** for those wishing to right justify strings and **typeset -RZ** for those wishing to strip trailing zeros from strings.

```
USAGE="usage: leftjust.ksh" # typeset -L and typeset -LZ
# Declare three strings with -Ln attribute.  This will not influence
# the read statement, but will influence the print statement.
 typeset -L10 first_name    # output width will be 10 characters
 typeset -L8  middle_name   # output width will be 8 characters
 typeset -L15 last_name     # output width will be 15 characters

# Gather input names from a file and write them to standard output in
# three neat columns.  The first column will use up 10 characters, the
# second column 8, and the third 15.
 while read first_name middle_name last_name
 do
   print "$first_name$middle_name$last_name"
 done < file_of_names

# Another use of left justification is to isolate a substring and
# assign it to another string.   Here, we declare a string variable
# named middle_initial.  If we try to assign a string value to
# middle_initial, only the leftmost character in the string value will
# actually be assigned.
 typeset -L1 middle_initial
 print -n "\nEnter a middle name: "
 read middle_name
# Assign to middle_initial the first character of middle_name.
 middle_initial=$middle_name
 print "Middle initial -- $middle_initial"

# Finally, we can use typeset -LZ to strip leading zeros.
 typeset -LZ month day year
 print -n "\nEnter today's date in numerical form: "
 read month day year    # North American-style date
 print "$month-$day-$year"
```

Executing This Script

Using a text editor, place some names inside of a file named **file_of_names**.

```
$ cat file_of_names          # here's my file of names
Hugo Killer Whale
Flipper The Dolphin
Cher Melissa Stanislawski
Liberace Rosencrantz Smith
Incredible Howard Hulk
```

Notice that these names aren't formatted into nice, neat columns, so let's ask the script to do that for us:

```
$ leftjust.ksh
Hugo      Killer  Whale
Flipper   The     Dolphin
Cher      Melissa Stanislawski
Liberace  RosencraSmith
IncredibleHoward  Hulk

Enter a middle name: Joyce
Middle initial  -- J

Enter today's date in numerical form: 01 05 91
1-5-91
```

Notice that the input word "Rosencrantz" was truncated to "Rosencra" because "Rosencrantz" was longer than 8 characters.

Concatenating Strings I

You can concatenate (append) multiple strings to create a new string. The following script concatenates four strings into a new string named **complete_name**.

```
USAGE="usage: apndstr1.ksh"    # concatenate one string to another

 read first_name?"Enter first name: "
 read middle_name?"Enter middle name: "
 read last_name?"Enter last name: "

# Concatenate this information and provide appropriate prefixes and
# white space. The white space will become part of complete_name.
 complete_name="Ms. $first_name $middle_name $last_name"
 print "Full name -- $complete_name"
```

Executing This Script

```
$ apndstr1.ksh
Enter first name: Marilyn
Enter middle name: Joyce
Enter last name: Tucker
Full name -- Ms. Marilyn Joyce Tucker
```

Concatenating Strings II

Surprisingly, you can concatenate the values of two strings even if there is no white space between them. In fact, you can also concatenate a string variable to a string constant without any intervening white space. If there's no white space, you may be wondering how the KornShell knows when one string starts and the constant begins. For example, how does the KornShell know to concatenate the constant **.new** to the value of variable **old_string** in the following assignment?

```
new_string=$old_string.new
```

Put another way, how come the KornShell doesn't try to assign the value of a variable named **old_string.new** to **new_string**? The reason is that KornShell variables can only contain certain characters. (See Chapter 2 for a list of those characters.) So, in the previous example, the KornShell knows that the variable name ends at the **g** in **old_string** because variable names cannot contain periods. Therefore, the KornShell assumes that **.new** is a constant that should be concatenated to **$old_string**.

```
USAGE="usage: apndstr2.ksh"      # concatenate one string to another
 relative_directory='/final_exam'
# Concatenate two strings without any intervening white space.
 actual_directory=$HOME$relative_directory
 cd $actual_directory      # change current directory
 print "$full_pathname"

# Create backup files of every regular file in the current directory.
 for file in !(*.backup)  # don't back up the .backup files
 do
   if [[ -f $file ]]       # is object a regular file?
   then   # concatenate value of variable ($file) to constant (.backup)
          # and assign result to new variable (name_of_backup_file)
      name_of_backup_file=$file.backup
# If cp command works correctly, tell the user about it.
      if cp $file $name_of_backup_file  # cp is UNIX copy command
      then
         print "Copied $file to $name_of_backup_file"
      fi
   fi
 done
```

Executing This Script

```
$ apndstr2.ksh
/usr/users/daniel/final_exam  # assume that HOME=/usr/users/daniel
Copied a to a.backup
Copied b to b.backup
Copied c to c.backup
```

Removing the Leftmost Characters in a String with

The following script demonstrates the **#** operator, which starts at the beginning (the left side) of a string and deletes a substring from it. Actually, the **#** operator doesn't really change the value of the string. Essentially, you use **#** to find out what a certain string would look like if a chunk of it were removed.

```
USAGE="usage: remove1.ksh"  # demonstrates the substring operator #
 animal="tiger"
# The following two lines are synonymous:
 print "The full string -- $animal"
 print "The full string -- ${animal}"
# Delete substrings from the left portion of the string.
 print "Remove the 't'  -- ${animal#t}"
 print "Remove the 'ti' -- ${animal#ti}"
 abbrev="tig"
 print "Remove the '$abbrev' -- ${animal#$abbrev}"
 print "Try (unsuccessfully) to remove the 'iger' -- ${animal#iger}"
 # You can also delete a pattern.
 print "\nRemove the first two characters -- ${animal#??}"
 print "Remove up to and including the first 'e' -- ${animal#*e}\n"
# Remove tokens (words) from the string.
 cats="lions and tigers"
 print "The full string -- ${cats}"
# Pattern "* " matches everything up to and including the first space.
 print "Remove the first token -- ${cats#* }"
 print "Remove the first two tokens -- ${cats#* * }"
```

Executing This Script

```
$ remove1.ksh
The full string -- tiger
The full string -- tiger
Remove the 't'  -- iger
Remove the 'ti' -- ger
Remove the 'tig' -- er
Try (unsuccessfully) to remove the 'iger' -- tiger

Remove the first two characters -- ger
Remove up to and including the first 'e' -- r

The full string -- lions and tigers
Remove the first token -- and tigers
Remove the first two tokens -- tigers
```

Removing the Rightmost Characters in a String with %

Use the % operator to remove a substring from the end (the right side) of a string.

```
USAGE="usage: remove2.ksh"   # demonstrates the substring operator %

 animal="tiger"
 abbrev="ger"

 print "The full string -- ${animal}"
 # Delete substrings from the right characters in a string.
 print "Remove the 'r'  -- ${animal%r}"
 print "Remove the 'er' -- ${animal%er}"
 print "Remove the '$abbrev' -- ${animal%$abbrev}"
 print "Try (unsuccessfully) to remove the 'tige' -- ${animal%tige}"

# You can also delete a pattern.
 print "\nRemove the last two characters -- ${animal%??}"
 print "Remove the characters beginning with 'g' -- ${animal%g*}"

 cats="lions and tigers"
 print "\nThe full string -- ${cats}"
 print "Remove the last token -- ${cats% *}"
 print "Remove the last two tokens -- ${cats% * *}"
```

Executing This Script

```
$ remove2.ksh
The full string -- tiger
Remove the 'r'  -- tige
Remove the 'er' -- tig
Remove the 'ger' -- ti
Try (unsuccessfully) to remove the 'tige' -- tiger

Remove the last two characters -- tig
Remove the characters beginning with 'g' -- ti

The full string -- lions and tigers
Remove the last token -- lions and
Remove the last two tokens -- lions
```

An Application of %

Filenames are themselves strings, so you can use the substring deletion operators to parse filenames. For example, you can use the **%** operator to help you change filenames. The following script changes all filenames ending in **.shd** to the **.shadow** suffix.

```
USAGE="usage: rename.ksh"     # using % to parse filenames

 for old_file_name in *.shd  # list all objects ending in '.shd'
 do
  # Strip '.shd' suffix and replace it with '.shadow'.
   new_file_name=${old_file_name%.shd}.shadow
  # mv is the UNIX command that renames a file.
   mv $old_file_name $new_file_name
   if (($? == 0))  # examine error status of mv command
   then      # mv was successful
     print "Changed $old_file_name to $new_file_name"
   else      # mv was unsuccessful
     print "Could not change $old_file_name to $new_file_name"
   fi

 done
```

Executing This Script

```
$ rename.ksh
Changed jean_marc.shd to jean_marc.shadow
Changed mick.shd to mick.shadow
Changed tim.shd to tim.shadow
```

versus

The following script demonstrates the difference between **#** (delete first occurrence) and **##** (delete up to and including last occurrence).

```
USAGE="usage: remove3.ksh"  # difference between # and ##

 simple="abcdabcd"
# If your pattern does not contain any wildcards, then the # and ##
# operators produce identical outcomes.
 print "The full string -- ${simple}"
 print "Remove the 'ab' with #  -- ${simple#ab}"
 print "Remove the 'ab' with ## -- ${simple##ab}"

# However, if the pattern does contain wildcards, then the # and ##
# operators may produce different results.  Notice that the letters
# 'ab' appear twice in 'simple'.  The following use of # causes the
# KornShell to delete the first occurrence of *ab.
 print "\nRemove '*ab' with # -- ${simple#*ab}"
# However, using ## causes the KornShell to remove all characters
# through the last occurrence of *ab.
 print "Remove '*ab' with ## -- ${simple##*ab}"

# The pattern '* ' matches any group of characters that ends with
# a blank space.  It is a very useful pattern for dividing a sentence
# into words.
 phrase="I always get the last word."
 print "\nThe full string -- ${phrase}"
 print "Removing the first word yields -- ${phrase#* }"
 print "Removing all but the last word yields -- ${phrase##* }"
```

Executing This Script

```
$ remove3.ksh
The full string -- abcdabcd
Remove the 'ab' with #  -- cdabcd
Remove the 'ab' with ## -- cdabcd

Remove '*ab' with # -- cdabcd
Remove '*ab' with ## -- cd

The full string -- I always get the last word.
Removing the first word yields -- always get the last word.
Removing all but the last word yields -- word.
```

% versus %%

The following script demonstrates the difference between % (delete last occurrence) and %% (delete up to and including first occurrence).

One of the trickier parts about working with % and %% is that it's hard for most people to visualize strings moving from right to left.

```
USAGE="usage: remove4.ksh"  # difference between % and %%

 phrase="I always get the first word."
 print "The full string -- ${phrase}"

# This next use of % tells the KornShell to start at the end of
# the string and delete the first occurrence of the pattern ' *'.
# That is, working backwards (from right to left), delete every
# character until the first blank space in the string.
 print "Removing the last word yields -- ${phrase% *}"

# Using %% instead of % tells the KornShell to delete the longest
# occurrence of ' *'.
 print "Removing all but the first word yields -- ${phrase%% *}"

 oz="Lions and tigers and bears"
 print "\nThe full string -- ${oz}"
 print "Delete from last 'and*' to end of line  -- ${oz%and*}"
 print "Delete from first 'and*' to end of line -- ${oz%%and*}"
```

Executing This Script

```
$ remove4.ksh
The full string -- I always get the first word.
Removing the last word yields -- I always get the first
Removing all but the first word yields -- I

The full string -- Lions and tigers and bears
Delete from last 'and*' to end of line  -- Lions and tigers
Delete from first 'and*' to end of line -- Lions
```

Using # on Numbers

Remember that unless numbers are explicitly declared as integers, the KornShell treats the numbers as a string. Therefore, you can use the substring deletion operators (**#**, **##**, **%**, and **%%**) on a numerical string.

Here's a script that takes longer to explain than to execute. In the United States, phone numbers are 10 digits long, where the first 3 digits are an area code. If the caller and person called are within the same area code, the caller must dial only the last 7 digits of the phone number. If the caller and person called are within different area codes, then the caller must dial all 10 digits. We'll use the **#** operator to analyze a 10-digit string of numbers.

```
USAGE="usage: remove5.ksh < phone_numbers"  # parsing numerical strings

 while read a_phone_number  # read in one phone number at a time
 do
  # Assume that the caller is within the 617 area code.
  # Delete leading '617-'; leave all other area codes intact.
   print "Please dial ${a_phone_number#617-}"
 done
```

Executing This Script

Use a text editor to enter some 10-digit phone numbers into a file named **phone_numbers**. Here's my list:

```
$ cat phone_numbers   # cat is the UNIX command to display a file
 929-555-4567
 617-555-3598
 427-555-4322
 909-555-0082
 617-555-1298
```

Now redirect standard input so that the script reads in **phone_numbers**:

```
$ remove5.ksh < phone_numbers
Please dial 929-555-4567
Please dial 555-3598
Please dial 427-555-4322
Please dial 909-555-0082
Please dial 555-1298
```

Deleting a Substring from the Middle of a String

Since you can delete the left or right parts of a string, you may wonder if you can also delete a substring from the middle of a string. While the KornShell does not support an operator to do this, you can use **#**, **%**, and a little trickery to accomplish this feat. The **remove6.ksh** script shown below uses the following algorithm to remove the substring " and tigers" from the middle of the string "Lions and tigers and bears."

`Lions and tigers and bears`	Original string
`Lions` ~~`and tigers and bears`~~	After %
~~`Lions and tigers`~~ `and bears`	After #
`Lions and bears`	Concatenate the remaining strings

The UNIX operating system provides several string replacement utilities (like **awk**, **sed**, **ed**, and **ex**). As the following example demonstrates, you can also use the KornShell to substitute one string for another.

```
USAGE="usage: remove6.ksh"      # delete middle part of string
 oz="Lions and tigers and bears"
 words_to_remove=" and tigers"
 print "The full string -- ${oz}"
# Delete everything from $words_to_remove until the end of the string.
 remaining_left=${oz%$words_to_remove*}

# Delete everything up until $words_to_remove.
 remaining_right=${oz#*$words_to_remove}

# Concatenate the remaining left and right parts to form a new string.
 safer_oz="$remaining_left$remaining_right"
 print "The string minus \"$words_to_remove\" -- $safer_oz"

# For fun, we can substitute $new_text in place of $words_to_remove.
 new_text=" and tofu"
 new_age_oz="$remaining_left$new_text$remaining_right"
 print "A new version of the string -- $new_age_oz"
```

Executing This Script

```
$ remove6.ksh
The full string -- Lions and tigers and bears
The string minus " and tigers" -- Lions and bears
A new version of the string -- Lions and tofu and bears
```

Deleting Branches of Pathnames

A pathname is itself a string. Therefore, you can use the substring deletion operators on pathnames. These operators are very useful for isolating branches (directories) in a long pathname. Each operating system uses different pathname naming rules. (The examples in this book use UNIX pathnames.)

So you can better understand the following example, I'd better mention that the KornShell variable **PWD** holds the pathname of the current directory and the KornShell variable **HOME** holds the pathname of the home (login) directory.

```
USAGE="usage: remove7.ksh"                    # using # on pathnames

 print "Home directory -- $HOME"
 print "Current directory -- $PWD"

 relative=${PWD#$HOME/}
 print "Same dir. relative to HOME -- $relative"
```

Executing This Script

```
$ remove7.ksh
Home directory -- /usr/barry
Current directory -- /usr/barry/book/text/ch9
Same dir. relative to HOME -- book/text/ch9
```

In the following example, I've changed the current directory so that **PWD** does not start with the pathname of the **HOME** directory. Therefore, the phrase **${PWD#$HOME/}** won't be able to delete anything.

```
$ remove7.ksh
Home directory -- /usr/barry
Current directory -- /seuss/samiam
Same dir. relative to HOME -- /seuss/samiam
```

Finding the Length of a String

Use the following syntax to find the length of a string:

length=${*#string*}

"Length" means the number of characters in the string.

The following script reads each line from a file, one line at a time. The script then calculates the length of each line. For extra information, see the readability example in Chapter 16.

```
USAGE="usage: strlen.ksh"  # finding string length

# By setting IFS to a null string, we are ensuring that read won't
# ignore leading white space in the input line.
 IFS=""

 while read -r line   # read one line at a time from the input file
 do
  # Write length of line, then a tab, and then the text of the line:
   print "${#line}\t$line"
 done
```

Executing This Script

Use a text editor to enter the following atrocious verse into a file named **bad_poetry**:

```
$ cat bad_poetry
   Haiku: Ode to Autumn

Crimson crackling leaves.
Pumpkins on a frosty fence.
Rotting grapes smell sweet.
```

Now we'll preface each of these lines with a character count:

```
$ strlen.ksh < bad_poetry
22  Haiku: Ode to Autumn
0
25  Crimson crackling leaves.
27  Pumpkins on a frosty fence.
27  Rotting grapes smell sweet.
```

Parsing Strings into Words

Sometimes it's nice to parse input text into words. This dandy little script parses a text file into words and then tells you how many unique words were used. Although the script is fairly short, the algorithm is kind of complicated; here it is:

1. Read in a line of text from the input file and store it in a variable named **line**. Since **line** has the lowercase attribute, the script will convert all input uppercase letters to lowercase.
2. If the input line was blank, ignore it. If the input line did contain text, use the statement **set $line** to parse the text into tokens and store each token as a positional parameter.
3. Write each positional parameter (each token) to an output file such that each token is on a separate line. We accomplish this feat with the statement **print** **"$*"**. This statement writes all the positional parameters, one at a time, and separates each positional parameter with the first character in **IFS**. Since the first character in **IFS** is a newline, each positional parameter will be stored on a separate line.
4. Return to Step 1 until the script finishes reading all the lines of text.
5. Use the UNIX **sort** utility to place all the words in the output file into lexical order.
6. Use the UNIX **uniq** utility to remove redundant words. That is, if a word appears more than once in the output file, then **uniq** will remove all but the first occurrence.
7. Use the UNIX **wc -l** utility to count the number of lines in the output file. Since each line contains exactly one word, the number of lines should equal the number of unique words.

```
USAGE="usage: parsewrd.ksh"        # parse strings into words
 typeset -l line  # line's text will be stored in lowercase
 read input_filename?"Pathname of file to analyze: "
 read words_file?"Pathname of file to store words: "

# Set IFS equal to newline, space, tab, and common punctuation marks.
# Notice that this assignment takes up two lines (due to the newline).
 IFS="
     ,.;!?"
 while read line  # read one line of text file and assign it to line
 do
   # Parse $line into individual words and assign each word
   # to a different positional parameter.
    if [[ "$line" != "" ]]  # ignore blank lines
    then
      set $line     # parse the line into words
      print "$*"    # print each word on a separate line
    fi
 done < $input_filename > $words_file

 sort $words_file | uniq | wc -l  # UNIX utilities
```

Executing This Script

Using a text editor, write some text into a file. Here's what I used:

```
$ cat bad_poem                # cat is the UNIX utility that displays a file
         Why, Oh Why?
Why, oh why,
Do we never hear ourselves snore?
```

Now run the script to find out how many unique words were used in **bad_poem**:

```
$ parsewrd.ksh
Pathname of file to analyze: bad_poem
Pathname of file to store words: words_in_file
8
```

What's inside file **words_in_file**?

```
$ cat words_in_file
why
oh
why
why
oh
why
do
we
never
hear
ourselves
snore
```

Parsing Strings into Characters

You can divide a passage of text into individual characters. To do this, start by declaring a variable as follows:

```
typeset -L1 one_char
```

Now, whenever you try to assign a string of characters to **one_char**; for example:

```
one_char=$line
```

the KornShell will assign the very first character (the leftmost character) in that string to **one_char**.

The following example counts the occurrences of lowercase **y** in an input file.

```
USAGE="usage: parsechr.ksh [< input_file]"  # parse string into chars
 typeset -L1 one_char           # declare a one-character string
 integer character_counter
 integer y_counter=0

 while read -r line # read in the next line
 do
   length_of_this_line=${#line}  # how many chars does it contain?
   character_counter=0
   while ((character_counter < length_of_this_line))
   do  # go through line, character by character
     one_char=$line   # get next character from the line and assign
                      # it to variable one_char
     line=${line#?}   # delete that character from line
     if [[ "$one_char" = "y" ]]
     then
        ((y_counter=y_counter+1))
     fi
     ((character_counter = character_counter + 1))
   done
 done

 print "This passage contains $y_counter y's."
```

Executing This Script

```
$ parsechr.ksh < bad_poem
This passage contains 4 y's.
```

Specifying Default Values

The KornShell supports four string operations called *parameter expansion modifiers.* These modifiers examine strings to see if they are set, null, or unset and then take an appropriate action depending on the outcome. In this context, *string* means any string variable or positional parameter. A *null* string is a positional parameter or string variable whose value is "" (an empty string), for example:

```
str1="Rain"              # str1 is not null
str2=""                  # str2 is null
```

An *unset* string is any of the following:

- A positional parameter whose value has not been set.
- The name of a variable that has never been explicitly or implicitly declared.
- A string variable explicitly unset by the **unset** statement.

for example:

```
# Set positional parameters $1, $2, and $3:
 set apple banana carambola
# Any positional parameter greater than $3 is now unset.

# Set (assign) the value of a variable named str3:
 str3="Snow and Sleet."
# Explicitly unset the value of str3
 unset str3
```

Table 16 summarizes the parameter expansion modifiers. Here is an example that explores the first parameter expansion modifier in the table: *var*=${*string*:–*expr*}. Given that variable **str1** is set to "Rain" and that **str2** is null, compare the following results:

```
r1=${str1:-"Dry"}   # assign "Rain" to r1; don't change str1
r2=${str2:-"Wet"}   # assign "Wet" to r2; don't change str2
```

Table 16. Parameter Expansion Modifiers

Operation	If string is unset or null, then...	If string is set and is not null, then...
var=${*string*:–*expr*}	*var*=*expr*	*var*=${*string*}
var=${*string*:=*expr*}	*string*=*expr* *var*=*expr*	*var*=${*string*}
var=${*string*:+*expr*}	*var* becomes null	*var*=*expr*
var=${*string*:?*expr*}	the KornShell writes *expr* to standard error	*var*=${*string*}

By the way, if you're testing a string to see if it's unset, then the colon after the string is optional. If you're testing a string to see if it's null, the colon is required.

```
USAGE="usage: prom_mod.ksh [shoe_color]" # {-}, {=}, {?}
# If user enters an argument on the command line, then $1 will be set.
# If user does not enter an argument on the command line, then $1 will
# be unset.  If $1 is set, then the KornShell will assign $1 to color,
# but if $1 is unset, the KornShell will assign "white" to color.
 color=${1-"white"}
 print "You have selected $color shoes"

 read choice?"Enter corsage choice (or press <RETURN> for default): "
# If user enters <RETURN>, then choice will be null.
# If choice is null, then the KornShell assigns "gardenia" to choice.
# If choice is not null, then the KornShell leaves choice alone.
 flower=${choice:="gardenia"}
 print "You have selected a $flower"
# NOTE: The preceding parameter expansion modifier will also modify
#       the value of variable choice.

 read music_choice?"Enter your choice of music: "
# If user enters <RETURN>, then music_choice will be null.
# If music_choice is null, the KornShell prints an error message
# and then exits the script.  If music_choice is not null, then the
# KornShell assign $music_choice to variable music.
 music=${music_choice:?"You have to pick something!  Bye."}
 print "You picked $music"
```

Executing This Script

```
$ prom_mod.ksh              # pick all the defaults, go with the flow
You have selected white shoes
Enter corsage choice (or press <RETURN> for default): <RETURN>
You have selected a gardenia
Enter your choice of music: <RETURN>     # uh oh, not a good choice
prom_mod.ksh[23]: music_choice: You have to pick something!  Bye.

$ prom_mod.ksh purple       # avoid defaults, be creative
You have selected purple shoes
Enter corsage choice (or press <RETURN> for default): thorny rose
You have selected a thorny rose
Enter your choice of music: The Beatles
You picked The Beatles
```

Parsing PATH

The KornShell variable **PATH** (and its cousins **CDPATH** and **FPATH**) holds a set of directories. For example, the following statement assigns a set of three directories to **PATH**:

```
PATH=/bin:$HOME/bin:.
```

Notice that the colon (:) separates the directory names.

How would you parse **PATH**? After all, its assigned value does not contain any white space. Actually, there are many ways to parse **PATH**. One way is to use the substring deletion operators. Another way, shown in the following script, is to rely on the fact that the **for** statement uses **IFS** to parse a string into individual list items.

```
USAGE="usage: path_ex.ksh"  # influence of IFS on for loops
PATH=.:/bin:$HOME/bin   # assign three dirs to PATH

# By default, IFS consists of white space characters.  Since there is
# no white space in $PATH, the for statement cannot parse $PATH.
 print "IFS equals white space"
 for directory in $PATH
 do
   print "$directory"
 done

# By adding the colon to the list of IFS characters, the for statement
# can parse $PATH into its constituent directories.
 IFS=':'$IFS  # add the colon character to IFS
 print "\nIFS contains the colon plus white space"
 for directory in $PATH  # for will parse PATH based on IFS
 do
   print "$directory"
 done
 print

# Now we'll do something useful with $PATH. We'll find out how many
# objects are stored in each directory of $PATH.  Theoretically, the
# more objects, the slower the search.
 print "\nIFS still contains the colon plus white space."
 for directory in $PATH
 do
   cd $directory                       # change current directory
   names_of_objects_in_directory=*     # * expands to the names of all
                                       # objects in current directory
   set $names_of_objects_in_directory # assign positional parameters
   print "$directory contains $# objects"  #
 done
```

Executing This Script

```
$ path_ex.ksh
IFS equals white space
.:/bin://node_2707c/barry/bin

IFS equals the colon plus white space
.
/bin
//node_2707c/barry/bin

IFS still equals the colon plus white space
. contains 35 objects
/bin contains 111 objects
//node_2707c/barry/bin contains 13 objects
```

Chapter 14

KornShell Reserved Variables

This chapter details all of the KornShell's reserved variables.

If You're New to Programming...

You've probably noticed that certain words (for example, **print**, **for**, **while**, etc.) have special meaning to the KornShell. These words are KornShell statements. The KornShell also reserves many variable names (for example, **OPTARG** and **OPTIND**) and gives these variables special meaning.

You don't have to memorize every reserved KornShell variable. Just browse through the chapter quickly and take a few mental notes. Then, as your experience grows, you can return here and find what you need. For now though, the only really essential variables to learn are **PATH** and **PWD**.

This book focuses on KornShell scripts rather than the KornShell command line. Many reserved variables have limited use within scripts and are primarily intended to make the KornShell command line easier to use.

Notice that all the reserved variables have uppercase names. To contrast them, you should probably give user–defined variables, the **x**'s and **y**'s of your scripts, lowercase names. Then, the reserved variables will be easier to spot.

If You're an Experienced Programmer...

The KornShell supports several dozen reserved variables. The reserved variables fall into two classes:

- Variables whose values the KornShell automatically sets and updates. For example, the KornShell automatically updates the value of the reserved variable **SECONDS** so that it contains the number of seconds since the current KornShell was invoked.

- Variables whose values the KornShell does not automatically set. Instead, KornShell users or system administrators set the values of these variables. For example, the reserved variable **HOME** contains the name of the login directory. The KornShell user or system administrator will assign a directory to **HOME**.

The fourth column of Table 17 tells you who sets the value of the variable. For example, the **SECONDS** variable is marked "KSH" to tell you that the KornShell sets it. On the other hand, the **ENV** variable is marked "U or SA" to tell you that the user or system administrator sets this value.

For many variables (indicated in the rightmost column of the table), unsetting the variable removes its special meaning. For example, if you unset **SECONDS** as follows:

```
unset SECONDS
```

then **SECONDS** loses its magic. That is, even if you try to reset the value of **SECONDS**, the KornShell will no longer automatically write the number of seconds since the current KornShell was invoked into **SECONDS**. Note that unsetting a variable is not the same thing as assigning a null string to a variable.

Table 17. KornShell Reserved Variables

Variable	What this variable holds (detailed later in this chapter)	Default	Who sets?	Unsetting removes meaning?
CDPATH	directories that **cd** searches	none	U	no
COLUMNS	terminal width	80	S	no
EDITOR	pathname of command line editor	**/bin/ed**	U or SA	no
ENV	pathname of start-up script	none	U or SA	no
ERRNO	error number of most recently failed system call	none	KSH	yes
FCEDIT	pathname of history file editor	**/bin/ed**	U or SA	no
FPATH	path of autoload functions	none	U	no
HISTFILE	pathname of history file	**$HOME/.sh_history**	U or SA	no
HISTSIZE	number of accessible commands in history file	128	U or SA	no
HOME	login directory	none	SA	no
IFS	set of token delimiters	white space	U	no
LINENO	current line number within script or function	none	KSH	yes
LINES	terminal height	24	SA	no
MAIL	pathname of master mail file	none	SA	no
MAILCHECK	frequency at which the KornShell checks for receipt of new mail	600 (seconds)	U or SA	yes
MAILPATH	pathnames of master mail files	none	SA	no

Variable	What this variable holds (detailed later in this chapter)	Default	Who sets?	Unsetting removes meaning?
OLDPWD	previous current directory	none	KSH	no
OPTARG	name of argument to a switch	none	KSH	yes
OPTIND	option's ordinal position on command line	none	KSH	yes
PATH	pathname of directories the KornShell searches for commands, scripts, or programs	**/bin:/usr/bin**	U or SA	no
PPID	PID of parent	none	KSH	no
PS1	command line prompt	**$**	U	no
PS2	prompt for command that extends more than one line	**>**	U	no
PS3	prompt of **select** statement	**#?**	U	no
PS4	debug mode prompt	**+**	U	no
PWD	current directory	none	U	no
RANDOM	random integer	none	KSH	yes
REPLY	input repository	none	KSH	no
SECONDS	number of seconds since the KornShell was invoked	none	KSH	yes
SHELL	controls creation of restricted KornShell	none	SA	no
TERM	type of terminal you're using	none	SA	no
TMOUT	turn off (time out) an unused KornShell	0 (unlimited)	KSH	yes
VISUAL	command line editor	**/bin/ed**	U or SA	no
$	PID of current process	none	KSH	no
!	PID of background process	none	KSH	no
?	exit status of most recent KornShell statement, OS command, or user program	none	KSH	no
_	miscellaneous data	none	KSH	yes

The remainder of this chapter details these reserved variables.

ENV

The **ENV** variable holds the pathname of a start-up script that the KornShell will call every time you

- Start up a new KornShell
- Run a KornShell script

For details, see Chapter 11.

ERRNO and $? – Error Information

Every KornShell statement, every KornShell script, every operating system command, and every user program returns an *error status* into variable **$?**. The error status is an integer that symbolizes the success or failure of the statement, script, command, or program. Generally speaking, an error status of 0 indicates success and a nonzero error status indicates failure. Unfortunately, some commands are careless in setting the error status, so you can't always depend on **$?** being an accurate barometer of success or failure.

Most users can ignore **ERRNO**. The KornShell automatically sets the value of **ERRNO** equal to the error number of the most recently failed system call executed by the KornShell. So, to make sense of **ERRNO**, you probably need some knowledge of KornShell internals.

HISTSIZE, HISTFILE, and FCEDIT – History File

Chapter 17 details command line editing and the history file. The KornShell supports three variables—**HISTFILE, HISTSIZE,** and **FCEDIT**—to control the creation and use of the history file.

The **HISTFILE** variable holds the pathname of the history file. The default value of **HISTFILE** is **$HOME/.sh_history**. So, for example, if your login (**HOME**) directory is **/usr/julie**, then the history file will be stored in pathname **/usr/julie/.sh_history**.

If you are working on a terminal that does not support windows, there is seldom any reason to change the value of **HISTFILE.** However, if you are working on a terminal that supports multiple windows, you might want to create multiple history files, one for each window running a KornShell. If you do not create separate history files, then the commands you execute in different windows will all be archived in one central history file. Some users like this, but others find it rather confusing. If you'd like a different history file for each window, then put the following two lines in your KornShell start-up file:

```
HISTFILE=$HOME/.history$$
export HISTFILE
```

The **HISTSIZE** variable holds an integer representing the number of commands that you can access from the history file. For example, if you specify the following:

```
HISTSIZE=50
```

in your **$HOME/.profile** start–up script, then the KornShell allows you to read, edit, or execute any of the 50 most recently issued commands. If you don't specify a value of **HISTSIZE**, then the KornShell allows you to read, edit, or execute any of the 128 most recently issued commands. By the way, after the KornShell has been invoked, modifying the value of **HISTSIZE** won't alter the number of commands that you can access.

You can use the **fc** command (or its alias, **r**) to edit commands from the history file and then re–execute them. Of course, in order to edit a command, you'll need a text editor. You may specify the text editor when you invoke the **fc** command; for example, the following command tells **fc** to use the text editor stored at pathname **/usr/ucb/vi** when editing command number 238:

```
$ fc -e /usr/ucb/vi 238
```

When editing a lot of commands, it may become annoying to keep reminding **fc** to edit with **/usr/ucb/vi**. Therefore, KornShell lets you "set it and forget it" with the **FCEDIT** variable; for example, the following command will tell KornShell to do command line editing with **vi**:

```
$ FCEDIT=/usr/ucb/vi
```

Now that **FCEDIT** is set, you can edit command number 238 in a more civilized manner, to wit:

```
$ fc 238
```

In case you're wondering, **fc –e** takes precedence over the value of **FCEDIT**. For example, if you set **FCEDIT** to **vi** and specify **fc –e /usr/ucb/emacs,** the KornShell will use **emacs** (not **vi**) to edit the command line.

IFS – Parsing Lines into Tokens

IFS is an acronym for internal field separator. Its primary purpose is to define what a token is for those statements (**read, set, for, select**) or commands that need to parse information into tokens.

We detail **IFS** in Chapter 12. Briefly, **IFS** holds a set of characters, where each character is a token delimiter. The default set of characters is all three white space characters (space, tab, newline). For many KornShell scripts, the default set of characters is just fine. However, here's an example of a possible reassignment to **IFS:**

```
IFS='Zz'     assign IFS the two letters Z and z
```

Given this definition of **IFS** and the following line of input:

```
Zebras in zoos go zzoom.
```

here's how the **read** statement would parse the line:

```
first token:   ""           # everything from start of line to first Z or z (nothing)
second token:  "ebras in "  # everything after Z until next Z or z
third token:   "oos go "    # everything after z until next Z or z
fourth token:  ""           # everything after z until next Z or z (nothing)
fifth token:   "oom."       # everything after z to end of line
```

When writing the values of the positional parameters with the following statement:

```
print "$*"
```

the first character in **IFS** separates the values. See Chapter 9 for an example.

LINENO – Current Line Number

The KornShell sets **LINENO** to the current line number within the script. However, if you place **LINENO** inside a function, the KornShell sets **LINENO** to the current line number relative to the beginning of the function.

Note that all lines, even blank lines and comments, are included in **LINENO**'s count. Furthermore, if you put multiple statements (separated by semicolons) on one line, then **LINENO** still counts that as only one line.

```
USAGE="usage: LINENOex.ksh"      # LINENO reserved variable

 function kerry
 {
   print "Greetings from Line $LINENO of $0"
 }

 function anne
 {
  # Comments and blank lines are also included in the count.

   print "Hello again."
   print "Greetings from Line $LINENO of $0"
 }

kerry    # call function kerry
anne     # call function anne
print "Greetings from Line $LINENO of $0"
```

Executing This Script

```
$ LINENOex.ksh
Greetings from Line 2 of kerry
Hello again.
Greetings from Line 5 of anne
Greetings from Line 18 of LINENO_ex.ksh
```

MAIL, MAILCHECK, and MAILPATH – Electronic Mail

Ahh yes, the rustling of electromagnetic waves on your front doorstep, the barking of electronic dogs, the crackling of bits as you excitedly tear open the envelope...there's nothing quite like getting fresh electronic mail.

There are two basic kinds of mail storage systems. In one, the mail system appends all incoming mail to the user's master mail file. In the other mail storage system, each piece of incoming mail gets stored in its own separate file. If your mail storage system is the latter, then **MAIL**, **MAILPATH**, and **MAILCHECK** do not have any influence. (The remainder of this section assumes that you are using the master mail file storage system.)

If all your electronic mail ends up in one master mail file, then the system administrator or user should set **MAIL** equal to the pathname of that master mail file; for example:

```
MAIL=/usr/spool/mail/paul
```

On the other hand, some users belong to multiple mail systems and have multiple master mail files. For these users, the system administrator or user should set **MAILPATH** equal to the pathnames of all of your master mail files. For example, if user "paul" has two different master mail files, then the following assignment tells **MAILPATH** about both of them. (Use a colon to separate each pathname.)

```
MAILPATH=/usr/spool/mail/paul:/uucp/paul
```

If both **MAIL** and **MAILPATH** are set, **MAILPATH** has precedence over **MAIL**.

Assuming that **MAIL** or **MAILPATH** have been set, you can assign an integer value to **MAILCHECK**. The **MAILCHECK** variable determines how often (in seconds) the KornShell will check for new mail. For example, the following command tells the KornShell to check the mailboxes or mail files every 5 minutes (300 seconds):

```
MAILCHECK=300
```

If no new mail arrived during those 300 seconds, the KornShell keeps quiet about it. However, if mail did arrive, KornShell announces its arrival with a jolly:

```
You have mail in $_
```

where KornShell replaces **$_** with the name of the master mail file that received the mail.

OPTARG and OPTIND – Values Associated with getopts

Chapter 9 explores both of these variables. Briefly, **getopts** automatically sets **OPTARG** equal to the following:

- The name of an invalid switch
- The name of an argument to a valid switch

The value of **OPTIND** is usually an argument to a **shift** statement. See the **getopts6.ksh** example in Chapter 9 for details.

PATH, CDPATH, and FPATH – Search Directories

Each of these three variables—**PATH**, **CDPATH**, and **FPATH**—holds a different list of directories. Under certain circumstances, the KornShell will search through these lists in order to find:

- A certain program or shell script to execute (**PATH**)
- A certain directory to move to (**CDPATH**)
- A certain autoload function (**FPATH**) (see Chapter 10)

Permit me a short digression. **PATH**, **CDPATH**, and **FPATH** only influence implicit pathnames; they have no influence over explicit pathnames. On UNIX systems, an *explicit* pathname begins with any of the following:

```
/  //  ~  .  ..
```

and an *implicit* pathname does not; for example:

```
/usr/ucb/vi              # explicit pathname, begins with /
vi                       # implicit pathname
~/bin/myscript           # explicit pathname, begins with ~
myscript                 # implicit pathname
./games                  # explicit pathname, begins with .
games                    # implicit pathname
```

An explicit pathname can also begin with any variable name that expands to an explicit pathname; for example, assuming that the value of **HOME** is **/usr/mar**, then:

```
$HOME/heart/is           # explicit pathname, $HOME starts with /
heart/is                 # implicit pathname
```

Now that we've gotten that out of the way, we can concentrate on **PATH.** Let's start by setting **PATH** equal to three directories: **.** (the current directory), **/bin,** and **$HOME/bin.** Here's the assignment:

```
$ PATH=:.:/bin:$HOME/bin
```

If we try to execute a script by typing its explicit pathname, for instance:

```
$ /usr/quentin/title.ksh
```

then the KornShell will try to execute whatever is stored at **/usr/quentin/title.ksh** and ignore **PATH.** However, if we type the following implicit pathname:

```
$ goo
```

then the KornShell will search through the directories of **PATH** one by one until it finds **goo.** The quest is illustrated in Figure 5.

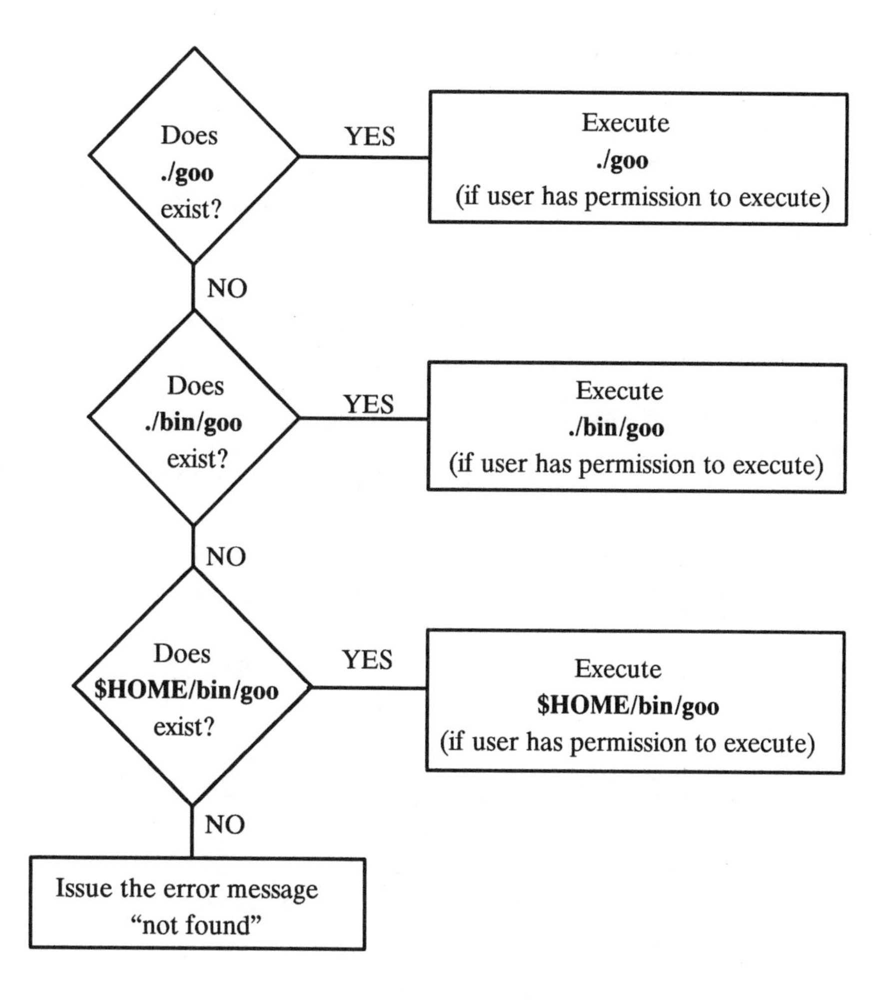

Figure 5. The KornShell searches the directories of PATH for an implicit pathname

CDPATH is similar to **PATH** in that it holds a list of directories; however, **CDPATH** only influences the **cd** (change directory) statement. (Unlike other UNIX shells, **cd** is built into the KornShell; it is not an external command.) The **cd** statement takes an explicit or implicit pathname as an argument. If you specify an explicit pathname, **cd** ignores **CDPATH**. If, however, you specify an implicit pathname, **cd** looks for a subdirectory by that name in the list of directories of **CDPATH.**

Let's explore **CDPATH** through some examples. First, let's assign a list of directories to **CDPATH** as follows:

```
$ CDPATH=:..:$HOME/my_book:/usr/jan
```

If you issue an explicit pathname like:

```
$ cd /usr/beth
```

then **cd** ignores **CDPATH** and simply tries to change the current directory to **/usr/beth**. Suppose though, that you specify an implicit pathname argument instead, like:

```
$ cd chapter8
```

In this case, **cd** will search for directory **chapter8** in the following order:

1. Does **./chapter8** exist? If yes, change current directory to it.
2. Does **$HOME/my_book/chapter8** exist? If yes, change current directory to it.
3. Does **/usr/jan/chapter8** exist? If yes, change current directory to it.

There is no default value for **CDPATH**. If **CDPATH** isn't set and you issue a **cd** statement, then the KornShell searches for implicit directories underneath **.** (the current directory).

If you do specify a list of directories for **CDPATH,** it is almost always a good idea to include the **.** directory in that list.

See also **MAILPATH.**

PS1, PS2, PS3, and PS4 – Prompts

The KornShell supports the following four prompts:

- **PS1** holds the command line prompt.
- **PS2** holds the prompt for command lines continued on another line.
- **PS3** holds the prompt for **select** statements.
- **PS4** holds the debug mode prompt.

The KornShell uses the value of the variable **PS1** as the command line prompt. When you first invoke the KornShell, the prompt stares back at you. After every command finishes running, the command line prompt greets you. The command line prompt is set to the value of **PS1.**

The default KornShell command line prompt is a dollar sign (**$**) followed by a space; however, a system administrator may decide to assign a different default prompt for your system. If you don't like the default prompt, you can change it by assigning a new value to **PS1**. Typically, KornShell users specify the command line prompt in their start-up script (see Chapter 11); however, you can redefine the prompt at any time. For example, if you find the dollar sign a little too boring, you can change it by assigning a new value to **PS1;** for example:

```
$ PS1='Hey There Good Looking: ' # change PS1
Hey There Good Looking:          # here's the new prompt
```

Go ahead and try it—make up your own witty prompts. Come on back when you've gotten the urge out of your system.

Welcome back. Did you have a good time? Yes, I'm sure you did, but let's get serious. Most beginners treat the prompt as a lifeless lump of clay, an inert (and frequently profane) text string. Yet, the prompt can be a lot more than that. The prompt can contain all sorts of interesting dynamic information. For example, here's how to get the prompt to display the current directory:

```
$ PS1='$PWD> '                        # change PS1

/usr/mel> x=3                         # the prompt contains the current directory

/usr/mel> cd /usr/joan/teach          # whenever you change the current directory...

/usr/joan/teach>                      # the prompt changes
```

Notice how the prompt changed whenever we changed directories. See "Some Popular Command Line Prompts" later in this section for some more ideas.

! BEWARE: Common Mistakes Setting Prompts !

The assigned value, if it contains variables, should be enclosed in single quotes; compare the following assignments:

```
PS1=$SECONDS       # wrong
PS1='$SECONDS '    # right
PS1="$SECONDS "    # wrong
```

It is a good idea to specify at least one character of white space at the end of the prompt. Remember that the KornShell will ignore trailing white space unless you enclose it within quotes:

```
PS1='prompt '      # right
PS1='prompt'       # okay, but resulting prompt could be confusing
```

The exclamation point (!), when used within a prompt, refers to the command number. If you want a literal exclamation point to appear as part of your prompt, specify two exclamation points in a row; for example:

```
PS1='Enter your command!! '
```

Assigning a value to **PS3** or **PS4** from your KornShell command line does not actually change the debug prompt when you debug your script. You must also export the assignment to **PS4.**

PS2 is the line continuation prompt. Its default value is the **>** character. The KornShell displays the line continuation prompt when you do not complete a command on one line. For example, the following **for** loop requires four lines, so the KornShell will display **PS2** three times:

```
$ for object in b*
> do
> print "\t$object"
> done
```

Just to get cute, I'll make **PS1** and **PS2** as literal as possible:

```
$ PS1='Command Starts Here: '; PS2='and continues here:
Command Starts Here: for object in b*
and continues here:  do
and continues here:     print "\t$object"
and continues here:  done
```

Sometimes, you *think* that you have completed the command on one line, but you really haven't. Often the culprit is an unmatched single– or double–quote; for example:

```
Command Starts Here: print "and here we are
and continues here: what?  I forgot to finish that line?"
```

PS3 is the variable controlling the prompt within a **select** statement. See Chapter 8 for some examples.

PS4 is the debug prompt. Actually, calling **PS4** a "prompt" is somewhat misleading because it doesn't actually prompt the user to enter input. Instead, when you debug your script (by specifying **set –x** or **ksh –x**), the KornShell precedes the name of the command being executed with the value of **PS4.** By default, the prompt is a plus sign (+). You may wish to change your debug prompt so that it equals **LINENO.** That way, the KornShell will display the line number of the command being executed. Another fun thing to do is to have **PS4** print the number of seconds elapsed since the script started running, like this:

```
SECONDS=0    # reset SECONDS
PS4='$SECONDS: '
```

(Remember to export the value of **PS4.** If you don't export it, the debug prompt won't change.)

Some Popular Command Line Prompts

Set the prompt to the current command number (see Chapter 17 for an explanation of command numbers):

```
$ PS1='! Korn> '      # change prompt
25 Korn> pwd          # prompt is now 25 Korn>
/usr/shannon/ftn/programs
26 Korn> cd /usr/shannon
27 Korn>              # the KornShell automatically increments command number
```

Set the prompt to the current directory relative to the **HOME** directory:

```
$ print $PWD                    # what's the current directory?
/usr/shannon/ftn/programs
$ print $HOME                   # what's the home directory?
/usr/shannon
$ PS1='${PWD#$HOME/}: '         # change prompt
ftn/programs/: print "hi"       # here's the new prompt
```

Set the prompt to the rightmost directory name:

```
$ print $PWD                    # what's the current directory?
/usr/shannon/ftn/programs
$ PS1='${PWD##*/}: '            # change prompt
programs: print "hi"            # here's the new prompt
```

Set the prompt to the number of seconds since you started up the KornShell:

```
$ PS1='$SECONDS: '      # change prompt
1341: print "hi"        # the new prompt tells us how old the KornShell is
hi
1343: print "hello"     # seconds are automatically updated
```

Set the prompt to the PID of the current process and the PID of the most recently invoked background process:

```
$ PS1='$$ $!: '         # change prompt
186 : print "hi"        # here's the new prompt; no background process yet
hi
186 : script&           # start a background process
[1] 215                 # 215 is the PID of the background process
186 215:                # prompt changes to include the background PID
```

PWD, OLDPWD, and HOME – Login, Current, and Previous Directories

PWD holds the name of the directory you're currently in. **OLDPWD** holds the name of the directory you just left. For example:

```
$ print $PWD                # print name of current directory
/usr/ignatov/clubs/seven

$ cd /rastelli/sticks       # change current directory

$ print $PWD                # print new current directory
/rastelli/sticks

$ print $OLDPWD             # print previous current directory
/usr/ignatov/clubs/seven

$ cd $OLDPWD                # change current directory to previous current directory
```

HOME holds the name of a special directory, typically the directory you log into. Usually, the system administrator sets the value of **HOME** for you; however, you may choose to redefine it. If you specify the **cd** statement without specifying an argument, **cd** sets the current directory to **HOME.** Also, on most UNIX systems, you can use the tilde (~) character to symbolize the **HOME** directory.

```
$ print $PWD                # what's the current directory?
/rastelli/sticks

$ cd $HOME                  # return to your login directory
$ cd                        # same as previous command
$ cd ~                      # same as previous command

$ print $PWD                # print new current directory
/usr/gatto
```

Don't confuse the **PWD** reserved variable with the **pwd** statement. Compare the following:

```
$ PWD                       # causes an error because PWD isn't a command
ksh: PWD:  not found

$ pwd                       # okay
/usr/ignatov/clubs/seven
```

It is legal to assign a value to **PWD,** but you really shouldn't do it. Changing the value of **PWD** does not actually change the current directory; it just causes confusion.

Note that changing the current directory within a script does not change the current directory of the shell or the process that called that script. For example, consider the following simple script:

```
USAGE="usage: PWD_ex.ksh new_dir" # PWD variable

  cd $1
  print "Current directory is $PWD"
```

```
$ print $PWD                    # find the current dir
/rastelli/sticks
```

Now let's run the script:

```
$ PWD_ex.ksh /usr/arthur/juggle # call the script
Current directory is /usr/arthur/juggle
```

Did the script change the current directory of the shell?

```
$ print $PWD                    # find the current dir after calling the script
/rastelli/sticks
```

No, it did not. See Chapter 11 for more information.

RANDOM – Random Integer Generator

The KornShell sets **RANDOM** to a random integer between 0 and 32,767. If you are accustomed to high-level languages, you might pretend that **RANDOM** is a function call that returns a random number. Experienced programmers should note that the KornShell uses a pseudo random number generator.

By default, the KornShell's random number generator is *seeded* to a random number. In other words, by default, **RANDOM** will contain a different value every time you run the script. However, when debugging a script, it is often helpful to work with the same value of **RANDOM** each time you run it. The following script explores random number seeding.

```
USAGE="usage: RANDOMex.ksh"  # RANDOM
 function throw_two_dice
 {
   ((dice1 = (RANDOM % 6) + 1))  # random number from 1 to 6
   ((dice2 = (RANDOM % 6) + 1))  # random number from 1 to 6
   ((total = dice1 + dice2))     # random number from 2 to 12
   return $total
 }
###################################################################
# Script starts executing at next statement.
# By default, RANDOM provides truly random numbers.
 throw_two_dice
 print "Truly random roll: $?"

# If you want to generate the same random number each time
# you run the script, set RANDOM to a constant.
 RANDOM=2 # seed random number generator to a constant
 throw_two_dice
 print "Same every time: $?"

# If you want to generate a different set of random numbers
# each time you run the script, then set RANDOM to $$ or to SECONDS.
 RANDOM=$SECONDS
 throw_two_dice
 print "Truly random roll: $?"
```

Executing This Script

```
$ RANDOMex.ksh
Truly random roll: 7
Same every time: 6
Truly random roll: 10

$ RANDOMex.ksh
Truly random roll: 5
Same every time: 6
Truly random roll: 2
```

REPLY and _ – Miscellaneous Input Repository

The KornShell sets the values of two reserved variables, **REPLY** and _, to hold various input information.

The KornShell sets the value of **REPLY** to the following:

- Whatever the user inputs in a **select** statement. See Chapter 8 for an example.
- Whatever the user inputs to a **read** statement that does not contain a target variable. See Chapter 12 for an example.

No other event can influence **REPLY.**

It looks like a typo, but _ is a KornShell reserved variable. The KornShell sets the value of _ to the following:

- The final token of the most recently executed KornShell statement, KornShell script, operating system command, or user program. In other words, every time you invoke anything (either in a script or on the KornShell command line), the KornShell automatically assigns a new value to _. For example, suppose that you are working in the KornShell and you issue the command **ls -l.** In this case, the KornShell automatically assigns **-l** to _ because **-l** is the last token on the command line. Suppose you issue another command, say, **read pints quarts.** Now the KornShell assigns the value "quarts" to variable _. Incidentally, the starting value of _ is the pathname of the script. In other words, before the KornShell executes any commands in a script, the KornShell assigns **$0** to _.
- The name of the master mail file that received mail. See the description of **MAILCHECK** earlier in this chapter.

SECONDS – Elapsed Time

The KornShell sets **SECONDS** to the number of seconds elapsed since you invoked the KornShell; for example:

```
$ print "I invoked this KornShell $SECONDS seconds ago."
I invoked this KornShell 1338 seconds ago.
```

As such, **SECONDS** counts the time wasted in front of the terminal when you could be doing something really meaningful with your life. However, you may choose to have **SECONDS** time a nontrivial event, as in this next script. Notice that you can assign a new integer value to **SECONDS** and the clock will restart at this value.

```
USAGE="usage: SECONDS.ksh"    # SECONDS

# Declare two integer variables.
 integer min
 integer sec


 SECONDS=0     # reset the clock to 0.
 print "How much is 173 x 19?"
 read answer
 elapsed_time=$SECONDS # how long did it take?
 ((min = elapsed_time / 60))
 ((sec = elapsed_time % 60))
 print "It took you $min minutes and $sec seconds to answer."
```

Executing This Script

```
$ SECONDS.ksh
How much is 173 x 19?
3287
It took you 2 minutes and 11 seconds to answer.
```

SHELL

(Most users can skip this variable.)

Ignore this variable unless you want to create a *restricted KornShell,* generally known as **rksh.** As the name implies, a restricted KornShell is a KornShell implementation that prevents (restricts) the user from doing certain things. Specifically, users running in a restricted KornShell are not allowed to do any of the following:

- Change the current directory. (In other words, the **cd** command won't work.)
- Change the value of the **SHELL, ENV,** or **PATH** variables.
- Invoke a program (including operating system utilities) by specifying the explicit pathname of that program.
- Redirect output with **>**, **>|**, **<>**, or **>>**.

However, if a user working in a restricted KornShell invokes a KornShell script, then the script will run normally. That is, a restricted KornShell does not restrict KornShell scripts.

Warning: setting up a bulletproof restricted environment is difficult! Do you really need to do it?

There are two ways to create a restricted KornShell. One way is to invoke the program named **rksh.** Another way is by setting the **SHELL** variable. This variable holds a pathname. If the leafname of this pathname contains the letter **r**, then the system invokes a restricted KornShell. Otherwise, the system invokes a regular (nonrestricted) KornShell. For those unfamiliar with this term, the *leafname* of a pathname is the last (rightmost) component of the pathname. For example, the following assignment in a start-up script will cause the system to invoke a restricted KornShell:

```
SHELL=/usr/bin/rksh       # leafname (rksh) contains letter r
```

However, the following assignment in a start-up script will cause the system to invoke a regular (nonrestricted) KornShell:

```
SHELL=/usr/bin/ksh        # leafname (ksh) does not contain letter r
```

By the way, many users think that the KornShell automatically assigns **SHELL** the pathname of the KornShell currently in use. However, the KornShell does not do this. If you're in the KornShell and want to find the pathname of the current KornShell, type the following:

```
$ print $0
/bin/ksh
```

TERM, COLUMNS, and LINES – Terminal and Window Characteristics

Each implementation of the KornShell provides several variables to define the shape, size, characteristics, and identity of the terminal or virtual terminals (windows) that you are using. The KornShell itself makes only scant use of these variables, but other software may depend on them.

The **COLUMNS** variable holds an integer value that specifies the virtual width of a KornShell command line when the KornShell is in **vi, emacs,** or **gmacs** editor mode. For example, the following:

```
$ COLUMNS=40
```

specifies a virtual width of 40 characters for command lines. Actually, you can still enter a command line longer than 40 characters. It's just that the KornShell will begin to left shift the command line after the 40th character.

Some programs read the value of **LINES** to determine how many lines of text can safely fit on the screen at one time. However, as terminals get smarter, the importance of **LINES** decreases.

On some implementations of the KornShell, the values of **COLUMNS** and **LINES** control how the **select** command outputs menu entries.

The **TERM** variable holds a string identifying the kind of terminal you are working on. For instance, the **TERM** variable on my terminal is set to the following:

```
apollo_1280_bw
```

which indicates that the terminal is Apollo style, has 1280 x-coordinate pixels, and is black and white. On UNIX systems, the file **/etc/termcap** lists literally hundreds of different possible values of **TERM**.

The KornShell ignores **TERM;** however, certain utilities, such as **vi,** ultimately depend on **TERM** for a description of the terminal's characteristics. Your system may support other terminal variables (for example, variables defining the number of x- and y-coordinate pixels) that may be valuable to certain graphics programs. However, the bottom line on most of these variables is that although you can use the KornShell to set or examine these variables, the KornShell doesn't depend on them.

TMOUT – Time Out an Unused KornShell

The default value of **TMOUT** is 0, meaning that the KornShell user can wait an infinite amount of time between entering commands. If you'd like to force users to, ahem, command or get off the shell, then assign an integer value to **TMOUT**. For example, let's set the time out period to two minutes (120 seconds) by issuing the following command:

```
$ TMOUT=120
```

If at any point during the KornShell session, the user goes two minutes without issuing a command, then the KornShell will issue the message:

```
shell will time out in 60 seconds
```

Once the message appears, the user has another minute to enter a command. If the user does not, the KornShell ends its session. If the user does enter a command, the KornShell time out clock starts ticking anew. Keep in mind that the clock starts when the user invokes the command; it does not start when the user simply begins *typing* a command. Something else to keep in mind—the KornShell has no qualms about timing you out of a session even when background processes are running.

On some systems, particularly systems with dumb terminals, the system automatically logs out users when the KornShell dies. Thus, **TMOUT** can be effective in automatically logging out users who've forgotten to log themselves out.

Some systems also support a screen time out variable, which temporarily darkens the monitor (to save electricity and wear-and-tear on the screen) when user input stops. Despite a certain conceptual resemblance, **TMOUT** and the screen time out variable are unrelated.

By the way, you cannot use **TMOUT** within a shell script to force users to type faster.

VISUAL and EDITOR – Command Line Text Editors

Use **VISUAL** or **EDITOR** to specify a text editor for KornShell command lines. (See Chapter 17 for an explanation of command line text editors.)

The **VISUAL** variable confuses a lot of users. First of all, some users think they have to specify the full pathname at which the text editor is stored; for example, **/usr/ucb/vi.** In reality, the KornShell command line text editors are built into the KornShell itself. In other words, if you do assign **VISUAL** the value **/usr/ucb/vi**, the KornShell will not actually use the **vi** editor stored at **/usr/ucb/vi.** Instead, the KornShell interprets only the last few characters of the value of **VISUAL.** If the last two characters are **vi**, the KornShell will use **vi**–style command line editing. If the last five characters are **emacs**, then the KornShell will use **emacs**–style command line editing. Finally, if the last five characters are **gmacs**, the KornShell will use **gmacs**–style command line editing.

The second cause of confusion concerns the potency of **VISUAL**. Once you specify a value of **VISUAL** that loads **vi**, **emacs**, or **gmacs**–style editing, then changing the value of **VISUAL** does not always move you to a different editor.

The third cause of confusion is that you don't have to specify a value of **VISUAL**. The KornShell on your system will default to a particular editor, which isn't necessarily **vi, emacs,** or **gmacs.** If you are used to this default editor, then you probably shouldn't change **VISUAL.**

The fourth cause of confusion is that the value of **VISUAL** does not restrict your choices for regular text editing. For example, if **VISUAL** is set to **emacs,** you can still use **vi** (or any other text editor) to edit a text file. In other words, **VISUAL** only influences the KornShell command line itself; it does not influence file editing.

The fifth cause of confusion is that **EDITOR** serves exactly the same purpose as **VISUAL**; however, **VISUAL** has precedence over **EDITOR.** In other words, if you assign a value to both **VISUAL** and **EDITOR**, the KornShell will ignore the value of **EDITOR.** Given that, I'd suggest that you ignore **EDITOR.** Note that **EDITOR** defaults to **/bin/ed,** but **VISUAL** has no default.

$, !, and PPID – Process ID

Casually speaking, a *process* is an executing program. (Refer to a textbook on operating systems for a more formal definition.) Operating systems keep track of processes by associating a unique identification number (usually called a *PID*) with each process. The PID is more than just an interesting piece of trivia; certain statements (for example, **kill**) require a PID as an argument.

The KornShell provides the following three reserved variables to help you find PIDs:

$$ is the PID of the current process.

$PPID is the PID of the current process's parent. The parent process is the process that invoked the current process.

$! is the PID of the most recently invoked background process (even if that process isn't currently running). See Chapter 15 for more information on background processes.

Here's a script that exercises these three variables:

```
USAGE="usage: pid_ex.ksh"  # demonstrates $$ and $PPID

 print "The PID of the current process is $$"
 print "The PID of the parent process is $PPID"
```

Executing This Script

Before invoking **pid_ex.ksh,** let's find out what the PID of the KornShell is. (Remember, an executing KornShell is itself a process.)

```
$ print "The PID of my KornShell is $$"
The PID of my KornShell is 225
```

Now, we'll invoke the script from the KornShell, thus making the KornShell into the script's parent:

```
$ pid_ex.ksh
The PID of the current process is 234
The PID of the parent process is 225
```

UNIX users can use the **ps** command (with appropriate switches) to obtain PIDs and PPIDs. However, parsing the complicated **ps** output format from within a script can be a bit of a chore. (Also, the SysV and BSD versions of **ps** take different switches, so writing a portable shell script with **ps** is downright tricky.)

Chapter 15

Foreground, Background, and Signaling

This chapter explains the difference between foreground and background, and then details signaling. Beginners can probably skip over this chapter, especially the signaling parts.

Background and Foreground

Consider the following session on the KornShell command line:

```
$ ls -Rl         # UNIX utility
. . .
$ stats          # program to average five billion floating-point numbers
. . .
$ my_script      # a KornShell script
```

You may think to yourself, "Hey, those three commands ran in the KornShell." However, it would be more accurate to think, "Hey, those three commands ran in the KornShell's *foreground*." It is an easy mistake to make because, by default, all commands run in the *foreground*. The foreground can execute only one command at a time.* When that command finishes executing, the KornShell prompts you to enter another one, and so you do until you end the KornShell session.

---

* One could argue with this assertion and say that a pipeline (that is, a command line containing a pipe operator) executes multiple commands at one time.

The problem with the foreground is that a lengthy program can tie up your terminal for hours or even days. For example, if you invoke **stats** on Monday, you might not be able to invoke **my_script** until Tuesday. To solve this problem, the KornShell lets you run commands in the *background.* Background commands run off in their own little world without disturbing the foreground. When the background command finishes running, the KornShell can send you a short message to tell you that it's done. By running time-consuming commands in the background, the foreground is freed up for interactive commands.

Although only one command at a time can run in the foreground, you can concurrently run multiple background commands.*

To run a command in the background, simply append an ampersand (**&**) to the end of it; for example:

```
$ stats&                    # run stats in background
```

If you want **stats** to continue running after you log out (yes, it's possible), preface the entire command with the word **nohup** (which is short for do **not hang up**); for example:

```
$ nohup stats&              # run stats in background even after log out
```

As a script writer, you should be aware that scripts run in the foreground can be interactive, but scripts run in the background cannot. That is, a background script has to take all of its input from a file or from a pipe; background scripts cannot gather input from the terminal. Also, you should usually redirect standard output and standard error so that they write their output to a file or to a pipe, not to the terminal. So, it would probably be better to use a command like the following to invoke **stats**:

```
$ stats < input_data > the_answer 2> errors&
[1] 405
```

When you invoke a command (script, operating system utility, or user program), whether it's running in the foreground or background, the command becomes a *job.* For each job, the KornShell assigns a job number (for example, **[1]**) and the operating system assigns a process identifier (for example, **405**). You can use either value as input to a group of statements collectively known as the *job control statements.* Here is a list of the job control statements.

bg moves a foreground job to the background. You can only do this if the foreground job is stopped. To stop a foreground job, you have to send it a STOP signal, usually by typing a certain <CONTROL> sequence (perhaps <CONTROL>s).

fg moves a background job to the foreground. You can only do this if the background job is *stopped.* To stop a background job, you have to send it a STOP signal, usually by typing **kill -STOP** *job_name.*

jobs lists the job numbers and job identifiers of all current background jobs.

kill sends a signal to a background job. (We detail signals in the next section.) One common use of **kill** is to terminate a background job.

wait waits for a certain background job to finish executing. For example, suppose that **scriptA** depends on the results of **scriptB.** Therefore, you could use **wait** to tell the KornShell to hold off executing **scriptA** until **scriptB** finishes.

---

* Not all KornShell implementations support job control. Generally speaking, if your operating system supports job control, so will your KornShell.

The job control statements are *not* a standard part of the KornShell. In other words, your version of the KornShell may or may not support the preceding statements.

You can have the KornShell send you a message when your background job finishes executing. To do so, you must turn on the *monitor* option by issuing the following statement:

```
$ set -o monitor             # turn on the monitor option
```

The following statement turns off the monitor option:

```
$ set +o monitor             # turn on the monitor option
```

When Should I Run a Job in the Background?

Terminals that support multiple windows are rapidly replacing single–window dumb terminals. If your terminal does support multiple windows, chances are good that you can run multiple KornShells concurrently. If that's the case, then you may not want to run your scripts, even the time–consuming ones, in the background at all. Instead, you might find it easier to run your time–consuming scripts in separate windows. However, if you're still singing those VT100 blues, the background will help you get a lot more work done.

Up until now, we've concentrated on running time–consuming programs in the background. However, there are other kinds of programs known as *servers* or, in UNIX slang, *daemons,* that typically run in the background. A server provides a resource (a service) to other processes (called *clients*) running on the system. Generally speaking, clients access servers sporadically. The servers lurk in the background and listen for service requests from clients. For example, most UNIX systems run a server called **tcpd.** This server runs quietly in the background using minimal system resources until a client makes a TCP/IP request. When that happens, the **tcpd** server temporarily uses a lot of resources.

The operating system probably starts several servers based on the information inside its login scripts. Other software packages, such as X windows, may also start up servers. Users may be asked to start up servers before running certain kinds of programs.

Another use of the background is for running scripts that need to access information sporadically. For example, once a minute, the following script requests information about disk space and writes it to a file named **/tmp/disk_log.**

```
USAGE="usage: sporadic.ksh" # loop once a minute

 while :     # loop until system administrator kills script
 do
   df >> /tmp/disk_log    # write disk usage to /tmp/disk_log
   sleep 60  # halt script for 60 seconds
 done
```

This would be an ideal script to run in the background even after you log out; here's how to invoke it:

```
$ nohup sporadic.ksh&
```

Signaling

Usually, once you start a script, you want it to run to completion. Oh sure, the script may pause from time to time to wait for input, but the general flow of a script is from start to finish.

But suppose you start the script and suddenly realize, "Wait a second. I didn't want to run that script. It could disrupt the whole balance of power in Europe." Or perhaps after starting a script you think to yourself, "I need to temporarily halt the script so I can see what happened to Andorra and Liechtenstein." In both cases, you need to send a *signal* to the script.

A signal is a number that you send to a script. Since numbers are a little tricky to remember; every system provides an English–like name that corresponds to the number. The number symbolizes your intentions on a scale ranging from "I think there might be a slight problem here" to "Stop that thing no matter what!" Each operating system supports a different set of signals. To find out the signals that your operating system supports, issue the **kill –l** statement. Here's what happened when I used it on my system:

```
$ kill -l          # list all the signals that my operating system supports
 1) HUP              12) SYS                  23) CHLD
 2) INT              13) PIPE                 24) TTIN
 3) QUIT             14) ALRM                 25) TTOU
 4) ILL              15) TERM                 26) TINT
 5) TRAP             16) USR1                 27) XCPU
 6) IOT              17) USR2                 28) XFSZ
 7) EMT              18) CLD                  29) VTALRM
 8) FPE              19) APOLLO               30) PROF
 9) KILL             20) STOP                 31) URG
10) BUS              21) TSTP                 32) WINCH
11) SEGV             22) CONT
```

How to Send a Signal to a Script

The method you use to send a signal to a script depends on whether the script is running in the foreground or in the background.

You usually send signals to foreground scripts by typing a particular key or keys. In order for this to work, the key (or keys) must have been predefined to correspond to a signal. Unfortunately, each system predefines keys in a different way. Oftentimes though, if you are working on a UNIX system, you can generate:

- a **QUIT** signal by typing **<CONTROL>**
- an **INT** signal by typing **<CONROL>c** or by pressing **<DELETE>**
- a **STOP** signal by typing **<CONROL>s**
- a **CONT** signal by typing **<CONROL>q**

I want to reemphasize that your system might not support the preceding key definitions. Also, many applications change the way that the system handles special keys. For example, pressing the

<DELETE> key or <CONTROL>c after you've entered an **emacs** or **vi** session will not cause the foreground process to terminate.

Some systems permit you to create your own key definitions. If you're working on the UNIX operating system, you can use the **stty** command to define keys. Unfortunately, the syntax of **stty** is not standard across different versions of the UNIX operating system.

To send a signal to a background script, use the **kill** statement.

The syntax of the **kill** statement is as follows:

kill *-signal job_name*

The *signal* can be either the name of the signal (for example, **QUIT**) or the signal number (for example, **3**). For *job_name,* enter the job number (preceded by a **%**), the PID of the background process, or the name of the script (preceded by a **%**). For example, suppose that you invoke **scriptA** in the background as follows:

```
$ scriptA&
[1]  405
```

Here are several ways to send a **QUIT** signal to this job:

```
$ kill -QUIT 405          # 405 is the PID
$ kill -3 405             # -3 is the number corresponding to QUIT
$ kill -QUIT %1           # 1 is the job command number
$ kill -QUIT %scriptA     # specify the full name of command...
$ kill -QUIT %sc          # ...or just the start of it
$ kill -QUIT %%           # sends signal to most recently invoked job, which
                          # may or may not be scriptA
```

Sending a signal is only half the battle. The other half is doing something with that signal.

Writing Scripts That Respond to Signals

By default, every signal (except for **STOP** and **CONT**) received by a script will terminate the script. However, you can use a **trap** statement to "catch" a specific signal and take appropriate action. The action your script takes is completely up to you. You might ignore the signal altogether or you might do something elaborate such as call a secondary signal-handling script.

You can set traps on more than one signal. Perhaps your script will take one action if it receives a **QUIT** signal and another if it receives a **HUP** signal.

You may be wondering if it's possible to set up so many traps that it becomes impossible to kill your script. In fact, it is always possible to kill a script (as long as you *own* the job running it) by sending it a **KILL** signal. The KornShell will ignore any traps that you set for the **KILL** signal. The **KILL** signal is a kind of programming back door, or, to pick another metaphor, a way to prevent painting yourself into a corner.

Catching Signals

The following script sets traps on two different signals, **INT** and **QUIT.**

```
USAGE="usage: trap_ex1.ksh"  # setting traps on INT and QUIT

# The script will respond to an INT signal by printing the value of c.
 trap 'print "Received INT signal; c = $c"' INT
# The script will respond to a QUIT signal by printing the value of rt.
 trap 'print "Received QUIT signal; rt = $rt"' QUIT

 integer c=0
 integer rt=0

 while ((c < 10000))
 do
   ((c = c + 1))
   ((rt = rt + c))
 done
 print "The final answer is $rt"
```

Executing This Script

We could run **trap_ex1.ksh** in either the background or foreground, but running it in the background makes the demonstration a little easier to follow. Here goes:

```
$ trap_ex1.ksh&                 # start up script in background
[1] 6551                        # KornShell assigns it job number 1
$ kill -INT %1                  # send INT signal to trap_example1
Received INT signal; c = 1578
$ kill -QUIT %1                 # send QUIT signal to script
Received QUIT signal; rt = 17931066
$ The final answer is 50005000
```

Start it again; this time send it a **HUP** signal. Since **trap_ex1.ksh** doesn't trap the **HUP** signal, the script will immediately die.

```
$ trap_ex1.ksh&
[1] 6552
$ kill -HUP %1                  # send a BUS signal to script and job dies
[1] + Hangup                          trap_ex1.ksh&
```

A Trap That Calls Another Script

The following script named **trap_ex2.ksh** sets a trap on the **INT** signal. If the script is running and you send it an **INT** signal, then **trap_ex2.ksh** calls (as a dot script) another script named **interupt.ksh**. The **interupt.ksh** script asks the user whether or not to continue running the script. If the user says yes, **trap_ex2.ksh** starts running again (right where it left off before the **INT**erruption). If the user says no, then both **trap_ex2.ksh** and **interupt.ksh** stop running.

```
USAGE="usage: trap_ex2.ksh" # call another script in response to signal
 integer c=0
 integer rt=0
 print "The PID of this process is $$"
# Invoke interupt.ksh as a dot script; pass it these two arguments:
#    1) the PID of this process
#    2) the value of variable c
 trap '. interupt.ksh $$ $c' INT
 while ((c < 5000))
 do
   ((c = c + 1))
   ((rt = rt + c))
 done
```

```
USAGE="usage: interupt.ksh PID number" # script called by trap_ex2.ksh

 print "The script is now stopped and the current value of c is $2"
 print "Do you want to continue? "
 read response
 if [[ $response = [Yy]* ]]
 then
   print "Okay then, the script will continue where it left off."
   kill -CONT $1          # send signal to trap_example1 to continue
 else
   print "I'll stop then."
   kill -KILL $1          # send signal to trap_example1 to terminate
 fi
```

Executing This Script

Let's run **trap_ex2.ksh** in the foreground. Running it in the background will make it difficult for **interupt.ksh** to correctly perform the **read response** statement.

```
$ trap_ex2.ksh              # run script in foreground
<CONTROL>c                  # send an INT signal
The PID of this process is 1175
The script is now stopped and the current value of c is 753
Do you want to continue?
Yes
Okay then, the script will continue where it left off.
<CONTROL>c                  # send another INT signal
The script is now stopped and the current value of c is 1392
Do you want to continue?
No
I'll stop then.
Killed
```

Trapping User Errors

So far, we've seen how to trap signals. However, you can also trap errors within your script. In other words, you can tell the KornShell to execute an error routine whenever something goes *wrong* inside your script. By wrong, I mean that the value of the error status variable **$?** becomes nonzero.

As you may recall, every operating system command, user program, KornShell statement, and KornShell script sets the value of **$?** to some integer value. By convention, setting **$?** to **0** means that the command executed properly and setting it to a nonzero value means there was an error. If you set a trap on **ERR,** then the KornShell will execute your choice of error status routine whenever **$?** becomes nonzero.

Unfortunately, when the value of **$?** becomes nonzero, it does not always mean that there is a mistake. For example, the **while read** statement returns a nonzero value in **$?** upon reaching the end of input.

```
USAGE="usage: trap_ex3.ksh"  # trapping on ERR (error)
# Redirect standard error to /dev/null (the UNIX system garbage can).
# If we don't do this, the KornShell will write its own cryptic
# error messages to the screen.
 exec 2> /dev/null
# Set a trap on ERR.  This trap will be triggered whenever the value of
# $? becomes nonzero.
 trap 'print "Sorry, but you did not enter a legal integer."' ERR
 integer number
 while :     # keep looping until break is executed
 do
   print -n "Please enter an integer: "
   read number # if user does not enter an integer, $? becomes nonzero
   if (($? == 0))
   then
      break
   fi
 done
 print "Twice $number is $((number * 2))"
```

Executing This Script

```
$ trap_ex3.ksh                    # run this script in the foreground
Please enter an integer: five
Sorry, but you did not enter a legal integer.
Please enter an integer: 5e0
Sorry, but you did not enter a legal integer.
Please enter an integer: 5
Twice 5 is 10
```

trap — respond to signals, errors, and exits.

Syntax:

trap [*response*] [*event1* ... *eventN*]

Where:

response — can be either one of the following or can be omitted altogether. If you omit it, the KornShell ignores *event*.

- *'command'* — is the name of any program, shell script, or KornShell statement. For example, a "command" could be a user-written program like **a.out,** a UNIX utility like **sort,** or a KornShell **print** statement. Enclose *command* inside a pair of single quotes.
- – — a minus sign tells the KornShell to restore the prior trap actions for *event1...eventN.*

event1...eventN — is one or more of the following. (If you specify more than one, separate them with blank spaces.)

- *signal* — any of the signal numbers or signal names returned by the **kill –l** command. The KornShell executes *response* when one of the *signals* is received.
- **DEBUG** — The KornShell executes *response* after every command. You can use **DEBUG** to create a do–it–yourself debugger.
- **ERR** — The KornShell executes *response* whenever **$?** is nonzero. You can use **ERR** to produce your own error messages or perhaps to take corrective action on certain errors.
- **0** or **EXIT** — The KornShell executes *response* whenever a function, a script, or the KornShell session itself ends. For example, you can use **EXIT** to delete the history file at the end of your KornShell session.

Quick Summary:

Use **trap** to define a *response* to certain kinds of *events.* If you specify **trap** without any arguments, the KornShell lists the names of all *events* for which a trap has been set.

Chapter 16
KornShell Applications

This chapter contains six complete KornShell scripts—some useful, some frivolous, all educational. Here's a list of those examples:

- Simple numeric guessing game
- Moo
- Card Dealing
- Readability index
- Copy comments in C source code to another file
- Disk hogs

The first three examples are games. These examples perform a lot of math. Then, we come to two examples that really show off the KornShell's facility with strings. We conclude with an example that uses a recursive function.

This chapter also discusses KornShell script performance.

Simple Numerical Guessing Game

Many programmers like to try out a new language by writing simple games. Here's a really easy one. The following KornShell script picks a random number between 1 and 100 and then gives hints to help the user guess the number.

```
USAGE="usage: guessnum.ksh"  # simple guessing game
# If you want to make the game easier or harder, just adjust the
# value of the constant max_random_number.
typeset -r max_random_number=100

 ((n = (RANDOM % max_random_number) + 1))  # n is between 1 and 100
 print "I've picked a number between 1 and $max_random_number."

 while true  # loop until user guesses correct number
 do
   print -n "\nEnter your guess: "
   read guess
   if ((guess == n))
     then
        print "Correct!"
        exit 0                           # leave script
     elif ((guess > n))
     then
        print "Your guess is too high."    # a hint
     else
        print "Your guess is too low."     # another hint
   fi
 done
```

Executing This Script

```
$ guessnum.ksh
I've picked a number between 1 and 100.

Enter your guess: 50
Your guess is too high.

Enter your guess: 25
Your guess is too low.

Enter your guess: 37  # have to be pretty lucky to guess it this quickly
Correct!
```

The Game of Moo

Here's a guessing game that's a little more challenging than **guessnum.ksh.** It's **moo**—a game that tests a player's logic skills. **Moo** is available on many UNIX systems as an executable C program. The next two pages show a KornShell version of the game.

Moo generates a random four–digit number, which the user attempts to guess in as few tries as possible. The script gives clues in the format "*m* bulls; *n* cows," where *m* indicates the number of correct digits in the correct position and *n* indicates the number of correct digits in incorrect positions. So, for example, if the clue is "2 bulls; 1 cows," then you know that 2 digits in your guess are in precisely the correct position, 1 digit is in the wrong position, and 1 digit isn't part of the answer at all.

Executing This Script

```
$ moo.ksh
Enter your guess: 1234
1 bulls; 2 cows

Enter your guess: 5678
0 bulls; 0 cows

Enter your guess: 9123
1 bulls; 1 cows

Enter your guess: 0124
1 bulls; 2 cows

Enter your guess: 0134
2 bulls; 2 cows

Enter your guess: 0431
1 bulls; 3 cows

Enter your guess: 4130
4 bulls; 0 cows

You guessed the number in 7 guesses.
```

```
USAGE="usage: moo.ksh"      # a game of logic
integer number_to_guess[4]  # declare an array of integers
integer cows
integer bulls

####################################################################
# Start by generating a random four-digit number in which each digit
# is unique; for example, 0392 is an appropriate number, but
# 2393 is not appropriate because the digit 3 appears twice.
function generate_random_digits
{
 (( number_to_guess[1] = RANDOM % 10 ))  # pick first digit
 for count in 2 3 4
 do
    (( number_to_guess[$count] = RANDOM % 10 ))
    c=1
    while (( c < count ))
    do
      if (( number_to_guess[$count] == number_to_guess[$c] ))
        then
          (( number_to_guess[$count] = RANDOM % 10 ))
          c=1
        else
          (( c = c + 1 ))
      fi
    done
 done
}

####################################################################
# Figure out the number of cows and bulls in the user's guess.
function give_the_poor_user_a_clue
{
 bulls=0
 for pos in 1 2 3 4  # count the number of bulls
 do
   if (( number_to_guess[pos] == user_guess[pos] ))
   then
     ((bulls = bulls + 1))
   fi
 done
```

The script continues on the next page

```
 cows=0
 for npos in 1 2 3 4     # count the number of cows
 do
   for upos in 1 2 3 4
   do
     if (( number_to_guess[npos] == user_guess[upos] ))
     then
       ((cows = cows + 1))
     fi
   done
 done
 (( cows = cows - bulls ))

 print "$bulls bulls; $cows cows\n"
}
####################################################################
# The shell script begins execution at the next line.
typeset -L1 one_char
integer number_of_guesses=0

generate_random_digits  # call function to generate a number

until (( bulls == 4 ))  # user keeps guessing until correct
do
   read guess?"Enter your guess: "

  # Is the user's guess a four-digit number?
   if [[ $guess = [0-9][0-9][0-9][0-9] ]]
   then  # Yes!
     ((number_of_guesses = number_of_guesses + 1))
   else  # No!
     print "You entered an improper guess."
     continue
   fi

 # The user's guess is a four-digit string; we need to convert it into
 # individual digits, assigning each digit to array user_guess.
    for pos in 1 2 3 4
    do
      one_char=$guess
      user_guess[$pos]=$one_char
      guess=${guess#?}
    done
    give_the_poor_user_a_clue
done   # ends the until loop
print "\nYou guessed the number in $number_of_guesses guesses."
```

Dealing Cards

The script on the next two pages shuffles a deck of cards and then deals some of those cards to two players: Jake and Fats. The script provides more educational value than entertainment value. In other words, it isn't really a game. However, you might use the code as the beginning of a real card game (such as blackjack).

Executing This Script

```
$ deal.ksh
Deal how many cards to each player? 3
Jake has: 8 of Diamonds;     6 of Spades;        9 of Spades;
Fats has: 6 of Hearts;       9 of Clubs;         Ace of Spades;
```

```
USAGE="usage: deal.ksh"  # shuffle and deal cards
# Declare a couple of global variables.  The variable deck is
# being declared as an integer.  Later, it will become an array
# of integers.  The variable position_within_deck marks the
# next card to deal.  A value of 1 indicates the top of the deck.
 integer deck
 integer position_within_deck=1
#######################################################################
function shuffle_the_deck_of_cards
{
 integer count=1
 integer switch_this_card
   while ((count <= 52))  # initialize the deck
   do
       deck[$count]=$count  # deck[1]=1 deck[2]=2 ... deck[52]=52
       ((count = $count + 1 ))
   done

   count=1
   while ((count <= 52))
   do    # "shuffle" the deck with a simple switching algorithm
     ((switch_this_card=(RANDOM % 52) + 1))
     temp=${deck[$count]}
     deck[count]=${deck[$switch_this_card]}
     deck[$switch_this_card]=$temp
     ((count = $count + 1))
   done
}
#######################################################################
function deal_a_card
{
 typeset -L18 complete_card  # to make cards align nicely
# Convert an integer into a value and a suit.
   ((value_as_a_number = (${deck[$position_within_deck]} % 13) + 1))
   ((suit_as_a_number  =  ${deck[$position_within_deck]} / 13     ))
# Determine the card's name:
   case $value_as_a_number in
          1) card_name='Ace';;
      [2-9]) card_name=$value_as_a_number;;
         10) card_name=10;;
         11) card_name='Jack';;
         12) card_name='Queen';;
         13) card_name='King';;
          *) print "misdeal";;  # this isn't likely to happen
   esac
         # The script continues on the next page
```

```
# Determine the card's suit:
   case $suit_as_a_number in
          0) card_suit=Hearts;;
          1) card_suit=Diamonds;;
          2) card_suit=Spades;;
          3) card_suit=Clubs;;
   esac

   complete_card="$card_name of $card_suit; "

   if [[ $1 = "to_jake" ]]
   then
      jakes_hand=$jakes_hand$complete_card   # add card to Jake's hand
   else
      fats_hand=$fats_hand$complete_card     # add card to Fats' hand
   fi

   ((position_within_deck = position_within_deck + 1))
}
####################################################################
# The script begins execution at the next line:
 shuffle_the_deck_of_cards

 jakes_hand=""    # clear Jake's hand
 fats_hand=""     # clear Fats' hand

 read how_many?"Deal how many cards to each player? "

   while ((how_many))  # deal this many cards to each player
   do
      deal_a_card to_jake
      deal_a_card to_fats
      ((how_many = how_many - 1))
   done

# Display each player's hand:
   print "Jake has: ${jakes_hand%;}"
   print "Fats has: ${fats_hand%;}"
```

Readability Index

Readability formulas return a number that allegedly indicates how easy or hard it is to read a given passage of text. I recently ran this book through a well-known readability formula and it received a score equivalent to the dialog in "Gilligan's Island." Please, don't get me started.

Prominent literaticians use all sorts of complicated parameters in their readability formulas. For example, average number of syllables per word is a popular parameter. However, we're not interested in anything that fancy; we simply want to have a little fun with the KornShell. I have, therefore, devised a simple formula, humbly entitled the "Rosenberg Readability Reaction." (Well, it had a nice alliterative quality.) Here it is:

$$RRR = (5 * awl) + asl + plw$$

where:

awl = the average number of characters per word.
asl = the average number of words per sentence.
plw = the percentage of words in the passage that are 7 or more letters long.

The higher the RRR, the more difficult the passage.

A KornShell script that calculates the RRR of one or more text files is shown on the next two pages.

Executing This Script

What is the RRR of files **chapter1**, **chapter2**, and **chapter3**?

```
$ readable.ksh chapter[1-3]
Now analyzing chapter1
Now analyzing chapter2
Now analyzing chapter3

The RRR is 32
```

```
USAGE="usage: readable.ksh file1 [file2...fileN]"   # readability index

# Declare four global variables.
integer total_words=0
integer total_letters=0
integer total_long_words=0
integer total_sentences=0
#######################################################################
# This function reads each line of text in the file in order to count
# all its words, long words (> 7 letters), and total letters.
function count_words_and_long_words_and_letters
{
 integer length_of_this_word
# The following characters will be excluded from the count of letters.
# Any of the following characters mark the end of a word.
 IFS="\"\',.?!;:- \011"      # 011 is the octal ASCII value of a tab

   while read -r line         # read in the next line of text
   do
     if [[ -z $line ]]        # skip blank lines
     then
       continue
     fi
# Divide line into words; store words as positional parameters
     set $line
     words_in_this_line=$#        # how many words in this line?
     ((total_words = total_words + words_in_this_line))

     for words    # the list will expand to $*
     do
       length_of_this_word=${#words}
       ((total_letters = total_letters + length_of_this_word))
       if ((length_of_this_word >= 7))
       then   # increment total_long_words
          ((total_long_words = total_long_words + 1))
       fi
     done
   done  < $1
}
#######################################################################
# The following function estimates the number of sentences by counting
# periods, exclamation points, and question marks in the passage.
function count_sentences
{
   IFS='
            # assign white space to IFS
```

```
   while read -r line   # read in next line of file
   do
      while :           # while true
      do
         partial_line=${line#*[.!?]}     # chop line into sentences
         if [[ "$partial_line" = "$line" ]]
         then
           break
         else
           line=$partial_line
           ((total_sentences = total_sentences + 1))
         fi
      done
   done < $1
}
################################################################
# Here's where we calculate the readability coefficient.
function calculate_RRR
{
    ((awl_times_5 = ((total_letters * 5) / total_words) ))
    ((asl = total_words / total_sentences))
    ((plw = (total_long_words * 100) / total_words))
    ((RRR = awl_times_5 + asl + plw))
    print "\nThe RRR is $RRR"
}
################################################################
# The script starts executing at the next line:
return_an_answer=false
 for file  # take all objects on the command line
 do
   if [[ (-f $file) && (-r $file) ]]  # is object a readable file?
     then      # yes it is
        return_an_answer=true
        print "Now analyzing $file"
        count_words_and_long_words_and_letters "$file"
        count_sentences "$file"
     else      # no it isn't
        print "Cannot access $file"
   fi
 done
 if [[ $return_an_answer = "true" ]]
 then
    calculate_RRR
 fi
```

C Comments

The C programming language and the UNIX operating system go together like ants and picnics. Here's a script that shows off the substring deletion operators. Its purpose: to copy all the comments from a C source file into a separate file. (This script will not alter the contents of your C source code.)

Permit me to explain how this script works. About 15 lines down from the start of the script, you'll see the following intriguing line:

```
remainder_of_file=$(< $pathname)
```

This marvelous statement assigns the entire contents of file **$pathname** to variable **remainder_of_file.** That's right—the whole file. You can now parse the file into comments by parsing the string variable **remainder_of_file**. Here's how I did it:

- Find the start of a comment (**/***) with the following statement. It deletes everything from the beginning of the file to the start of the next comment:

  ```
  start_of_next_comment=${remainder_of_file#*\/\*}
  ```

  The pattern ***\/*** is very confusing; it means everything (*****) up to a slash (**/**) followed by an asterisk (*****). I wanted the slash and the second asterisk to be interpreted literally, so I preceded each of them with a backslash (****).

- Use the following statement to isolate the body of the comment. It deletes everything from the end of the file backwards to the end of the comment (***/**). The only thing left is the comment itself:

  ```
  comment=${start_of_next_comment%%\*\/*}
  ```

- Copy the comment to a separate file with this statement:

  ```
  print -R "$comment" >> $1.comment
  ```

I will not claim that this is the best possible algorithm for counting comments. The script's elegance seduced me. However, I must admit that as the input source code file grows larger, the script becomes painfully slow. The culprit is the line that uses **%%** to assign the comment. If you'd like to shoot for a little less elegance and a little more speed, then rewrite this statement.

Executing This Script

Hopefully, you have a file of C source code lying around the disk. I have a C source file named **math.c**, so here's how I invoked the script:

```
$ c_cmnts.ksh math.c     # copy comments from math.c into math.c.comments
Done!
```

The preceding script should have created a file named **math.c.comments.** This file should contain a copy of all the comments contained in **math.c.**

```
USAGE="usage: c_cmnts.ksh file.c"   # copy C comments into a file

# If user forgets to enter pathname of C file on command line,
# prompt for it:
 if (($# == 0))
 then
   read pathname?"Enter pathname of C source code: "
 else
   pathname=$1
 fi

# Make sure that $pathname is a readable regular file.
 if [[ (-f $pathname) && (-r $pathname) ]]
 then
   remainder_of_file=$(< $pathname)  # copy entire file into a variable
 else
   print "Cannot access $pathname"
   exit 1
 fi

integer length_after_comment_deleted=0  # declare variable

 while :
 do
  # Delete everything up to start of next comment
   start_of_next_comment=${remainder_of_file#*\/\*}
  # How large is the part of the file that's left?
   length_after_code_deleted=${#start_of_next_comment}
  # Determine when to end the loop.
   if ((length_after_code_deleted == length_after_comment_deleted))
   then
      break     # if there are no more comments, break out of loop
   fi
  # Isolate the comment and write it to .comments file.
   comment=${start_of_next_comment%%\*\/*}
   print -R "$comment" >> $1.comments
  # Remove the comment.
   remainder_of_file=${start_of_next_comment#$comment}
   length_after_comment_deleted=${#remainder_of_file}
done
print "Done."
```

Recursive File Hunt

Chapter 7 explained how to find objects *n* levels underneath the current directory through clever use of the * wildcard; for example, you could find all objects in the current directory and the next two directories underneath it by specifying the following:

```
for object in * */* */*/*
```

However, Chapter 7 never explained how to find every object at *every* level. Here, we solve this puzzle with a recursive function. (A recursive function is a function that calls itself.) Actually, this script goes a bit beyond a simple file hunt and returns a list of all the files in a given directory tree, from smallest to largest.

Executing This Script

Rank the size of all regular files underneath **/usr/users/swine** from the smallest file to the largest. Figure 6 shows the organization of this directory tree.

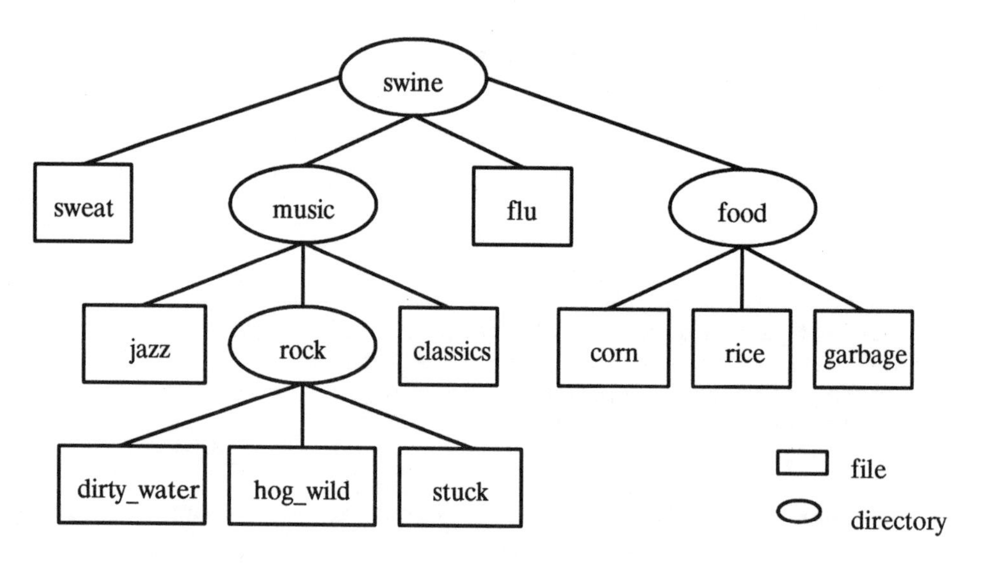

Figure 6. Organization of directory **/usr/users/swine**

```
$ disk_hog.ksh /usr/users/swine
4       /usr/users/swine/music/classics
4       /usr/users/swine/music/jazz
27      /usr/users/swine/food/rice
30      /usr/users/swine/flu
30      /usr/users/swine/food/corn
41      /usr/users/swine/music/rock/dirty_water
41      /usr/users/swine/sweat
44      /usr/users/swine/music/rock/hog_wild
57      /usr/users/swine/food/garbage
80      /usr/users/swine/music/rock/stuck
```

```
USAGE="usage: disk_hog.ksh directory"  # rank files by size

 temp_file=/tmp/filelist$$  # create a unique filename

########################################################################
# This function recursively descends a directory tree.
function expand_a_directory
{
 typeset object # object is a local string variable
 cd $1       # change directory
 for object in $PWD/*
 do
   # When the object is a directory, make a recursive call.
    if [[ -d $object ]]
     then
        expand_a_directory $object
  # When the object is a regular file, find out how big it is.
     elif [[ -f $object ]]
     then
        du -s $object >> $temp_file
     fi # ignore all objects except regular files and directories
 done
}
########################################################################
# The script starts executing at the next line.
# If the user does not enter a directory name on the command line,
# assume $HOME.
 expand_a_directory ${1:-$HOME}
 sort -n $temp_file # do a numeric sort
```

KornShell Performance

Once you get a KornShell script working, you will probably become obsessed with making it run faster. I feel obliged to tell you that if you really want something to run quickly, you probably should write it with a compilable language (such as C) instead of an interpreted language (such as the KornShell). Compiled programs just plain run faster than interpreted ones. The big advantage of interpreted languages is that you can usually write your code faster.

But enough of Computer Science 101. Here are a few helpful hints for turning a Kornsnail into a Kornschnell:

- Wherever possible, try to use KornShell statements instead of outside programs. By outside programs, I mean any executable binary files, including system commands and user programs. When you invoke an outside program, the operating system must load the program from disk to main memory before it can be run. The loading takes a comparatively long time. Using KornShell statements instead of system commands or user programs generally saves time. (In a sense, the KornShell statements are already loaded into main memory.)
- Math is fairly slow in the KornShell. However, if you must do math, declare your operands as integers.
- Avoid creating extra processes, even subprocesses.
- Keep your environment script as small as possible. Remember—the KornShell invokes that file every time you run a script.

The KornShell supports a statement called **time**, which measures the amount of time that a command, program, script, or pipeline takes. The **time** statement is a sort of software stopwatch. For example, to time a script named **turtle.ksh**, you'd issue the following command:

```
$ time turtle.ksh
real        0m0.50s
user        0m0.05s
sys         0m0.15s
```

The preceding **time** statement tells us that the script took a total of 0.50 seconds to run. During that 0.50 seconds, **turtle.ksh** itself used up 0.05 seconds. The **turtle.ksh** script required 0.15 seconds of kernel time. Presumably, the missing 0.30 seconds was used up by another process on the system. With these baselevel times recorded, you can experiment with **turtle.ksh**—changing this, removing that—and then retime **turtle.ksh** to see if it runs any faster.

By the way, if you specify **time** followed by a pipeline; for example:

```
$ time ls -l | grep 'rwx'
real        0m6.43s
user        0m0.23s
sys         0m0.46s
```

then **time** measures the amount of time it takes to run *all* the commands in the pipeline, not just the first one.

Chapter 17

Command Line Editing and the History File

Although the focus of this book is KornShell scripts, much of your work will actually be with the KornShell itself, typing in commands and such. This short chapter describes two features of the KornShell that simplify command line sessions:

- Command line editing
- The history file

We'll detail both of these features, describe the **fc** command, and then finish up with a few sample command line sessions.

What Is Command Line Editing?

It's a pleasure to edit a file with a good text editor. For this reason, a typewriter is no match for a computer. Nevertheless, when it comes to editing the command line itself, many computer systems with dumb terminals are about as ineffective as a typewriter. That is, although most computer systems let you edit text files, many don't let you edit the command line very gracefully.

The KornShell supports "command line editing" features, which allow you to edit the command line in much the same way as you would edit a text file. If you already know how to edit a text file with **vi**, **emacs**, **gmacs**, or **ed**, then you're all set. You can select any of these to be your command line text editor. Actually, if you select one of them, say **vi**, you don't get *all* the features of **vi**, but you do get enough of **vi** to comfortably edit command lines as you would edit text files.

There are two aspects of command line editing. You can edit the current command line and you can edit previously issued commands stored in a history file.

What Is a History File?

Every time you enter a command on the KornShell command line, the KornShell automatically stores a copy of that command in the *history file*. In other words, the history file contains a record of all the commands that you have invoked.

As the name implies, the history file is, in fact, a file. However, the history file is not a regular text file; for instance, unlike a regular text file, you cannot edit the history file with a text editor. In fact, the only way to access the information in the history file is with the **fc** statement (detailed on the next page).

You control the pathname of the history file through the **HISTFILE** variable. The **HISTSIZE** variable controls the number of commands that **fc** can access. (See Chapter 14 for more information on **HISTFILE** and **HISTSIZE**.)

What If You're on an Intelligent Terminal?

You may be lucky enough to work on an intelligent terminal that already supports command line editing features. For instance, your windowing system might provide a modern, mouse-oriented command line editor. To put it bluntly, what do you do if you're used to working with something that's a whole lot better than **vi**?* Frankly, if you're used to editing the command line in a certain way, you don't have to select **vi**, **emacs**, **gmacs**, or **ed**; you can stick with the command line editor that's built into your system. In fact, if that's the case, this chapter may hold little value for you.

---

* Dentist appointments are a whole lot better than **vi**.

Listing Previous Commands

This page illustrates how to use the **fc** command (or its alias, **history**) to get a listing of previously issued commands. I've changed the command line prompt to '! $' in order to have the KornShell print the current command number as part of the prompt. (See Chapter 14 for details on how to change prompts.) Note that the examples on this page reflect the state of my history file at the moment I was writing this page; your history file will undoubtedly contain different commands and numbers.

```
173 $ history                # list the 15 most recent commands (and the current one)
158         print ${x#*e}
159         pwd
160         cd s
161         script
162         print $RANDOM
163         history
164         cat list_of_chapters
165         cd ..
166         y="bon jour"
167         print $x$y
168         print "hello $x $y"
169         set -A array dog mouse elephant
170         print ${array[*]}
171         print ${#array[*]}
172         set --
173         history

174 $ history 166 168        # list commands 166 through 168
166         y="bon jour"
167         print $x$y
168         print "hello $x $y"

175 $ history -r 166 168     # list commands 166 through 168 in reverse order
168         print "hello $x $y"
167         print $x$y
166         y="bon jour"

176 $ history -2             # list the previous two commands (and the current one)
174         fc -l 166 168
175         fc -rl 166 168
176         fc -l -4

177 $ history set            # list commands from most recent set command to present
172         set --
173         history
174         fc -l 166 168
175         fc -rl 166 168
176         fc -nl 166 168
177         fc -l set
```

Re-Executing Previous Commands

This page illustrates how to use the **fc** command (or its alias, **r**) to re-execute a previously issued command. We'll start off by issuing a few UNIX commands just to fill up the history file:

```
214 $ cc main.c math.c io.c strings.c        # compile some C code

215 $ grep 'func' list_of_chapters           # search for a pattern
10 -- functions

216 $ grep 'strings' list_of_chapters        # more pattern searching
13 -- strings
```

With commands tucked away in the history file, we can use **r** to re-execute some of them:

```
217 $ r                         # repeat execution of the last command (216)
grep 'strings' list_of_chapters   # this was the last command
13 -- strings

218 $ r cc                      # repeat most recent command starting with cc
cc main.c math.c io.c strings.c

219 $ r grep                    # repeat most recent command starting with grep
grep 'strings' list_of_chapters
13 -- strings

220 $ r 215                     # repeat command number 215
grep 'func' list_of_chapters
10 -- functions

221 $ r math.c=cond.c 214  # repeat command 214, but substitute cond.c for math.c
cc main.c cond.c io.c strings.c
```

By the way, you cannot use **r** to re-execute multiple commands; for example, this won't work:

```
222 $ r 214 215                 # attempt to re-execute command numbers 214 and 215
ksh: fc: bad number             # you can only re-execute one command at a time
```

However, you *can* re-execute multiple commands by placing the commands in edit mode first. (See the next page for examples.)

Editing, Then Re-Executing Previous Commands

This page illustrates how to use the **fc** command to edit, then re-execute, a previously issued command or group of commands. Before editing a command, you should set the value of **FCEDIT** to the appropriate editor. In fact, **FCEDIT** should really be set inside one of the KornShell login scripts. For example, if you want to edit commands with **vi**, put the following line inside a KornShell login script:

```
FCEDIT=vi; export FCEDIT
```

Editing previously issued commands makes the most sense when the commands are detailed, so suppose you put a few elaborate commands, like the following, inside the history file. You can place any command or statement on the command line that you could place inside a KornShell script, even commands or statements that don't fit on one line.

```
270 $ read str?"Enter your name: "            # prompt for input, assign input to str
Enter a string: Eric Eldred

271 $  length_of_name=${#str}                 # find length of str

272 $ if [[ $length_of_name > 25 ]]           # an if/then/else statement spanning 6 lines
> then
>    print "You have a very long name."
> else
>   print "You don't have a very long name."
> fi
You don't have a very long name.
```

Suppose that after issuing command number 272, you'd like to make a few minor modifications to it, then re-execute it. Here's what you'd do:

```
273 $ fc                       # edit a copy of last command
```

This command will place you in the **vi** editor, but instead of editing a file, you'll be editing the six lines that originally appeared in command number 272. You can add, delete, or modify any of the text just as you would any text stored in a file. End your session as you would end any **vi** session (usually, by typing **ZZ**). After you end the editing session, the KornShell will store the results as command number 273 of the history file. The KornShell will then attempt to execute command number 273. Note that **fc** cannot change the contents of command number 272. Once a command is stored inside the history file, it cannot be changed.

The three commands—270, 271, and 272—are related. In a sense, they are like a KornShell script. You can edit any one of them individually; for example:

```
274 $ fc 271                   # edit, then re-execute command number 271
```

or you can edit them collectively; for example:

```
275 $ fc 270 272               # group command numbers 270, 271, & 272, edit, re-execute
```

---

fc, r, history

list, edit (and re–execute), or re–execute a previously issued command or commands.

Syntax:

re–execute most recent command	**r**
re–execute specific command	**r** *cmd_id*
edit, then re–execute most recent command	**fc**
edit, then re–execute specific command(s)	**fc** *cmd_id_range*
edit (with specific editor), then re–execute most recent command	**fc –e** *editor*
edit (with specific editor), then re–execute specific command(s)	**fc –e** *editor cmd_id_range*
list 16 most recently issued commands	**history**
list 16 most recently issued commands in a certain way	**history** *display_options*
list specific commands	**history** *cmd_id_range*
list specific command in a certain way	**history** *display_options cmd_id_range*

Where:

editor (optional) is the pathname of a command line editor. You can specify the pathname of any ASCII text editor on your system. If you omit *editor,* then **fc** uses the command line editor stored at variable **FCEDIT.** If **FCEDIT** is not set, then **fc** uses the editor stored at **/bin/ed.** If you specify – for *editor,* then **fc** will suppress editing of the command line.

display_options (optional) are none, any, or all of the following options:

–n suppresses command numbers in output listing. The history file labels each command with a unique number. If you do specify **–n, fc** won't display this number. If you don't specify **–n, fc** will display this number.

–l lists recently issued commands.

–r reverses the order in which **fc** displays commands. By default (if you don't specify **–r**), **fc** displays commands from oldest to newest. Specifying **–r** causes **fc** to display them from newest to oldest.

cmd_id_range (optional) identifies the command or group of commands to which **fc** applies. The influence of *cmd_id_range* depends on whether you are using **fc** to list commands or whether you are using **fc** or **r** to edit or re–execute commands. If you are using **fc** or **history** to list commands and you omit *cmd_id_range,* then **fc** applies to the 16 most recently issued commands. If you are using **fc** to edit or re-execute commands and you omit *cmd_id_range,* then **fc** only applies to the most recently issued command. If you don't like these defaults, then you can specify a *cmd_id_range* consisting of one or two values, where either value can be a

(unsigned) *number* — identifies a specific command number. (The history file labels each command with a unique number.)

(negative) *number* — identifies the command number equal to the current command number minus *number*. For example, if current command number is 100, then specifying a *number* of –5 means that you want to act on command number 95.

string — identifies the most recent command beginning with *string.*

Quick Summary:

Use the **fc** command or its aliases to access commands stored in the history file. You can do any of the following with **fc**:

- List previously executed commands.
- Re-execute previously executed commands.
- Edit, then re-execute, previously executed commands.

An alias for **fc –l** is **history.** In other words, you can use **history** or **fc –l** interchangeably. The alias **r** (short for "repeat" or "redo") stands for the command **fc –e –**.

Appendix

Statement and Alias Quick Reference

alias [**–tx**] *name* = ´ *value* ´

–t	establish a tracked alias between *name* and the program at pathname *value.* Most users can ignore this option. The KornShell can find *value* faster if it is a tracked alias than if it is not a tracked alias. You can only establish a tracked alias if 1) the trackall option is on (use **set –h** to turn it on), and 2) the directory in which *value* is stored is part of your **PATH.**
–x	export this alias. This is not a true export because you cannot export an alias from parent to child. If you're declaring aliases in an environment file and want those aliases to be accessible to a KornShell script, you must specify the **–x** option.
name	the name of the alias.
value	any string. Usually, *value* is the name of an operating system command or a KornShell statement.

Use **alias** to create aliases or to display a list of all known aliases. An alias is a nickname (or shorthand) for *value*.

```
$ alias                        # list names and values of all aliases
$ alias input='read -r'        # create alias named input that expands to read -r
$ alias doit='print "Directory is $PWD"; ls -l'  # create alias named doit
$ alias -t mygame='$HOME/games/mygame'  # create tracked alias named mygame
```

autoload

autoload is an alias for **typeset –fu.** Use **autoload** to specify a function defined in a file stored in a **FPATH** directory.

bg *job_name*

job_name the job you want to restart. See "job_name" listing later in this appendix.

Use **bg** to resume execution of a stopped *job.* The *job* will run in the background.

```
$ bg %1       # resume job number 1; run it in background
$ bg 145      # resume job having PID of 145; run it in background
```

break [*number*]

number number of nested (enclosing) loops to which **break** applies. Default value of *number* is 1.

Use **break** within loops only. Use it to leave the current loop (if *number* = 1) or the current loop plus any enclosing loops (if *number* > 1).

```
break         # leave current loop
break 1       # same as above
break 2       # leave current loop and loop surrounding it
```

case *value* **in**
pattern1) command1
...
commandN;;
pattern2) command1
...
commandN;;
...
patternN) command1
...
commandN;;
esac

value — is any value. Typically, *value* is the name of a variable.

pattern — is any constant, pattern, or group of patterns. Use the | symbol to separate patterns within a group of patterns.

command — is the name of any program, shell script, or KornShell statement (except **case** or **esac**).

Use **case** to compare a *value* to one or more *patterns.* If *value* matches a *pattern,* the KornShell executes *command1* through *commandN.* Compare **case** to **if.**

```
case $string in    # compare value of string to three patterns
  [a-z]*) print "$string starts with a lowercase letter.";;
  [A-Z]*) print "$string starts with an uppercase letter.";;
  *) print "$string does not start with a letter.";;
esac
```

cd *dir_name*
cd –
cd

dir_name is the pathname of any directory. If you specify an explicit pathname, then the KornShell attempts to change the current directory to *dir_name.* If you specify an implicit pathname, then **cd** uses the directory list of **CDPATH** to find the appropriate current directory. (See the description of **CDPATH** in Chapter 14.) By the way, a *dir_name* that begins with **..** means the directory above the current one.

– is equivalent to **cd $OLDPWD; pwd.** In other words, the – puts you back into the previous directory and then prints the name of this directory.

Make *dir_name* the current directory. Specifying **cd** without any arguments is equivalent to specifying **cd $HOME**.

```
$ pwd                           # what is the current directory?
/usr/users/bina
$ cd /usr/users/per/programs    # change current directory
$ pwd                           # what is the current directory now?
/usr/users/per/programs
$ cd -                          # go back to previous directory
/usr/users/bina                 # cd - automatically prints new directory
$ cd ..                         # go up one level
$ pwd                           # what is the current directory now?
/usr/users
```

cd *change_this to_this*

change_this is a string within the current directory name that you want to change.

to_this is the string you want to change *change_this* to.

Use this form of **cd** to change the current directory by changing *change_this* to *to_this.* After making the change, **cd** prints the new current directory.

```
$ pwd                           # what is the current directory?
/usr/users/roger/programs
$ cd quentin nancy              # change current directory
/usr/users/nancy/programs       # it automatically prints new current directory
```

continue [*number*]

number number of nesting loops to which **continue** applies. Default value of *number* is 1.

Use **continue** within loops only. If *number* = 1, **continue** skips current iteration of loop. If *number* > 1, **continue** skips current iteration of loop and *number* enclosing loops.

```
continue     # skip rest of current iteration of innermost loop
continue 1   # same as above
continue 2   # skip rest of current iteration of innermost loop and loop surrounding it
```

do

Use **do** to mark the beginning of the body of a **for, while, select,** or **until** loop.

done

Use **done** to mark the end of the body of a **for, while, select,** or **until** loop.

echo *text*

echo is an old Bourne shell output statement. You should use the **print** statement instead of **echo.**

elif

Use **elif** to precede the second through *N*th conditions of an **if** statement. See **if.**

else

Use **else** to introduce the default actions of an **if** statement. In other words, if all previous conditions are false, then the KornShell executes the commands between **else** and **fi.** See **if.**

esac

Use **esac** to mark the end of a **case** statement. See **case.**

eval [*arg1* ... *argN*]

arg any value.

eval is short for "evaluate." This statement works in three steps. Step 1: The KornShell expands *arg1* through *argN*. Step 2: The KornShell catenates the results of Step 1 into a single command. Step 3: The KornShell executes the command formed in Step 2.

```
$ x=10; y=12; z=8                    # assign values to a few variables
$ read mystery_variable?"What variable would you like to examine: "
What variable would you like to examine: y
$ eval print '$'$mystery_variable    # execute the command print $y
12
```

exec *numberaction target*

number an integer. Enclose numbers greater than 9 within braces; for example, {12}. The number 0 corresponds to standard input, the number 1 corresponds to standard output, and the number 2 corresponds to standard error.

action an I/O redirection operator.

target the pathname of a file, the *number* of another stream, or a minus sign (–).

Use **exec** to open or close a stream. Don't put any white space between *number* and *action.*

```
$ exec 3< data          # open file data for reading, assign it stream number 3
$ exec 4<& 3            # open stream 4 as a redundant copy of stream 3
$ read -u3 line         # read first line of data
$ exec 3<&-             # close stream 3; stream 4 is still open
$ read -u4 line         # read second line of data
```

exec *program*

program the pathname of a program.

Use this version of **exec** to replace the current KornShell with *program,* and do so such that *program* occupies the same process space now occupied by the KornShell.

```
$ exec myscript         # run myscript in KornShell's process space
```

exit [*number*]

number integer that KornShell will return to the caller. There is no default value of *number.*

Use **exit** to leave a KornShell script or to quit a KornShell session.

```
exit          # leave KornShell script and return to KornShell
exit 2        # same as above, but assign the value 2 to $?
```

export [*name* = [*value*]]

name the name of a variable.

value the starting value assigned to the variable.

Use **export** to make variable *name* and its *value* accessible to children. If you specify **export** within a function, *name* won't be a local variable. If you specify **export** without any arguments, then the KornShell lists the names of all exported variables.

```
$ export sam              # allow children of current process to access variable sam
$ export sam='hello'      # as above, but initialize sam to 'hello'
```

false

false is an alias for **let 0.** Use it to create a condition that always evaluates to false.

fc [*cmd_id_range*]
fc [–e *editor*] [–lnr] [*cmd_id_range*]

–e *editor*	specify pathname of *editor* to use when editing *cmd_id_range.* If you omit *editor,* **fc** uses the command line editor stored at variable **FCEDIT.** If **FCEDIT** is not set, then **fc** uses the editor stored at **/bin/ed.** If you specify – for *editor,* **fc** will suppress editing of the command line.
–n	suppress command numbers in output listing.
–l	list recently issued commands.
–r	reverse the order in which **fc** displays or edits commands.
cmd_id_range	is the command or group of commands to which **fc** applies.

Use **fc** to list recently issued commands, re–execute them, or edit a list of recently issued commands and then re–execute them.

```
$ fc -l          # list 16 most recently issued commands
$ fc -e -        # re-execute most recently issued command
$ fc             # edit, then re-execute, most recently issued command
```

fg *job_name*

job_name	the job you want to restart. See "job_name" listing later in this appendix.

Use **fg** to resume execution of a stopped *job.* The *job* will run in the foreground.

```
$ fg %1          # resume job number 1; run it in foreground
$ fg 145         # resume the job having PID of 145; run it in foreground
```

fi

Use **fi** to mark the end of an **if** statement. See **if.**

for *variable* [**in** *list*]
do
 command1
 ...
 commandN
done

variable	is any variable name.
list	is a list of strings, numbers, or filenames. If the list contains any KornShell wildcards, the KornShell expands the wildcards into filenames before beginning the loop. The default value of *list* is "$@".
command	is the name of any program, any shell script, or any KornShell statement (except for **done**).

Use **for** to loop through all the elements of *list.* The first time through the loop, **for** assigns *variable* the first item in *list.* The second time through the loop, **for** assigns *variable* the second item in *list,* and so on until all the elements in *list* are used up. The loop runs as many times as there are elements in *list.*

```
for object in a*   # generate a list of all objects in current
do                 # directory that start with the letter a
  print "$object"
done
```

function *name*
{
 body
}

name	is the name of the function.
body	is the *body* of a function. It can contain any code that any other part of a KornShell script could contain. However, you cannot specify another function within the *body;* that is, you cannot nest functions. Recursive function calls are legal, though.

Use **function** to define a named routine that can be called from within the script. An autoloaded function is a function stored in a separate file; an autoloaded function can be called from the KornShell or from any KornShell script.

```
function triangle_area   # define a function named triangle_area
{
  base=$1
  height=$2
  ((area = (base * height) / 2))
  print "The area of the triangle is $area"
}

triangle_area 10 6 # call function and pass it two arguments: 10 and 6
The area of the triangle is 30
```

functions

functions is an alias for **typeset –f.** Use it to find the names and definitions of all functions available in the current environment.

getopts *possible_switches var_name* [*data1 ... dataN*]

possible_switches is a list of legal one–letter switch names, possibly including one or more colons. A colon (**:**) indicates that the preceding switch requires an argument. However, if a colon is the first character in *possible_switches,* then the KornShell will respond to illegal command line switches by setting the value of *var_name* to **?** and the value of **OPTARG** to the name of the undefined switch.

var_name is any variable name.

[*data1 ... dataN*] is one or more strings separated by white space. If you do not specify *data,* **getopts** will analyze the current set of positional parameters (usually set by the command line). If you do specify *data,* **getopts** will evaluate *data* instead of the positional parameters.

Use **getopts** to analyze command line switches. A command line switch is a **+** or **–** followed by a single letter. A switch may be optionally followed by a switch argument.

```
while getopts lh argument
do
   case $argument in
      l) amplitude=10;;
      h) amplitude=25;;
   esac
done
```

hash

hash is an alias for **alias –t.**

history

history is an alias for **fc –l.** (Use it to display the "history" of your command line session.)

if *condition*
then
    command1
    ...
    commandN
[**elif** *condition*
    command1
    ...
    commandN]...   # you can specify multiple **elif** statements
[**else**
    command1
    ...
    commandN]
fi

condition	is usually a numerical comparison, string comparison, or object test; however, *condition* can be the name of any program, operating system command, or KornShell statement (except **if, then, elif,** or **else**).
command	is the name of any program, shell script, or KornShell statement (except **if** or **then**).

Use **if** to evaluate one or more *conditions* and take an action depending on the outcome.

```
if [[ $flower = rose ]]
then
  print "A rose would express sweet love."
else
  print "A $flower would smell just as sweet."
fi
```

in

Use **in** as a modifier within a **for** or **case** statement. See **for** and **case.**

integer

integer is an alias for **typeset –i.** In other words, you use it to specify that a particular variable is to have the integer data type.

```
integer x            # declare x as an integer
```

job_name

The **bg, fg, kill,** and **wait** statements all require a *job_name* as an argument. The *job_name* can be the PID (process identifier) of the job. In addition, if the job was invoked from the KornShell (as opposed to being invoked from inside a script), then you can also specify *job_name* as any one of the following:

%%	is the current job.
%+	is another way of specifying the current job.
%–	is the previous job.
%number	is the job with this number. (When you invoke a background job, the KornShell returns the job *number* within square brackets; for example, **[1]**.)
%string	is the job whose invocation command begins with this *string.*
%?string	is the job whose invocation command contains this *string.*

jobs [*–lp*] *job_name*

–l	list usual job information as well as all PIDs.
–p	list PIDs only (omit usual job information).

Use **jobs** to find the names of all background and foreground jobs.

```
$ jobs        # list all jobs by job number
$ jobs -l     # list all jobs by job number and PID
$ jobs -p     # list PID of all jobs
```

kill *–signal job_name*
kill –l

signal	the name (such as **INT**) or number (such as **2**) of the signal.
job_name	the job you want to send a signal to. See "job_name" listing earlier in this appendix.
–l	list all signal names and numbers, but don't send a signal.

Use **kill** to send a signal to *job_name.* (See also **trap.**)

```
$ kill -INT %1 # send an INT (interrupt) signal to job number 1
$ kill -INT 145 # send an INT signal to job having a PID of 145
$ kill -2 145   # same as above, assuming INT corresponds to number 2
$ kill -l       # list names and numbers of all legal signals
```

let *expr*

The **let** statement evaluates *expr.* Use **((...))** instead of **let.**

print [–nprRs] [–u[*number*]] *text*

–n	suppress printing a carriage return after printing *text.*
–p	redirect *text* to co–process (instead of standard output).
–r	interpret the backslash (\) literally instead of as the escape character.
––	interpret the minus sign (–) literally rather than as a character that starts an option.
–R	interpret (\) and – literally (except when – is the first character in the **–n** option).
–s	redirect *text* to history file (instead of standard output).
–u[*number*]	redirect *text* to stream symbolized by *number.* Default value of *number* is 1 (standard output). If *number* is 2, then **print** writes *text* to standard error. See **exec** listing earlier in this appendix.
text	the *text* you want to output. You may want to enclose *text* within single or double quotes. The *text* can consist of any combination of variable names, literal values, and escape sequences. Here is a list of escape sequences:

\a	ring bell.
\b	output backspace character.
\c	suppress printing *text* following **\c.**
\f	output formfeed.
\n	output newline.
\r	output carriage return.
\t	output (horizontal) tab.
\v	output vertical tab.
****	output one backslash character.
\0*number*	output character whose octal ASCII value is *number.*

Use **print** to output *text.*

```
print              # print a blank line
print "hi"         # text consists of a literal value
print "$x"         # text consists of the value of a variable
print "hi\t$x"     # text consists of a literal value, an escape
                   # sequence, and a variable
```

pwd

Use **pwd** to print the name of the current (working) directory. Don't confuse the **pwd** statement with the **PWD** variable.

```
$ pwd          # what is the working directory?
/usr/users/bim
$ print $PWD   # another way of finding the working directory
/usr/users/bim
```

r

r is an alias for **fc –e –.** (Think of **r** as being an abbreviation for "repeat" or "redo.")

read [**-prs**] [**-u**[*number*] *variable?prompt*
read [**-prs**] [**-u**[*number*] [*variable1 ... variableN*]

-p read input from co-process (instead of standard input).

-r the input continues on the next line if the current line ends with a backslash (\).

-s store a copy of the inputted values inside the history file.

-u[*number*] read input from stream symbolized by *number.* Default value of *number* is 0 (standard input stream). See **exec** listing earlier in this appendix.

variable assign input to this variable (or variables).

prompt KornShell prints *prompt* before gathering input from user. Enclose prompt within single or double quotes.

Use **read** to gather input and assign it to one or more *variables.* The **read** statement uses the **IFS** variable to split input into tokens. The KornShell then assigns the first token to *variable1,* the second token to *variable2,* and so on. If there are more tokens than *variables,* the KornShell assigns remaining tokens to *variableN.*

```
read x       # gather input and assign it to variable x
read y z     # assign first token to y and all other tokens to z
read value?"Enter a value: "   # prompt, then assign input to value
```

readonly [*variable*[= *value*]]

variable the name of a variable you wish to declare as a constant.

value the value you wish to assign to *variable.*

Use **readonly** to declare constants. Once assigned, you cannot change the value of a constant.

```
x=7          # assign value to variable x
readonly x   # make x into a constant
x=9          # KornShell error --  x: is read only
```

return [*number*]

number (integer) value returned to caller. The default value of *number* is the current value of $?.

Use **return** to leave a function and return to the caller. If you specify **return** outside of a function, then **return** is equivalent to **exit.**

```
return 0    # leave callee and return to the caller; pass 0 back to $?
```

select *variable* [**in** *list*]
do
command1
...
commandN
done

variable	is any variable name.
list	is a list of strings, numbers, or filenames. If the list contains any KornShell wildcards, the KornShell expands the wildcards into filenames before beginning the loop. The default value of *list* is "$@".
command	is usually a **case** statement but could be any program, shell script, or KornShell statement (except **done**).

Use **select** to create a menu.

```
select language in espanol francais english
do
    case $language in
       espanol)  load_spanish;;
       francais) load_french;;
       english)  load_english;;
    esac
done
```

set [**–A** *name*][**–s**] [**––**] [*arg1*] ... [*argN*]

–A *name*	create an array called *name.*
–s	**–As** sorts the values of array *name;* **–s** (without **–A**) sorts the positional parameters.
––	unset all the positional parameters. If you use this option, do not specify any *args.*
arg	any number of numerical constants, string constants, or string patterns. If you don't specify **–A**, the KornShell uses the *args* to set the positional parameters. If you do specify **–A**, then the KornShell sets the cells of array *name* with *args.* The KornShell will try to glob wildcards into object pathnames.

Use **set** to assign and/or sort positional parameters. You can also use **set** to assign and/or sort array values. Finally, you can use **set** to unset positional parameters.

```
$ set -A nums 97 85 96 94  # create array named nums; assign four elements to it
$ set 97 85 96 94       # assign four positional parameters
$ set -s                # lexically sort the positional parameters
$ set *                 # KornShell will expand * to names of all objects in current
                        # directory and then make each object a positional parameter
$ set --                # unset positional parameters
```

set [±] *argument*
set [±][aefhmnoptuvx]

-o allexport or **-a**	export the value, data type, and attributes of every variable.
-o bgnice	run background jobs at a lower priority than foreground jobs.
-o emacs	run **emacs** as the command line editor; does not influence **FCEDIT.**
-o errexit or **-e**	issue an **ERR** trap if a command ends with a nonzero value of **$?**.
-o gmacs	run **gmacs** as the command line editor; does not influence **FCEDIT.**
-o ignoreeof	an end-of-file character won't kill the current KornShell session.
-o markdirs	append (/) to directory names resulting from wildcard expansion.
-o monitor or **-m**	print a message when a background job finishes.
-o noclobber	suppress overwriting of existing files caused by **>** redirection operation.
-o noexec or **-n**	don't execute the script; just check it for syntax errors.
-o noglob or **-f**	suppress expansion of patterns into pathnames.
-o nolog	suppress storing function definitions in history file.
-o nounset or **-u**	suppress expansion of unset variables; print error message.
-o privileged or **-p**	suppress execution of **$HOME/.profile** login script. Use **/etc/suid_profile** as the environment (**ENV**) file.
-t	halt execution of current script and return to KornShell.
-o trackall or **-h**	create tracked aliases for all subsequently executed binary objects that are stored in one of the directories in your **PATH.**
-o verbose or **-v**	echo all commands (without expanding them) to standard error as they are executed.
-o vi	run **vi** as the command line editor; does not influence **FCEDIT.**
-o viraw	run **vi** in single-character-at-a-time mode (as opposed to line mode).
-o xtrace or **-x**	run in debug mode. Expand all commands and echo them to standard error as they are executed. Precede each expanded command by value of **PS4** variable.
-o	report status (on or off) of above options.

Use **set** to control certain attributes of the KornShell. These attributes influence the KornShell command line or KornShell scripts. The minus sign (-) turns the attribute on and the plus sign (+) turns it off. The syntax for the **set** statement is a bit weird. You can either specify **-o** followed by a word *argument* or you can specify a one-letter switch. Be careful—the name of the one-letter switch is not always the first letter of *argument*. For example, **-h** and **-o trackall** are synonymous.

```
$ set -o allexport     # export subsequently defined variables
$ set -a               # same as above
$ set +a               # turn off allexport feature
```

shift [*number*]

number (integer) the number of positional parameters to eliminate. (Default is 1.)

Use **shift** to reduce the quantity of positional parameters by *number*. **shift** slides all remaining positional parameters to the left by *number*.

```
$ set a b c d e          # assign $1, $2, $3, $4, and $5
$ shift                  # left shift all positional parameters by 1 space
$ print $*               # print $1, $2, $3, and $4
b c d e
$ shift 2                # left shift all positional parameters by 2 spaces
$ print $*               # print $1 and $2
d e
```

test *expression*

test is an old Bourne shell statement that evaluates *expression*, returning true or false. You should use **[[...]]** instead of **test.**

then

See **if** earlier in this appendix.

time *command*

command an operating system command (like **ls**), a user program (like **a.out**), a KornShell statement, or a KornShell script. The *command* could also contain one or more pipe operators (**|**). If it does, **time** applies to the entire pipeline, not just the first element of it.

Use **time** as a stopwatch; **time** tells you how long it took to run *command*. Actually, **time** returns three pieces of information: **real** tells you the elapsed time of the command, **user** tells you how long *command* was actually running inside the CPU, and **sys** tells you how much kernel time *command* used. The value of **real** will usually be larger than **user** plus **sys**, with the missing time going to other processes running when *command* runs.

```
$ time myscript          # how long does it take to run myscript?
real        0m1.76s
user        0m0.15s
sys         0m0.35s
```

times

Use **times** to determine how much CPU time the KornShell and its child processes have used. **times** returns four values. The two values on the top line provide times for the KornShell itself, and the two values on the bottom line provide times for the children of the KornShell.

```
                          $ times
KornShell user  ——> 0m0.66s 0m2.21s <—— KornShell sys
Children user   ——> 0m2.86s 0m3.81s <—— Children sys
```

trap [*response*] [*event*]

response a command enclosed in single quotes, or a null string, or –. Null means ignore *event*. The – means restore the original *response* to the *event*.

event the name of a signal (for example, **INT**), **ERR** (nonzero value of **$?**), **DEBUG** (after every command), **0**, or **EXIT** (after leaving a function, script, or KornShell session).

Use **trap** to execute a *response* to an *event*.

```
trap 'wrap_up_script' QUIT  # run wrap_up_script upon
                            # receipt of a QUIT signal
trap                        # list all traps
```

true

true is an alias for the colon (:) statement. Use it to create a condition that always evaluates to true.

```
while true   # create an always-true loop
```

type *name*

name the name of any file, KornShell statement, function, or alias.

type is an alias for **whence –v.**

typeset [±][**f**][**ft**][**fu**][**fx**] [*func_name*]

-f display the code for *function_name*. If you don't specify *function_name*, then **-f** displays the code for all functions.

-ft turn on debug mode within *function_name*. (**typeset -ft** is equivalent to **set -x**.)

-fu tell the KornShell that *function_name* is externally defined; that is, the code for *function_name* is located in another file. In other words, use **-fu** to tell the KornShell that *function_name* is to be autoloaded.

-fx export *function_name* to children of the current process.

func_name is the name of the function to which the option applies.

Use **typeset -f** to research functions or to set certain attributes within them.

```
$ typeset -f            # display names and contents of all accessible functions
$ typeset -f funk       # display name and contents of function funk
$ typeset -ft funk      # go into debugging mode whenever funk is called
$ typeset +ft funk      # don't go into debugging mode when funk is called
$ typeset -fu clinton   # tell KornShell that clinton is the name of a function that
                        # is defined externally
$ autoload clinton      # same as above
```

typeset [±] [**Hilrtux**][**LZi**[*number*]] [*variable_name*[=*value*]]

-H the KornShell ignores this option if you are working on the UNIX operating system. If you aren't, **-H** converts the value of *variable_name* to a format consistent with pathnames on your system. The conversion formula is built into your KornShell implementation; you cannot change it.

-i declare *variable_name* as an integer.

-i*number* declare *variable_name* as an integer and specify that the *value* of *variable_name* will always be printed in base *number*.

-l whenever the KornShell expands *variable_name*, the KornShell temporarily changes any uppercase letters in *value* to lowercase.

-r make *variable_name* into a constant. That is, once you set its value, you cannot change it.

-t has no purpose to the KornShell. You can use this to "tag" certain variables for your own purposes.

-u whenever the KornShell expands *variable_name*, the KornShell temporarily changes any lowercase letters in *value* to uppercase.

-x export *variable_name* to children of the current process.

-L *number* left justify *variable_name*. The optional *number* specifies the field width.

-LZ*number* left justify *variable_name* and strip leading zeros from its value. The optional *number* specifies the field width.

-R *number* right justify *variable_name.* The optional *number* specifies the field width.

-RZ*number* right justify *variable_name* and strip trailing zeros from its value. The optional *number* specifies the field width.

variable_name the name of the variable you are declaring. If you don't specfiy *variable_name,* then the KornShell will display the names of all variables declared with the given attribute.

value the string or integer that will be the initial contents of *variable_name.*

Use **typeset** to declare the data type and/or attributes of *variable_name.* By default, all variables are automatically strings and you do not have to declare them before you use them. Specifying a minus sign (–) in front of one of the options turns on the feature, but specifying a plus sign (+) turns it off. Specifying **typeset** by itself will produce a list of all variables created with a **typeset** statement.

```
$ typeset -i q=7        # declare variable q as an integer
$ q=5                   # okay to do this
$ q="Hello"             # illegal to do this because "Hello" is not an integer
ksh: Hello: bad number
$ typeset +i q          # variable q is no longer an integer; it is now a string
$ q="Hello"             # now it's okay to do this
$ typeset               # list variables created with typeset or its aliases
$ typeset -x            # list exported variables
$ typeset -i            # list integer variables
```

ulimit [**-a**][**-cdfmst**][*number* | **unlimited**]

-a display all resource limits. You cannot specify a *number* with **-a.**

-c *number* set the size limit of a core dump at *number* blocks.

-d *number* set the size limit of the data area at *number* Kbytes.

-f *number* set the size limit of files created by child processes at *number* blocks. (This may prevent a child process from inadvertently filling up the disk.)

-m *number* set the size limit of physical memory that this process can access at any one time at *number* Kbytes.

-s *number* set the size limit of the stack at *number* Kbytes.

-t *number* set the real time limit of *number* seconds that any process can use.

unlimited tell the KornShell that you don't want a limit on the designated resource.

Use **ulimit** to set or display certain KornShell limits. If you specify *number*, then the KornShell sets a limit. If you don't specify *number*, then the KornShell displays the current limit. Some KornShell implementations prevent you from changing these limits. If you don't specify an option, then the default is **-f.** The options supported by **ulimit** vary between KornShell implementations. In other words, your version of the KornShell may support different **ulimit** options than those listed.

```
$ ulimit -a             # display all resource limits
$ ulimit -s 128         # set maximum size of stack at 128 Kbytes
$ ulimit -s             # just to make sure, check the size of stack 128
$ ulimit -f 20          # set size limit of children's files
$ ulimit 20             # same as above (because -f is default option)
```

umask [*mask*]

mask the file creation mask. This is a three–digit octal number. The first digit represents the rights of the owner, the second digit represents the rights of the group to which the owner belongs, and the third digit represents the rights of "others" (that is, users not in the group). Each octal digit provides read, write, and execute permissions as shown in the following table. For example, an octal digit of 3 indicates read permission, but no write or execute permission.

Octal digit	Read	Write	Execute
0	YES	YES	YES
1	YES	YES	NO
2	YES	NO	YES
3	YES	NO	NO
4	NO	YES	YES
5	NO	YES	NO
6	NO	NO	YES
7	NO	NO	NO

Use **umask** to set or display the default protections for all files that the current process creates.

```
$ umask 000  # everyone has complete access to created files
$ umask 007  # owner and group have access to created files; others have none
$ umask 077  # only the owner has access to created files
$ umask 222  # everyone can read from or execute created files, but no one
             # may write to them
$ umask 230  # owner can read and execute created files, group can read,
             # others have no rights
$ umask      # show current file creation mask
230
```

unalias *name*

name is the name of an alias.

Use **unalias** to delete *name* from the list of aliases.

```
$ alias doit='print "Directory is $PWD"'    # create alias named doit
$ unalias doit                              # cancel alias doit
```

unset *variable_name*
unset –f *function_name*

variable_name	the name of the variable you want to unset.
–f *function_name*	the name of the function you want to unset.

Use **unset** to remove *variable_name* from the list of variable names. You cannot unset constants (that is, variables that are declared as **readonly**).

```
$ str="Hello"          # create a variable named str
$ unset str            # delete str from list of variables
$ print "$str"         # print a blank line because str is no longer a variable
```

until *condition*
do
command1
...
commandN
done

condition	is usually a numerical comparison, string comparison, or object test; however, *condition* can be the name of any program, operating system command, or KornShell statement (except **while, do,** or **done**).
command	is the name of any program, any shell script, or any KornShell statement (except **done**).

Use **until** to create a loop. The loop will execute as long as *condition* is false.

```
$ count=1
$ until ((count > 5))  # create loop to count from 1 to 5
do
   print $count
   ((count = count + 1))
done
```

wait [*job_name1 ... job_nameN*]

job_name	the job or jobs you want to wait for. If you don't specify any *job_names*, then the KornShell waits for all the background jobs invoked by the current KornShell. See "job_name" listing earlier in this appendix.

Use **wait** when you need to hold off executing a command until one or more *jobs* finish running.

```
$ myscript1&                    # run myscript1 in background
$ myscript2&                    # run myscript2 in background
$ wait %myscript1; print "myscript is done!" # print something when script ends
$ wait %myscript2; myscript3    # run myscript3 when myscript2 finishes
$ wait; print "All over!"       # print "All over!" when myscript1, myscript2,
                                # and myscript3 finish running
```

whence [–v] *name*

–v return information about the class of object (for example, alias, function, etc.) that *name* is.

name the name of any file, KornShell statement, function, or alias.

Use **whence** to find the pathname of *name.* If *name* does not exist, **whence** returns nothing. If *name* does exist but is not a file, then **whence** simply returns *name.* Use **whence –v** to find out the class of object that *name* belongs to. In other words, is *name* a function? An alias? **whence –v** is particularly helpful in cases where *name* corresponds to several different objects and you aren't sure which one the KornShell is using. For example, suppose you create a function named **okra** and an alias named **okra.** When you type **okra,** will the KornShell invoke the function or the alias?

```
$ whence diff                  # at what pathname is diff stored?
/bin/diff
$ whence -v diff               # what kind of object is diff?
diff is /bin/diff              # diff is a file
$ whence -v kill               # what kind of object is kill?
kill is a shell builtin        # kill is a KornShell statement
```

while *condition*
do
command1

...

commandN
done

condition is usually a numerical comparison, string comparison, or object test; however, *condition* can be the name of any program, operating system command, or KornShell statement (except **while, do,** or **done**).

command is the name of any program, any shell script, or any KornShell statement (except **done**).

Use **while** to create a loop. The loop will execute as long as *condition* is true.

```
$ while read line      # loop to read the contents of myfile, line by line, and print it
> do
>     print $line
> done < myfile
```

Index

Symbols

A

B

I

J

K

L

P

T

U

Y

Z

80808 08080